Underdevelopment and Naxalism in India

Underdevelopment and Naxalism in India

Reflexive Discourse and Debates

Edited by

SMITA VERMA

RAWAT PUBLICATIONS

Jaipur • New Delhi • Bangalore • Guwahati • Kolkata

ISBN 978-81-316-0931-6

Published by
Prem Rawat for **Rawat Publications**
Satyam Apts, Sector 3, Jawahar Nagar, Jaipur 302 004 (India)
Phone: 0141 265 1748 / 7006 Fax: 0141 265 1748
E-mail: info@rawatbooks.com
Website: www.rawatbooks.com

New Delhi Office
4858/24, Ansari Road, Daryaganj, New Delhi 110 002
Phone: 011 2326 3290

Also at *Bangalore, Guwahati* and *Kolkata*

Typeset by Rawat Computers, Jaipur
Printed at Nice Printing Press, New Delhi

Contents

Acknowledgement

This edited volume is an outcome of a National Seminar on "Youth, Naxalism and Terrorism: The Politics of Development in Indian Sub-continent" organized by the P.G. Department of Sociology and Women Studies, Isabella Thoburn College, Lucknow (Uttar Pradesh) in February 2014 with financial support of Indian Council of Social Science Research, New Delhi and the Ministry of Tribal Welfare, Government of India, New Delhi. I express my sincere thanks to both the institutions for their financial support and co-operation.

I express my sincere thanks and gratitude to Professor Felix Padel, a renowned anthropologist for accepting to deliver the keynote address. I also express my heartfelt gratitude to Professor Partha Nath Mukherjee, former Director of Tata Institute of Social Sciences, Mumbai and former President of Indian Sociological Society, New Delhi for accepting to grace the occasion as the Guest of Honour. I am highly indebted to Dr Charles, President and Dr Prakash, Principal for their support and guidance in making this seminar a grand success.

Nearly 70 participants representing various parts of the country attended this conference and deliberated on the theme and sub themes of the conference for two days. However this volume contains only the eleven best papers. I express my sincere thanks to all the delegates for making the seminar a grand success. I wish to put on record my heartfelt thanks to my colleagues and my students in the department who tirelessly worked round the clock for months for preparation during the period of seminar days. They deserve all appreciations.

I owe a lot to my teacher Professor Maitrayee Chaudhuri for the continuous moral support and encouragement to engage myself in bringing out an edited volume. I am sure she will be happy to see this volume once it is out of press.

I remain indebted to my father, mother and other family members for their constant encouragement and moral support in my academic engagements. Last but not the least, I express my thanks to Mr Pranit Rawat, Rawat Publications, Jaipur for arranging the publication of this book in time with commitment.

Smita Verma

Contributors

Bikramaditya K. Choudhary, Secretary, JNUTA, Assistant Professor, CSRD/SSS, Jawaharlal Nehru University, New Delhi. E-mail: bkcjnu@gmail.com.

Biswajit Ghosh, Professor and Head, Department of Sociology, The University of Burdwan, Burdwan.
E-mail: bghoshbu@gmail.com.

Felix Padel, Visiting Professor, North East India Studies Programme, Jawaharlal Nehru University, New Delhi.

Mohammed Siirajuddeen, Doctoral Researcher, Centre for Political Studies, Jawaharlal Nehru University, New Delhi, E-mail: siraj.jnu1@gmail.com

Pallav Mukhopadhyay, Assistant Professor, Department of Journalism and Mass Communication, Department of Film Studies, West Bengal State University, Berunanpukuria, Kolkata, West Bengal.

Partha Nath Mukherji, Former President, Indian Sociological Society; Former Director, Tata Institute of Social Sciences, Mumbai; and Professor Emeritus, Institute of Social Sciences, New Delhi.

P.V. Ramana, Research Fellow, Institute for Defence Studies and Analyses, New Delhi. E-mail: alepuramana@gmail.com.

Rajat Kumar Kujur, Assistant Professor, Post Graduate Department of Political Science and Public Administration, Sambalpur University, Burla, Odisha.
E-mail: rajatkujur@gmail.com.

Rajneesh Kumar Gupta, Assistant Professor. Centre for Studies and Research in Diaspora (CSRD), Central University of Gujarat, Gandhinagar. E-mail: rajneeshkgupta@gmail.com.

S.N. Chaudhary, Rajiv Gandhi Chair in Contemporary Studies, Barkatullah University, Bhopal.
E-mail: rajivchairbpl@rediffmail.com.

S.N. Tripathy, Professor of Economics, 4th Vijoy Bihar, Berhanpur, Ganjam, Odisha.
E-mail: sn_tripathy2004@yahoo.com

Smita Verma, Associate Professor, Department of Sociology and Women Studies, Isabella Thoburn College, Lucknow.
E-mail: Verma.smita.lko@gmail.com.

1

Discourse on Underdevelopment and Naxalism

An Introduction

SMITA VERMA

The proposed book is based on a hypothetical assumption that the violent protests in terms of Naxal movements and brutal state responses are natural fallout of an unjust economic order that is being allowed to continue, operate and proliferate across many regions of the country over the years. An effort towards comprehending and debating some of the aspects of development paradigm through the analysis of nature, direction, quality and history on Naxalite movement has been attempted which has severe implications for the most ambitious project of modernization of India, its development and nation building.

Discourse on Development and Underdevelopment: Brief Reflection

The contemporary development literature seems to be depending on the slogan of large, more and quick. The outfall of such slogan does not always bring fruits to all and for sure not for nourishment for all. Some do get wealthy with such endeavour at the cost of majority who gets marginalized economically, socially and politically. Resources are localized in India as in any other part of the world and have been declared as national asset. These resources remain concentrated within the pockets of the so called backward state. After globalization, centrality of economic activities increased as all incentives for decentralized development seized to exist. These widening disparities and continuous marginalization often get manifested in the form of civil unrest at times of violent conflicts such as Naxal movements.

Genesis of the problem is related to underdevelopment of certain areas in India which are mostly dry parts of the country with undulating terrain and low water level. There is scarcity of fertile agricultural land. Forest resource was earlier excessively used in the name of locals by corporates taking *patta* in some of the regions. Mining-based industries do not consider the local inhabitants as skilled. There is hardly any effort to enhance the skill or improve the human resources of the region. It has been further observed that certain areas of the country moved very fast with the use of modern advance technology of electronics media and other resources while a vast majority of the countryside remained backward economically. The complex relationship between man and environment, uneven growth manifested over the years in the region and failure of successive governments implementing the various development and welfare programmes are some of the reasons enough for civil unrests and violent protests in the form of Naxal movements (Choudhary, 2017).

Further since 1990, the country allowed private players to use the national wealth and accrue profit at the unmatched level. This is contradictory to basic economic principles on two counts: first, with increasing level of production and export more complex product and production technology is liable to be better. India after 67 years of independence and much cited 'Shining India Campaign' started selling unprocessed minerals and second, the definition of national asset. How a private firm or individual within the territorial boundary or a MNC is allowed to sell the national wealth? And if the national wealth is to be sold in open market, how can they continue to remain as national asset for which indigenous community continues to sacrifice its interest. These two sets of questions do not have any ready answer because they are contradictory to the same economic principles that argue for initial disparity between persons and regions in the name of development. Ongoing development pattern vividly reveals the fact that rich mineral resource areas like the state of Odisha, West Bengal, Jharkhand and major sources of hydroelectricity in the seven sister states of North East has invited several corporate houses to establish heavy and medium scale industries to exploit the natural resources. The outcome of these lopsided elite focused development has been such that power is generated not for those whose water is used; minerals are extracted and exported by those who have nothing to do with the national building (ibid., 2017). The statement is liable to the state loyal elitist development economist saying that it is from that taxation and levy that the major social schemes like MNREGA and mid day meal and others are running by the government. The development induced displacement of population belonging to marginalized communities reveals horrible facts.

Ever since the country has adopted of economic and industrial development policy, the tribals have been making way for commercial forestry, construction of big and medium dams, allowing the mines to be open up for extraction of rich mineral resources. They are homeless because of the pressures and imperatives of development policy. Thus, apart from large dams and industrial townships, tribals have been rendered homeless by national parks and sanctuaries. How many tribals have lost their homes and lands as a result of conscious state policy? The estimates vary—they range from a few million to as many as twenty million. Even if we cannot come up with a precise, reliable number, to the question 'How many tribals have been involuntarily displaced by the policies of the Government of India', the answer must be: 'Too many'. Sociologist like Walter Fernandez estimates that "about 40 per cent of all those displaced by the government projects are of tribal origin. Since the tribals constitute roughly 8 per cent of India's population, this means that a tribal is five times as likely as a non-tribal to be forced to sacrifice his home and hearth by the claims and demands of development and/or conservation" (Guha, 2007).

The successive governments at the centre always made ambitious plan to have country's growth rate at 9 per cent or even more and strived to achieve it. Despite the best efforts, the government is unable to contain inequality, poverty and distribution of resources with justice. In fact, the inequality as far as resource distribution is concerned, a huge gap exists between towns and villages and so also between upper castes and under privileged. One can also see the unjust distribution of resources such as health, education, transport and other infrastructural facilities are concerned. India lives in two worlds of education, two worlds of health, two worlds of transport and two worlds of housing with a gap or divide in between. The globalization process and information awareness of opportunities has widened the entitlement needs which has ultimately expanded inequality gap further. The Constitution of India under Article 39 says that concentration of national wealth cannot be accumulated by a few individuals. This has been totally ignored by the policymakers. The government policy of neoliberalism and its primary conditions towards modernization and mechanization, export orientation, diversification to produce for the market, withdrawal of various subsidy regimes has been contributing to discontent amongst the poor sections of the society in several ways. The government commitment to Land Reform measures which provides ample opportunities to uplift the rural poor find no place in the agenda of governance. Moreover, the rural poor depended upon common property resources such as forests pastures, water sources and flora and fauna for fulfilment of their basic survival needs. With increasing tendency to derive maximum profit from these resources, the poor are being gradually thrown out of whatever access they had to such resources.

It has been put forth time and again that in order to empower the people belonging to indigenous communities, it is better to allow them to utilize the resources optimally both natural and physical available in their surroundings. The privatization policy of the government goes directly against the indigenous communities. As a result of that the society is witnessing sporadic discontents and protest movements of different forms both at micro and macro levels. The neoliberal policy pressures by the government may not be able to contain Naxalite movement in the country in the near future.

Contemporary development scenario in the country reflects on many contradictions. One major contradiction of

Indian democracy lies with its non-violent roots vs. the metamorphic growth of political violence across the country. It's difficult to understand why in the land of Gandhi, Maoism has become a rallying point. Today, Indian political system is facing a major threat to the stability of the nation-state which is an imperative feature of our democratic governance. The threats both internal and external in the form of naxalism (within the territorial boundaries of the state) and terrorism (all pervasive across boundaries) raises pertinent questions on the fragility of the socio-political institutions in providing equal access to all its citizens across castes/class/region and religion. It seems the state appears to be in a dual role of the 'perpetuator' as well as a 'victim' of violence on mass scale. The phenomenon has grown by leaps and bounds in the post-liberalization period.

Brief History on Naxalism

A close examination of the historical and ideological origin of the movement makes it clear that the movement thrives on the dissatisfaction of the marginalized and alienated population (Dixit, 2010). It began with a small peasant movement in a village called Naxalbari from West Bengal State with its leader Comrade Charu Majumdar and Kanu Sanyal and in due course of its journey produced many comrades with committed ideology who strongly believed in to capture power of the state by means of violent revolution and liberate the masses from rapacious exploitation by the state and the feudal lords. Indeed, the movement has come a long way and has now spread over to a wide areas affecting and influencing the lives of lakhs of people. The Government of India has estimated that the movement is now active in about 125 districts spread over 12 states (GoI, 2008). The main support for this movement covers the dalits and adivasis. Dalits and adivasis together comprise about one-fourth of the India's population. Dalits constitute around 16 per cent and adivasis, 8 per cent of the population. Most of them (80% of dalits and 92% adivasis) live in rural villages with natural surroundings. The high levels of rural poverty therefore are likely to indicate high distress among SCs and STs. The states like Bihar, Odisha, Madhya Pradesh, Uttar Pradesh and West Bengal are with highest rural poverty and they also account for high proportions of SC and ST poor. In addition, they suffer from multifaceted oppression and denial of justice, social, legal and political rights (GoI, 2008).

The table presented below speaks in volume of Maoist fear factor.

State-wise extent of Naxal violence during 2008 to 2012

States	*2008*		*2009*		*2010*		*2011*		*2012*	
	Incidents	*Deaths*	*Incidents*	*Deaths*	*Incidents*	*Deaths*	*Incidents*	*Deaths*	*Incidents*	*Deaths*
Andhra Pradesh	92	46	66	18	100	24	54	09	67	13
Bihar	164	73	232	72	307	97	316	63	166	44
Chhattisgarh	620	242	529	290	625	343	465	204	369	109
Jharkhand	484	207	742	208	501	157	517	182	479	162
M.P.	35	26	01	00	07	01	08	00	11	00
Maharashtra	68	22	154	93	94	45	109	54	134	41
Odisha	103	101	266	67	218	79	192	53	171	45
U.P.	04	00	08	02	06	01	01	00	01	00
West Bengal	35	26	255	158	350	256	92	45	06	00
Other States	14	04	05	00	04	00	06	01	08	00
Total	1591	721	2258	908	2212	1003	1760	611	1412	414

Source: Naxal Management Division, Ministry of Home Affairs, Government of India.

The naxalite movement too has witnessed a lot of ups and downs in its trajectory and always attracted youths purely for ideological reasons. But today, violent modus operandi of the movement raises serious questions about its ideological roots. Naxalites have been attacking common citizens, police establishments and infrastructures such as public transportation, causing insecurity and instability to the area. During the period 2006–2010 alone, there were nearly 9,000 incidents involving naxalites with over 3,000 civilians killed (Jha, 2014). In the recent past Naxalite lethal attack on a convoy of senior leaders in Chhattisgarh shows that the movement has lost its ideological credibility and is gradually losing sympathy of the civil society. The Naxalites are active in approximately 40 per cent of India's geographical area and control large portions of remote and densely forested areas which is called "Red Corridor". This area is known as the tribal belt where the tension between economic development and aboriginal land rights is continuing since long. Serious debates on the issue by intellectuals and policy makers blame the state for the survival of the movement for the last four decades and its policy framework of describing the issue as mere law and order transgression and need to be repressed and contained. The socio-economic perspective of naxalism talks about how the rebel movement is shaped due to the failure of the institutional mechanisms and framework to deliver socio-economic justice (Dixit, 2010). While the naxalite movement is mainly an internal threat, with globalization, external and internal security threats are inextricably linked. Of late, there has been a concern if there could be nexus between the Naxal-Maoist outfits and terror groups. The Naxal-Maoist modus operandi of beheading, slitting of throats and wanton killings of the innocents, blasting landmines on conveys and use of sophisticated firearms for attack creates space for fear in the minds of local community. Modernization process has provided potential instruments of destruction, means of transportation and communication and advanced technology. Along with it the glorification of violence and crime in films make the youths easy prey to such acts which justify violence on the ground of utilitarianism and ideology. Therefore it becomes important to understand the factors which have contributed to the growth of this wave of extremist acts mainly on the part of the youths.

It is also important to distinguish both Naxalism and Terrorism as a struggle for power. Societies which are experiencing a rapid economic development and expansion on the one hand and on the other hand a simultaneous static or declining rate of opportunities in the form of employment, education, infrastructural facilities besides basic amenities along with lopsided development, disparate social relationships, repressive state policies, corruption of those in power, social exploitation creates discontent, resentment. Along with it the perceived 'deprivation' and identity erosion fuels the movement ideologically.

Government Policy and Governance

The armed revolution of the backward poor and landless people is the result of under fulfilment of their basic rights and freedom which the Constitution of Indian guarantees them. Being aware about their rights, they are fighting to achieve the right to dignified life, right to livelihood and right against atrocities. Naxalite violence may not be the largest internal security threat rather lack of implementation of public policies, programmes, mal-governance or non-governance and delay in justice. Spread of Naxalism is the consequence of that what we see manifestation of public anger in different forms.

All evidence points to the fact that the Indian state has failed to understand the nature of revolutionary violence. The violent confrontation between the Naxalites and the Indian state has affected the political fabric of the entire society. The state agencies have given up all procedures under the rule of law on the pretext that forces of violence do not deserve it. The leaders of state assume that they can eliminate the influence of this ideology by liquidating the leaders, cadres and sympathizers of the movement. In May 2004, the common minimum programme of the United Progressive Alliance while expressing concern over the growth of extremist violence had said that "this is not merely a law and order problem, but a deeper socio-economic issue which needs to be addressed more meaningfully than has been the case so far (Mohanty, 2006).

The auspices of liberalization and globalization process in the recent times have had added salt to the injuries of tribals and marginalized communities who have been living a life with abject poverty and penury. The opening of natural resource economy to the private players and not providing gainful employment to the youths of that area added woes and many of them have joined Maoist's cadre. The largely "non-tribal leadership of the state has signed a series of leases with mining companies, both Indian and foreign. These leases permit, in fact encourage, these companies tc disposes the tribals from the land they own or cultivate, but under which lay rich veins of iron ore or bauxite" (Guha, 2007).

The World Bank Study (2005) titled *Voices of the Poor* concludes that the assessment of structural violence and not just physical violence essential for a better understanding of the security concerns of the poor. This security and development nexus is visible in one of the most serious security threats to the Indian State – Naxalism. The Ministry of Home Affairs Report of 2005–06 delineates three priority areas to deal with the Naxal menace. These are: (1) local capacity building of the affected states in terms of intelligence gathering and training po ice forces for effective military action; (2) making the administrative machinery more responsive, transparent and sensitive for effectively dealing with public grievances; and (3)encouraging peace dialogues between the affected states and the Naxal groups. As per the need for economic assistance, the Ministry has administered three schemes to strengthen the security apparatus at the state level, (1) Security Related Expenditure (SRE), (2) Police Modernization, and (3) Backward District Initiative (BDI). First two focus on combatting the Naxal threat from a military perspective while the third addresses the problems of development paradigm (GoI, 2008).

Accordingly, the Government of India released grant of ₹ 20 crores out of which ₹ 3,06,562 crore for police modernization, ₹ 2,475 crore for integrated development of affected regions. The above amounts were given as advance money. Further, the central government has advised the states to facilitate for the formation of informal groups like Village Defence Committees in the Naxal-affected areas to deal with public grievances and help expose the unlawful activities and misdeeds of Naxalites (Bisht, 2007).

Having all these policy prescriptions in place, the main challenge before the government is how to operationalize the strategies at ground level and contain expansion base of Naxalites. In fact the Naxalites in many areas stalled developmental initiative by the state. Amartya Sen has defined development as a process that encompasses the choices of the people. In other words, the people can manifest their full potentials and enhance their full capabilities and opportunities (1999). Going by this line of argument, no matter how much the government chants development slogans, it can be said that an insecure environment can not provide space for developmental objectives. What is needed at this critical juncture is a proactive conflict management and it's resolution strategy, in which development costs and a rigorous risk assessment analysis should be undertaken. Peace dialogues with Naxal groups should underline this key element and energy should be focused on creating innovative mechanisms for effective out come (Annexure to Lok Sabha Unstarred Question No. 2665, 2008).

Public perception on Naxalism and its various facets of activities varies. One group of intellectuals and even the Planning Commission of India seriously view Naxal activities with threat perception to national integrity and country's growth and development. Contrary to the above views, the other sections of intellectuals and sympathizers hold that Naxalism movement is a social movement of have-nots – excluded categories of the society – who have been fighting for their basic right to live a dignified life with their natural resource and livelihood. This debate needs a better understanding of this sensitive and delicate subject and perhaps could be resolved only through fear-free questions and some fair-frank answers such as: Is Naxalism a problem or is it the consequence of social and spatial disparity? Why has Naxalism mushroomed in the underdeveloped regions where tribals live in? Why has the government failed to address it and subsequently acknowledged Naxalism as a serious problem for national security? (Kumar, 2010).

Contribution of Authors to the Discourse

Let us take a brief review of the author's paper and how they have reflected on the issues of underdevelopment and Naxalism at micro and macro levels and contributed tangibly to the ongoing discourse.

Dr Padel begins with a trajectory narrative of his youth experience and raised a couple of questions on the philosophy and model of development the country has perused over the last six decades. Dr Padel narrates “thirty years ago when I used to travel on foot in some of the remotest parts of Bastar (now in South Chhattisgarh) I was afraid of meeting a tiger, elephant or bear but not of people. Sometimes I would meet a hunting party with bows and arrows but there was no reason to fear them and no rumours of Maoists. Now this beautiful area with people having indigenous culture has become a hell on earth, epicentre of civil war in the heart of India”. Dr Padel through his microscopic observation on Naxalite insurgency in Chhattisgarh and its surrounding areas has raised pertinent questions as to why the youths are getting oriented towards the philosophies of extremist movements. And why the development models have had failed to fulfil the aspirations of the majority. Dr Padel has tried to articulate the reasoning's in his paper.

The Inaugural Address of the Conference was delivered by Professor Partha Nath Mukherji, a renowned social scientists of the country. Professor Mukherji initiated the debate with remarks that I shall deal at the general abstract conceptual level of the phenomenon of terrorism and its relationship with social movements, followed by Naxalite Maoist Movements. At the end I will refresh my memories of my field visits in West Bengal, the time landmines were laid. Giving a historical narrative on Afghan Mujahedeen to whom President Ronald Reagan called them as freedom fighters because they raised war against Soviet troops. Two decades after, they were branded as terrorists by the President George W. Bush. The term terrorists, freedom fighters, and Shaheed (martyrs) have been used interchangeably in specific historical situations or contexts. Hence Mukherji argued placing the point formidably that it is too difficult to accept the definition of terrorism as one man's terrorists is another man's freedom fighter. Narrating on various social movements occurred across the history and geographical spaces, Mukherji opines that terrorism could be associated with liberation struggle or aims to capture state power through revolutionary movement or for formation of a separate state. Such movements seek to bring a social chance or transformation related social system.

Reflecting on the historical antecedents of Naxalite movement which originated from peasant uprisings in

Naxalbari, Khoribari and Phasidewa areas of Siliguiri sub-division of Darjeeling district of West Bengal under the leadership of Charu Mazumdar, Kanu Sanyal and many others split into many splinter groups due to ideological difference and spread into several areas with phenomenal growth as seen today with having areas named "Red Corridor". Whatever may be the facts the tribals are the worst victims of development policy of the government and Maoist insurgency in their areas. There is no hope of peace and tranquillity to prevail in their areas in near future. Giving concluding remarks Partha Nath Mukherji observed that nation-state has to respond to ongoing variety of social movements, be it gender-based, class-based, ethnic based and tribals are victims of various types of exploitation and oppression for too long in their natural surroundings. This is not good for a government which believes in democratic principle of governance.

Professor Ghosh observes that there has been rising trend of secessionist movements, terrorism and armed conflicts across societies and countries in the contemporary world. Based on review of relevant literature and secondary data, Professor Ghosh tries to explain the conditions that seem to promote terrorism and conflictual group mobilization particularly in the context of Maoist movement in India. He argues that terrorism or insurgency is not simply a product of socio-economic and cultural issues of the 'victims' against the 'oppressor'. While these 'necessary' conditions are certainly critical, they alone cannot explain the growth and persistence of anti-state movements and armed conflicts in many part of South Asia. One, therefore, needs to go beyond this conventional model to explain the phenomenon and look for 'sufficient' conditions. Such a wider perspective would allow us to introspect into different phases of Maoist or insurgency movements and take note of the flexible and changing character of conflictual group mobilization in the contemporary world.

Economic policies over last six decades have brought certain fundamental changes in social, economic and political life of the people. However, the development policies have generated contradictions and conflicts at various levels of the society and even at times these conflicts have had posed severe threat to the very existence of the nation-state. Economic liberalization has integrated rural resources with urban corporate and global market which produced new power structure based on minerals, forests, and water and land resources. And as a result of that new differentiation of rural classes and tribal deprivation has emerged. A community of academicians and policy makers strongly believe that development is said to bring opportunities to the people and new possibilities that seems to be proved as myth. Choudhary questions the basic premise of development. Why has development not reached the masses even after six decades of Independence with massive investment in technology of super quality. The society is now witnessing sporadic conflicts at micro levels over contestation of resources. Choudhary has tried to critique the ongoing essentialist paradigm of "Development–Displacement–Disparity" which would add further energy to the existing conflict across the regions commonly called Naxalism.

P.V. Ramana makes a departure in his paper and tries to understand the nature and direction of urban movements a product of faulty policies of urbanization and how the Tactical United Front operated in urban areas as centre of struggle by various classes under leadership of several leaders can be solicited their cooperation and sympathy making the Maoist struggle broad-based struggle. To begin with Ramana has defined the Communist Party as: (a) A party that requires a strong organization, (b) Army, a body of fighters, and (c) United front – that is an alliance or linkages with groups that would facilitate its ultimate goal. Urban movements across the country are now attracting students of reputed institute of higher learning who joins the cadre to build a strong working class movement. Ramana observes that Maoist could well exploit the emerging situation in the urban areas to their advantage.

R.K. Kujur observes that in a country like ours, women are still looked down upon, women experience greater violence of different kinds inside home and private spaces which reinforced the patriarchal values dominantly practiced in the society. Despite this, Naxal movement has been able to attract more and more young girls to Maoist cadre and many of them hold tactical positions. The CPI (Maoist) recently has come out with a volumes of writings on women liberation through Naxal movements. However, the field reality is different. Many women Maoist cadres have alleged sexual harassment by their fellow male counterparts. Such instances of sexual exploitation include rape, forced marriage and molestation by senior male cadres. It has been also reported that security forced deployed in the Maoist area indulge in such kind of activities. The consequences of sexual violence are physical, emotional and psychological having devastating effect on the victims. Kujur observes that Naxals never tried to claim liberating the women in the red territory but in fact brought more injuries to the life of women. He appeals to the government and policymakers to pay attention to this crucial area and evolve a conflict resolution mechanism to deal with Naxal movement.

Any scientific analysis social movement one cannot ignore history and the stages through the movement has passed through. Social movements of all types, whether it is primarily addressed to social and economic exploitations or ecological and environmental degradation, development or displacement and deforestation etc have become very popular particularly after 1991s. These movements are basically collective responses to the historical injustice committed on tribes and their socio-environmental heritage by external forces. Some have historical roots and some are recent in terms of its origin. Some of these movements are independent and autonomous and some have linkages with other social movements working in other parts of the country. Globalization has also added fuel to the fire to the ongoing development induced degeneration process. It has increased degree of exploitation of natural resources available in tribal areas in a massive scale without any relief to the tribals and the local environment observes Chaudhary in his paper. Injustice of all types has individually and collectively frustrated tribal masses. It appears that there is no ray of hope from any corner to restore their environment and human rights. S.N. Chaudhary tries to understand nature and dimensions of movements by raising a few questions as Why all these movements have arisen? What are the historical and contemporary roots of these movements? How Nation-State and its different institutions have addressed these movements? What is the nature and type of interface between civil societies and the social movements in tribal areas? and How these movements have been able to shape and re-shape the ongoing model and process of development?

Scheduled Tribe population constitutes around 8.2 per cent of the total population in India and forms one of the most economically impoverished and marginalized groups. The lopsided development process in the tribal areas has had caused discontent among the tribals which has culminated into the rise and spread of the Naxalite movement. The Government of India has estimated that the movement is active in about 125 districts spreading over 12 states. The Naxalite movement is almost more than four decades old now. The vulnerability of tribal population to exploitation by the government officials, money-lenders, landlords, and other agents of vested interests, and their illiteracy and poverty has intensified the movement. S.N. Tripathy observes that the Naxalite issues need not be treated as a mere law and order problem and tries to differentiate between Naxalism and terrorism. Terrorism is the violent and illegitimate thing which terrorizes the nation from outside and the Naxalism is something which engulfs the country from the inside. Naxalism is the outcome of socio-economic deprivation among the tribes and downtrodden and their manifestation of discontent. In the light of the above backdrop, S.N. Tripathy has tried to locate the factors that have contributed for the emergence of Naxalism and how the tribes fall prey to such activities and finally followed by some policy prescriptions to the government for the growth of tribes and their economy.

Siirajuddeen in his paper argues that the contestation of the state in India with Maoists and the consequent plight of the tribal population excluded from the political community have to be seen in a global context. He forth with blames the economic reform process and the governance practices which has created multifaceted deprivations. The people have raised voices through movements at micro level against these 'practices'. In fact these groups are branded as anti-establishment and anti-development and therefore anti-nationals who are deemed to be 'suspected'. The State's 'exceptionalism' in the areas of Maoist activity is operated by the configuration of the strategies necessitated by the neoliberalism and securitization. When securitization of governance in India has made the state more repressive and repression meted out to the constructed and perceived 'other' is intense exhibiting brute coercive will of state, neoliberalism as an exception permeated a paradigm of exclusion of the 'other' by privileging few. The paper discusses how contestation over new 'development model' has resulted 'otherization', 'suspectism' and 'counter-suspectism'. The conceptual variables of the debates on exceptions are analysed with respect to the multiple contradictions emerging in Indian society out of political economic anomalies thereby.

Rajneesh Gupta tries to contextualize the tribal issues emerging out of development projects. According to him Central India houses a large number of tribal communities and among them diversity in culture, religious believes, language and speech, customs and in terms of lifestyle is quite visible. Rajneesh Gupta laments to inform that the development process during the colonial period and even aftermath of Independence with successive governments at the centre and states, the tribals faced multiple problems like displacement, land alienation, usury, severe unemployment etc which gave a major blow to their livelihood and in fact many of them were forced to look into other avenues of survival. The emerging lopsided development has created huge amount of dissatisfaction and discontent among the tribal youths. The Naxalites now motivate the unemployed tribal youths to join the cadre and insurgency. Rajneesh Gupta observes that Naxalism is not at all a law and order problem but the cause of the problem is lack of people oriented development policies in general and addressing the tribal issues in particular.

In development politics media both print and electronics plays a major role. Media is considered as the fourth pillar of the society which keeps eye on the everyday happenings in the society and disseminate to the public for consumption. Dr Pallav tries to focus on the role of media telecasting on the issues of Naxalism and terrorism in the country. He emphasizes that a section of Media faces allegation that it tends to write about terrorists in the language provided by them. There is competition among journalists to have interviews with terrorist leaders in India to promote the commercial interests of their house. The media should also realize that they are becoming channels of communication between the terrorists and the public in the name of freedom to exhibit such statements of terrorists. The connection between terrorism and the media does not flow in a single direction rather it varies with the type of incident and is dependent upon many variables. In his paper, Pallav Mukhopadhyay has tried (a) to analyse the interaction of terrorism and the media, (b) to investigate how the media shape its role in covering the terrorist activities and (c) to focus how the media in a democratic society can devise new methods of fair and credible reporting of terrorist activities without jeopardizing their responsibilities to the people.

In Lieu of Conclusion

The lopsided development process in the tribal and backward areas has had caused severe discontents among the tribals and marginalized communities which has culminated into the rise and spread of the Naxalite movement in the country over the years. According to the Government of India the movement is active in around 125 districts spreading over 12 states. The Naxalite movement is almost more than four decades old now. The vulnerability of tribal and marginalized communities to exploitation by the government officials, moneylenders, landlords, and other agents of vested interests, and their illiteracy and poverty has intensified the movement. To me the Naxalite issue need not be treated merely as a law and order problem and needs to differentiate between Naxalism and terrorism. Terrorism is the violent and illegitimate thing which terrorizes the nation from outside and the Naxalism is something which engulfs the country from the inside. Naxalism is the outcome of socio-economic deprivation among the tribals and marginalized communities and their manifestation of discontents. I endorse the views of Shanti Munda who at the age of 74 says that I clearly remember the Naxalbari struggle of May 1967. "My younger daughter had been burn just fifteen days ago but nothing could stop me from being part of the huge gathering on May 24. Looking back at 1967 she remains convinced that Naxalbari was the right path to follow but the movement suffered after dalals and thieves sneaked in. The land will be centre of future struggle" (*Indian Express*, 2017). The neoliberal economic policy pursued by the government by inviting corporate players and handing over to them the rich, bountiful natural resources in the name of economic development has had complicated the issue further. I think so long as the government fails to seriously deal with land reforms and provide livelihood and employment opportunities to the youths of tribal and marginalized communities and their infrastructure development, the discontent or resentment will continue in one form or another. The intellectual discourse will continue on this vexed issue of nation's concern to find a way out to resolve in near future.

References

Annexure to Lok Sabha Unstarred Question No. 2665, 2008, Article: Understanding the Maoists.

Attacks on Infrastructure Politics, URL: http://essaymonster.net/politics/83366-understanding-the-maoists-attacks-on.html.

Bisht, Medha. 2007, Securitising Development and the Naxal Threat, The Institute for Defence Studies and Analyses (IDSA) URL- http://www.idsa.in/idsastrategiccomments/SecuritisingDevelopmentandtheNaxalThreat_MBisht_120207.

Choudhary, B K. 2017, Upward Movement vs. Outward Movement: Resource, Development and Indigenous People, *Transactions*, Vol. 39 (1).

Dixit, Raman. 2010, 'Naxalite Movement in India: The State's Response' in *Journal of Defence Studies*, Vol. 4 (2).

Government of India, 2008, Report of an Expert Group to Planning Commission on 'Development Challenges in Extremist Affected Areas'. URL: http://www.plagscan.com/highlight?doc=115563929&source=1&cite=7&hl=textonly#jum.

Guha, Ramchandra. 2007, Unacknowledged Victims, *Economic and Political Weekly*, Vol. 42 (32).

Jha, Mithilesh Kumar. 2014, *Technology for Revolution: Opportunity for a New Religion and a New Society*, Nayi Kitab.

Kumar, Pravesh. 2010, Naxalism: A Problem or a Voice for Social Justice? *Mainstream*, Vol. XL.

Mohanty, Manoranjan. 2006, Challenges of Revolutionary Violence: The Naxalite Movement in Perspective, *Economic and Political Weekly*, Vol. 41 (29).

Sen, Amartya. 1999, *Development as Freedom*, Oxford University Press, Oxford.

2

Youth, Naxalism, and Terrorism

The Politics of Development in Indian Subcontinent

FELIX PADEL

Thirty years ago when I used to travel on foot in some of the remotest parts of Bastar (now South Chhattisgarh), I was sometimes afraid of meeting a tiger, elephant, or bear, but not of people. Sometimes I would meet a hunting party with bows and arrows, but there was no reason to fear them, and no rumours of Maoists. Now this area of stunningly wild beauty and beautiful indigenous cultures has become a hell on earth, epicentre of civil war in the heart of India.

As many young people are getting drawn towards extremist movements and philosophies, we have to ask: why? Have the models of development on offer since independence lived up to their promise? Or is there a wide consensus that development has been lopsided and technocratic, raising up some while betraying the aspirations of the majority?

But Has the Promise of Maoism Been Any Different, Actually?

Just as corporations show a benign, seductive face through public relation (PR) and corporate social responsibility (CSR)

Keynote address delivered at the National Seminar on "Youth, Naxalism and Terrorism: The Politics of Development in Indian Sub-continent" organized by the P.G. Department of Sociology, Isabella Thoburn College, Lucknow in February 2014.

that contrasts utterly with the harsh reality of goondas and 'mafia raj' experienced by poor people whose land is taken under promise of low-level employment, so too Mao was an excellent propagandist, whose promise of liberation to thousands of peasants was betrayed by draconian regimes and mass starvation under the Great Leap Forward, when industrialization forced millions into starvation, and betrayals of comrades before and during the Cultural Revolution (both documented for example in Li, 1994). Similarly, are many of the youth joining India's Maoists finding their ideals betrayed in cycles of infighting and violence?

Nevertheless, Maoism in India today seems to be widely perceived by many people, including many young people, as one of the few valid alternatives to the mainstream.

Meanwhile, it seems that in the name of fighting terrorism and Naxalism, security forces often unleash a reign of terror that escalates an already inflamed situation, enrolling thousands more youths as adivasis recruited as 'Special Police Officers' – a recipe for civil war, as the Supreme Court has commented.

How to conceptualize this situation and reposition tribal policy to find an inclusive way forward? Is there a way to short circuit the polarization and bring back peace with justice and a rule of law in which rich and poor can expect equal treatment in the courts?

For real development, which would improve living standards for everyone, is it not necessary to ensure this equality before the law, while bringing about fundamental structural change, to stop abuses of power and endemic patterns of exploitation and corruption, at the same time as evolving techniques of conflict resolution and nonviolent resolution to bring about this change?

Terror on Both Sides

Arguably, the conflict between Maoists and security forces in eastern central India is one of the worst wars there has ever been in India, especially in the way it is impacting hundreds of tribal villages that have existed in forest areas since recorded history began. Correct figures for casualties and people displaced by the fighting are not available, but more than 600 villages burnt by *Salwa Judum* in South Chhattisgarh during

2005–2008 alone, producing more than 3,00,000 adivasi refugees, have been obtained from many sources (Bharadwaj, 2009). Also, this is a classic civil war in which adivasi SPOs recruited and trained by police are often fighting adivasis recruited by the Maoists.

At the dawn of India's history, the Kalinga War, as per the estimate made by Ashoka, whose attack on the Kalinga brought it about, killed 100,000 people, enslaved 150,000 and many more were killed because of famine and disease after the war was over (Thapar, 1961; Padel and Das, 2010: 55). The Telangana war in western areas of Andhra Pradesh from 1946–1952, during which 3,000 villages were 'liberated' and then recaptured, also killed and negatively affected a huge civilian population, and so did civil conflicts in Northeast India since 1950s, and Punjab and Kashmir since 1970s/1980s.

This pattern of insurgency/counterinsurgency warfare, effectively pitting security forces against insurgents who appear embedded in large civilian populations, is not only taking place in India of course but also a characteristic of the US-led 'War on Terror' as it has unfolded in Afghanistan, parts of Pakistan, Iraq, Libya, Syria, Yemen, and Somalia for example. Similar situation is well known in countries such as Columbia and Turkey, where the Revolutionary Armed Forces of Columbia (FARC) and Kurdistan Workers Party (PKK) Left-wing guerrilla groups have been fighting against security forces as well as Right-wing militants trained by security forces over many years – the pattern now escalating in central India.

Among several similar patterns, in most of these cases, terror is a tactic used by both sides – security forces and insurgents, though in different ways – 'hi-tech' terror by the security forces, including air power and drones in the 'War on Terror' affected countries, and lower-tech terror by insurgents. In the case of Afghanistan, Pakistan, Iraq, Yemen, and Somalia, it is clear that 'collateral killings' of civilians by drones and Joint Special Operations Command (JSOC) forces under direct command of the US President have radicalized huge segments of the civilian population of these countries, where Islamic terrorism previously had relatively little support (Mamdani, 2005; Scahill, 2008, 2013; Steele, 2012).

As the world's superpower, the United States sets the dominant paradigm that other countries tend to copy. The impunity of United States and other security forces to prosecution for the killing or torture of innocent civilians in these countries has clearly been a major factor in motivating recruitment to the Taliban or Al-Qaeda causes (Mamdani, 2005; Scahill, 2013). Sri Lanka also followed this paradigm in an extreme degree when an estimated 40,000 Tamil civilians were killed, including raping and torturing of many people, during and after the final assault on the Tamil Tigers in May 2009 (UN, 2011; Aneez and Sirilal, 2014).

A similar impunity is evident in the behaviour of Indian security forces in the 'Operation Green Hunt' against Maoists; and it is similarly evident that the injustice of this impunity is a major force in recruiting adivasis to the Maoist cause. The impossibility of bringing a successful prosecution against security forces for atrocities they commit against adivasis perpetuates a sense of injustice. The same applies in Northeast India and Kashmir for example (Pervez, 2013).

This is clear from Arundhati Roy's 'Walking with the comrades' (2010), which gives voice to young adivasi Maoists describing the horrors perpetrated on their friends and relatives by armed police that motivated their recruitment, and also from senior policeman E.N. Rammohan (Chaudhury, 2010), who describes a 'failure of leadership' among the armed police that fails to restrain them when they 'go berserk' in tribal villages, especially after suffering losses from the Maoists.

The leadership on both sides promotes violence and depicts the deaths of its own fighters, whether *jawans* or Maoist cadres, in terms of 'sacrifice' or 'martyrdom', to motivate further effort in a conflict that – like the larger 'War on Terror' – has no end in sight and cannot easily be 'won' by either side. Even if the violence from Maoists is much less than the violence from security forces, every time Maoists launch a successful attack on the police, in which police are killed, police tend to take revenge on the surrounding tribal villages suspected of supporting the Maoists (PUCL, 2006; CPJC, 2007; Chakravarti, 2008; Navlakha and Gupta, 2009; Pandita, 2011; Navlakha,

2012). Similarly, Maoist attacks on 'class enemies', following the original strategy promoted by Charu Mazumdar in West Bengal and Andhra Pradesh, lie behind the formation of *Salwa Judum* by members of Bastar's 'tribal elite', making them far more violent than they had ever been before (Choudhury, 2012).

Structural Violence

Armed police are being recruited and deployed in ever greater numbers to confront the Maoist threat. However, mass deployment is not only against Maoists, but also to force through a number of contentious projects in the face of local resistance. Within the last several years, hundreds of police at a time have been deployed in the following places, among many others: Tata Steel's Kalinganagar plant, on whose site police firings took place in January 2006 and in March–May 2010 (BIRSA, 2007; Samadrusti, 2010 March–May), the planned site of Posco's steel plant cum port on Odisha's coast, the sites of steel plants planned in South Chhattisgarh by Tata Steel and Essar Steel, at Singur and Nandigram in West Bengal, around the sites of planned power stations in Andhra Pradesh where several people were killed in police firings during 2010–2011 (Padel et al., 2013: 122), promoting several projects in Jharkhand, against nuclear power station protestors at Jaitapur (Maharashtra) and Kudankulam (Tamil Nadu), and against dam protestors in Arunachal Pradesh (Padel et al., 60).

The common point in these projects is large-scale financial investment: the vested interests involve very large sums of FDI (foreign direct investment) and money from Indian sources. This money can be seen as essentially what motivates or pays for the mass deployment of police to beat the local opposition. The fact of this process going on simultaneously with the war against the Maoists shows that underlying the latter is a resource war: an intense and escalating conflict over resources – land, minerals, water, and forest. This is what Marxists refer to as 'primitive accumulation', and in many ways, the process of land grabs and enclosure of common land – expropriated from small-scale farming communities, unfolding in India now, combined with rapid industrialization – follows the historical pattern of capitalist takeovers in Britain and Europe during the 19th century that Marx analysed in *Das Kapital*.

The situation in India's tribal areas today echoes a 500 year history of Europeans' conquest and annihilation of tribal societies that they perceived as 'primitive'. This perception of tribal people as 'primitive' justified the invasions and takeovers on the basis that these would 'civilize' them, even if the process involved great suffering. These ideas are still prevalent. The colonial era mindset that sees tribal societies as 'primitive' or 'backward' became entrenched on the Left as well as Right by seeing them as 'underdeveloped', after President Truman introduced this concept in his inaugural speech in 1949 (Esteva, 1992: 6–7; Padel et al., 2013: xvi–xvii). 'Social evolutionism' essentially applied the concept of evolution in nature, where thousands of species were evolving in a multitude of directions, to society in a mono-linear fashion, as if all societies necessarily evolve through the same stages (Padel, 2010: 243–287). This gave rise to an entrenched belief that all societies develop in the same way – an orthodoxy in some Marxist thought as well as throughout the discipline of economics, that has shaped the modern power structure of international relations: in particular the classification of countries into 'developed', developing', and 'underdeveloped', and the system that has enmeshed 'developing' and 'underdeveloped' countries into a burden of unrepayable debt through the World Bank loans or 'development projects' that created leverage through which the multinational corporations and financial institutions are expanding their takeovers of land and resources.

Throughout India's tribal areas a system of endemic exploitation has built up since British times that forces a large proportion of adivasis to live on the edge of starvation (Padel and Das, 2010: 419–454). Compounding this is an ideology of 'removing poverty through development and foreign aid' that has in fact facilitated a new scale of takeovers – and no real decrease in poverty levels – in the context of a new era of rapidly imposed industrialization masterminded from the world's financial capitals. In many ways, India's relatively high growth rate is a boom based on foreign investment entering the country with a view to looting its resources. In recent decades, India has witnessed rising rates of deforestation, extraction of minerals, and especially extraction and pollution of water by metal factories, which is unsustainable to an extreme degree. A crash in the near future is inevitable, even though for the moment, many of the youth in India are attracted by a 'brand new world' of constantly developing consumer items, in line with the IMF's characterization of India's high GDP as 'an engine for world growth'.

Today's techniques of capitalism, as a system of attracting the youth, are basically the same as those used by British administrators in India 170 years ago. The first high-ranking civil servants who interacted with Konds in Odisha proposed expanding markets as a way to facilitate 'the civilization of the wild tribes':

> Where they will have the opportunity of seeing articles from all over the world ... and by giving them new tastes and new wants will, in time, afford us the best hold we can have on their fidelity as subjects, by rendering them dependent on us for what will, in time, become necessities of life. (Report of G.E. Russell to the Government of Madras, 12 August 1836, quoted in Padel, 2010: 178–179)

The corporate drive to expand consumerism as a basis for dreams of a better life has never been so strong in India. Rationally, it can be countered when we understand that this consumerism is based on unsustainable levels of rapid resource extraction and depletion and on conflating wants with needs. Real necessities of life means adequate, nutritious food, clean water, adequate housing, and work, as well as justice and dignity for everyone. However, due to unequal distribution of food and wealth a large proportion of the population – in India and most other countries – is deprived of these necessities, while nearly all of us are swept up into the desire for the latest fashions for mobiles, motorbikes, cars, modern houses, foods, clothes, and much more. Films are one medium of promoting these desires, and the violence in films inserts a subliminal message into the collective unconscious that only by fighting and winning can you get what you want.

This message is reinforced by the behaviour of today's superpower. Since the Vietnam War, the United States has behaved with extraordinary aggression towards people in other countries. Herman and Chomsky characterize this behaviour as 'the real terror network' and 'manufacturing consent' through manipulation of media reporting (Herman, 1983; Herman and Chomsky, 1988). The techniques of using terror on civilian populations have been perfected above all by the US military and intelligence agencies. Herman and Chomsky highlight the history of this in Vietnam, Laos, Cambodia, Indonesia, and Latin America, including the examples of napalm and agent orange in Southeast Asia, CIA support for some of the most brutal dictatorships – such as Suharto's in Indonesia and Pinochet's in Chile and much more – culminating in today's use of 'targeted assassinations' by JSOC and drone attacks, under direct command of the US President, in many countries, in clear contravention of international law.

What is especially ironic in the 'War on Terror' – as many critics have pointed out – is that many of the terrorist groups have been built up by the United States in a pattern of alternately funding and fighting them. Osama bin Laden is one of many *mujahedin* commanders in Afghanistan financed by the CIA via Pakistan's secret services in order to force the Soviets out of the country (Steele, 2012). That he and many others turned against the United States after it invaded Afghanistan and other countries has an air of inevitability.

So is the US policy based simply on stupidity? To an impartial observer, it seems obvious that the countless attacks on civilians during the Afghan and Iraq wars, including the jailing, torture, and humiliation of hundreds of innocents, culminating in the 'collateral damage' of hundreds of drone and other attacks that have killed or injured innocent people, is a primary factor fuelling resistance and insurgency. Is it just that the military mindset does not perceive this? Or considers it unimportant compared to an overall strategy of enforcing US hegemony through superior firepower? Or is there actually an addiction to war in this mindset, and to use of maximum firepower, even when it is obvious that this is provoking an unstoppable backlash? Certainly the arms industry and trade are at the centre of the economy of 'developed countries', and in economic relations between countries, and a key source of financial corruption infecting governments. They also constitute an obvious investment in war (Feinstein, 2011).

The danger, and tragedy, is that US policies have promoted civil wars in an increasing number of 'failed states'. This has happened in Afghanistan and Iraq through direct invasion by the United States and allied forces, who have often formed alliances with some of the most reactionary and repressive warlords and factions; in Pakistan, Yemen, and Somalia through indirect intervention including drone attacks; and in Libya and Syria through support for 'democracy' movements that swiftly got hijacked by Al Qaeda-linked elements. In the two latter countries, it is apparent that the United States has been in effect supporting Al Qaeda elements with the aim of forcing regime change. The civil wars set in motion during this process cannot easily be brought to a peaceful conclusion, to put this mildly.

In other words, is the United States and its allies seems to have been promoting 'failed states', warlords, and civil war in order to facilitate the takeover and extraction of resources by their corporations and financial institutions. Naomi Klein (2007) shows this is precisely what happened in the aftermath of the invasion of Iraq, following the pattern promoted through the IMF and the World Bank in many other countries, and she shows how the same pattern is visible in the manipulated conflict presently unfolding in Ukraine (Klein, 2014).

In other words, most wars today are basically over control of resources (Klare, 2002), dressed up as ideological wars – for 'democracy' according to the US administration and media, for Islamic or communist ideals according to opponents. The pressures towards conflict therefore fall hardest on the areas richest in natural resources – the 'resource curse' (Padel and Das, 2010: 343–347, 399–402; Padel et al., 2013: 92–96). This is why the mineral-, forest- and water-rich adivasi regions of central India are particularly affected, and what appears on the surface as an ideological conflict between Maoism and the mainstream is fundamentally a resource conflict.

Maoists are obviously correct in their critique of existing patterns of structural violence based on exploitation and dispossession. But perhaps they mirror the mainstream in more ways than they differ. Mao's 'Great Leap Forward' gave a blueprint for extremely rapid raising of a country's steel output, regardless of the human cost; the precise blueprint that defines today's trajectory in the resource-rich states of eastern central India where adivasis predominate. This is one reason why, whether or not reports of Maoists get a large proportion of their funding through covert payments from mining companies are true, we are unlikely to get a proper critique of the mining industry from the Maoists. Fundamentally, the Maoist ideology is based on the same materialist exploitation of resources as capitalism, and the same disregard for community well-being and natural systems, and arguably, a similar structural violence, which was certainly a characteristic of China under Mao.

Utsa Patnaik (2007: 115–121) has questioned whether Mao's 'Great Leap Forward' caused the massive mortality that a large range of scholars have established. While she is clearly right on the manipulation of poverty statistics in India and much more, the manipulation of statistics of steel production as well as deaths in Mao's China is attested from a huge range of sources; and the estimates of death through famine by a much larger range of authors than she names vary between 18 million and 46 million, making it almost certainly the world's worst famine (Mirsky, 2012, a review of Yang, 2012, whose estimate of the death toll is 36 million, based on research covering confidential official accounts of famine deaths and the killing of protesters). Mao showed no remorse for famine victims, making clear that he saw their deaths as an acceptable price for the socialist system he believed he was promoting (Li, 1994; Yang, 2012). His 'great sparrow campaign' during 1958–1960 incited the killing of sparrows and other small birds, blamed for eating grain. Killing these birds, that actually ate insect pests, upsets the ecological balance and was a factor in the locust swarms that contributed to China's famine. Like other famines, from Ireland in the 1840s to British India in the 19th century and early 1940s, to Ukraine under Stalin in the 1920s and numerous African famines, grain growing regions in China were forced to export their produce even as people were dying of starvation in large numbers, and anyone who questioned the Great Leap was punished severely, including Mao's former comrade Peng Dehuai in 1959. Mao's sparrow killing campaign, like his plan for the Three Gorges Dam (built years after his death), exemplifies the materialistic attitude to nature and blindness to ecosystems intrinsic to his ideology, at variance with many of the beautiful nature-centric aphorisms in his writings.

Middle Ground

Yet if the aim is to promote grassroots democracy in India's tribal areas, it also has to be admitted that many policies that India's Maoists have promoted are in accordance with the following: ensuring a fair price for forest produce and excluding middlemen, shutting down illegal liquor shops and confronting the liquor mafia, a democratic style of local meetings and organizations, with emphasis on women as men's equals (Navlakha, 2012).

When everyone admits that the PESA (Panchayat [Extension to Excluded Areas]) Act (1996) has not been properly implemented and is difficult to implement, surely the answer has to be finding middle ground with grassroots initiatives brought in by the Maoists, rather than trying to exterminate all trace of them.

The twin strategies of 'security' and 'development' in the Integrated Action Plan (IAP) for defeating the Maoists offer nothing new. 'Security' and 'development' for whom? Mass police deployment in dozens of areas to force through large-scale 'development' projects in the face of grassroots resistance shows that both concepts are in service to capitalist aims and against the interests of village communities. Moreover 30 crore for each Maoist-affected district under the IAP acts as an incentive towards conflict (Padel et al., 2013: 222–223). Odisha's Industrial Security Forces Act of 2012 shows how 'security' for big corporations is placed above the interests of workers as well as of communities threatened with displacement. In many ways, what the Maoists are opposing is a system of extreme capitalism, similar to and even much worse than the 19th century system that Marx analysed, while opposing the Maoist insurgency is the mask assumed by the mainstream in vastly expanding its security presence in rural areas.

In this context, how we are going to find middle ground and make peace attractive, especially for young people, who are getting drafted into security forces in large numbers or joining the Maoists? If the development process becomes mature, both sides will admit mistakes and search for middle ground based on the well-being of local citizens.

Middle ground also needs to be found between the interests of economy and ecology – two words derived from similar meanings that have become separated by an ideological wall. The concept of sustainable development attempts to link them. But in most definitions, when 'economy' is put first, ahead of 'society' and 'environment', this makes a nonsense out of the real meaning of sustainability, which is exemplified in how adivasi and other indigenous or tribal societies have sustained over centuries, basically by basing their economies on ecological principles of restraint in what is taken from nature. Markets and the economy surely need to be reconfigured as soon as possible to serve society rather than the other way round and to ensure the long-term health of the ecosystems that life depends on, rather than their rapid exhaustion.

Putting the economy first allows the concept of 'sustainable development' to be deployed in CSR schemes, advertised by PR firms in a way that makes a nonsense out of the concept, reducing it to mean development that can produce financial profit in the immediate future, with no long-term safeguards at all (Padel and Das, 2010: 539–545).

Truly sustainable development, rather than depleting natural resources drastically and masking this through 'greenwash', needs to start by learning from adivasi economic systems that emphasize cooperation and sharing, and restraint in what is taken from nature.

Rethinking Real Development

When the twelve Niyamgiri villages selected to hold gram sabhas according to the Supreme Court's Judgement in April 2013 voted unanimously against Vedanta's mining project, they also voted against receiving individual *patta* under the Forest

Rights Act, laying claim instead of communal traditional rights over the whole mountain – in line with the communal rather than private property based values that Marx and Engels highlighted in tribal societies.

Many in the mainstream equated mining with development. In February, Justice Gogol in the Supreme Court asked Sanjay Parikh, the lawyer representing the Dongria Konds, 'Why are you fighting shy of giving them development? Do you want them to lead a life of abject poverty for the next 100 years?' (Balaji, February 2013).

Dongria answered this question. As one of them said to a reporter after the vote:

> I produce enough to meet the needs of my 18-member family throughout the year and sell the surplus grain, vegetables and spices in the local market to earn ₹ 2,000 every week … . The mining will dry up the perennial streams coming down from the hills and irrigating our land throughout the year. (Satapathy, October 2013)

In many ways the Niyamgiri outcome represents real development, even though it contradicts the narrowly materialist concept of development promoted by the mining lobby. The functioning of the gram sabhas was overseen impartially by the Odisha government, and villagers made sure they were an expression of real grassroots democracy at work of the kind envisaged in legislation such as the PESA and Forest Rights Acts.

The above exchange shows how often people assume that traditional adivasi economies are 'uneconomic' and the cause of poverty, when very often the reverse is the case (Padel et al., 2013: xv–xx, 21–46). As a tribal group still in control of their natural resources, Dongria do not see themselves as living in poverty at all. They do not have or need modern 'conveniences' and look at the 'development' Vedanta has brought to the Lanjigarh area (where the alumina refinery was built from 2003 in defeated expectation of mining bauxite from Niyamgiri) with horror – hundreds of deaths in road and work accidents and from goondas, terrible pollution and police repression, and appalling condition of villagers who lost their lands or saw their water sources drying up and getting polluted.

Here in Lucknow people should know that development is not always in a single direction. In many ways, India in the 18th century was more highly developed than the British society, which imposed its rule through the East India Company. The British were more developed militarily, and in terms of manipulating law and finance to extend their conquests. But in terms of manufacturing skills, hygiene (the British did not even have the custom of daily baths!), sophistication of musical and many other aspects of culture and what today we call a multicultural society, India was far more developed than Britain, which only allowed Christians of certain denominations to hold high office. When the British took over more and more of India, including the kingdom of Awadh in 1856, they cut off indigenous lines of development. Manufacturing industries got gradually killed off that in quality were far beyond that of cloth or even coinage being produced in Britain and promoted in India.

Similarly, we are confident of the ways we are 'more developed' than tribal societies – in our technology above all, or literacy. But are we aware of areas where they are far more developed than us? This is based on the principle of sustainability and the knowledge of forest plants and natural species; on community spirit, which privileges sharing over competition, and the sense of democracy that accompanies this; on a system of law that seeks reconciliation rather than categorizing outcomes in terms of right and wrong, so that very often a case ends with both parties being fined which include paying for a feast to reconcile the contestants; on extremely highly developed systems of dance and song, and a religion that remains in control of communities rather than brahmin priests, and that promotes a sense of sacredness in nature.

It is not romanticizing tribal societies to say that they are already more highly developed than the mainstream in many areas of life and that displacement or invasion by 'development projects' undermines many years of development. Where we would all agree perhaps is that real development needs to ensure food and water security, justice, and work for everyone. Clearly these basic needs have not been taken care of by following the World Bank-dictated models of increasing economic growth, funding dams, and coal mines and displacing of vast majority of adivasis by dams, mining, and industrializing areas that have witnessed a drastic decline in their quality of life (CSE, 2008).

Real development will take place when an impartial rule of law is assured, so that adivasis and dalits can expect equality before the law in courts, with outcomes not dependent on lawyers' fees and no 'false cases' languishing in jails. At present, numerous 'false cases' slapped against adivasi and other protestors against imposed 'development projects' contrast with the impunity enjoyed by corporations that infringe the law, and by members of the security forces who commit rapes and other atrocities, including 'false encounters' (Iqbal, 2009; Padel, 2013; Shakil, 2013; Padel et al., 2013: 222–236).

Real development will take place if we, the human species, can develop to a stage that Abdullah Öcalan characterizes as a 'democratic civilization', based on an enduring peace and proper distribution of resources (Padel, 2012; Öcalan, 2012) – develop beyond the primitive urge to settle differences by war and to deplete the earth's remaining resources rapidly by using them to build weapons of mass destruction and fight each other (Padel, 2008; Klare, 2002).

So in many ways, India's indigenous movements against resource grabs by big corporations, protecting ecosystems at the same time as their own livelihoods, represent the cutting edge of development worldwide, in line with 'transition towns' in 'developed countries' that aim to reduce their carbon footprint, and an 'Economics of Happiness' (ISEC, 2013) based on a return to community and involvement in growing food.

References

Aneez, Shihar and Ranga Sirilal (7 April 2014). 'Sri Lanka Won't Cooperate UN War Crime Probe: Foreign Minister'. *Reuters*. Available at: http://www.reuters.com/article/2014/04/07/us-sri-lanka-un-rights-idUSBREA3616520140407

Balaji, R. (20 February 2013). '100 Year Poverty Poser on Vedanta'. *Telegraph*. Available at http://www.telegraphindia.com/1130221/jsp/nation/story_16587643.jsp

Bharadwaj, Sudha (2009). 'Gravest Displacement, Bravest Resistance: The Struggle of Adivasis of Bastar, Chhattisgarh against Imperialist Corporate Landgrabs'. *Sanhati.* 1 June. Available at http://sanhati.com/excerpted/1545/

BIRSA (2007). *Tata Landmines Adivasis.* Documentary. 18 September. Available at http://www.youtube.com/watch?v=Lj9 MAOqBFQw

Campaign for Peace and Justice in Chhattisgarh (CPJC) (August 2007). *Salwa Judum: Civil War in Chhattisgarh.* Delhi: CPJC.

Centre for Science and Environment (2008). *Rich Lands, Poor People: Is Sustainable Mining Possible?* Delhi: CSE.

Chakravarti, Sudeep (2008). *Red Sun: Travels in Naxalite Country.* Delhi: Viking/Penguin.

Chaudhury, Shoma (12 June 2010). 'Bringing on the Army against the Naxals Will Be a Disaster: Interview with E.N. Rammohan'. *Tehelka.* 7(23). Available at http://archive.tehelka. com/story_main45.asp?filename=Ne120610bringing_on.asp

Choudhury, Shubranshu (2012). *Let's Call Him Vasu: With the Maoists in Chhattisgarh.* Delhi: Penguin.

Esteva, Gustavo (1992). 'Development'. In Wolfgang Sachs (ed.) *The Development Dictionary: A Guide to Knowledge as Power* 6–25. London: Zed.

Feinstein, Andrew (2011). *Shadow World: Inside the Global Arms Trade.* London: Farrar, Straus and Giroux.

Herman, Edward S. (1983). *The Real Terror Network: Terrorism in Fact and Propaganda.* South End Press.

——. and Noam Chomsky (1988). *Manufacturing Consent: The Political Economy of the Mass Media.* New York: Pantheon Books.

Iqbal, Javed (2009). 'Rape as a Weapon of war'. *The New Indian Express.* 9 June. Available at http://moonchasing.wordpress.com/2010/06/09/rape-as-a-weapon-of-war/

International Society for Ecology and Culture (ISEC) (2013). *The Economics of Happiness.* Documentary. Available at http://www.theeconomicsofhappiness.org/

Klare, Michael T. (2002). *Resource Wars: The New Landscape of Global Conflict.* New York: Henry Holt and Co.

Klein, Naomi (2007). *The Shock Doctrine: The Rise of Disaster Capitalism.* New York: Metropolitan.

——. (10 April 2014). 'Why US Fracking Companies Are Licking Their Lips over Ukraine'. *The Guardian*. UK. Available at http://www.theguardian.com/commentisfree/2014/apr/10/us-fracking-companies-climate-change-crisis-shock-doctrine

Li, Zhisui (1994). *The Private Life of Chairman Mao*. London: Chatto and Windus.

Mamdani, Mahmood (2005). *Good Muslim, Bad Muslim: Islam, the USA and the Global War Against Terror*. Delhi: Permanent Black.

Mirsky, Johnathon (7 December 2012). 'Review of Jushen 2012'. *New York Times*. Available at http://www.nytimes.com/2012/12/09/books/review/tombstone-the-great-chinese-famine-1958-1962-by-yang-jisheng.html?_r=0

Navlakha, Gautam and Gupta, Ashish (28 August 2009). 'Bastar: The Real Divide behind the Impending Dirty War'. *Radical Notes*.

Navlakha, Gautam (2012). *Days and Nights in the Heartland of Rebellion*. Delhi: Penguin.

Öcalan, Abdullah (2012). *Prison Writings. The Road Map to Negotiations*. Translated by Havin Guneser. Cologne: International Initiatives.

Padel, Felix (2008). 'Mining as a Fuel for War'. *The Broken Rifle*. 77: 1. Available at www.wri-irg.org/node/3576

——. (2010). *Sacrificing People: Invasions of a Tribal Landscape*. Delhi: Orient BlackSwan.

——. (2012). 'Kurdish Quest of Countering Capitalism to Build a Democratic Civilisation'. Review of Abdullah Ocalan's Prison Wrings. *Economic and Political Weekly*. 13 October. Available at http:/peaceinkurdistancampaign.wordpress.com/resources/abdullah-ocalan/road-map/the-kurdish-quest-of-countering-capitalism-to-build-a-democratic-civilisation/

——. (2013). 'Rapists, Uniformed'. *Hard News*. February. Available at http://www.hardnewsmedia.com/2013/02/5804

——. and Das, Samarendra (2010). *Out of This Earth: East India Adivasis and the Aluminium Cartel*. Delhi: Orient BlackSwan.

Padel, Felix, Dandekar, Ajay and Unni, Jeemol (2013). *Ecology, Economy: Quest for a Socially Informed Connection*. Delhi: Orient BlackSwan.

Pandita, Rahul (2011). *Hello Bastar: The Untold Story of India's Maoist Movement*. Chennai: Tranquebar Press.

Patnaik, Utsa (2007). *The Republic of Hunger and Other Essays.* Delhi: Three Essays Collective.

People's Union of Civil Liberties (PUCL) (June 2006). *When a State Makes War on Its Own People: A Report on Violations of People's Rights During the Salwa Judum Campaign in Dantewada, Chhattisgarh.* Available at http://www.pucl.org/Topics/Human-rights/2006/slawajudum.htm

Pervez, Ayesha (2013). 'Securing Justice for Rape Survivors from Kashmir and Northeast Is an International Human Rights Crisis'. *Kafila.* Available at http://kafila.org/2013/10/15/securing-justice-for-rape-survivors-from-kashmir-and-northeast-is-an-international-human-rights-crisis/

Roy, Arundhati (2010). 'Walking with the Comrades'. *Outlook.* 29 March. Available at http://www.outlookindia.com/article.aspx?264738-1

Samadrusti (6 March 2010). 'LALA 76 – Weapon of Mass Repression'. Bhubaneswar: Samadrusti. Available at http://www.youtube.com/watch?v=LWob7fHKzLQ

——. (31 March 2010). 'Victims of Kalinga Nagar Attack'. Available at http://youtu.be/ePI50DbinDA

——. (2 April 2010). 'Police Firing in Kalinga Nagar'. Available at http://www.youtube.com/watch?v=ADUQQAn9zBA&feature=youtu.be

——. (27 April 2010). 'No One Here Gets Out Alive'. Available at http://youtu.be/eeYiHN7ZE4A

——. (14 May 2010). 'Chandia Police Firing'. 1–5. Available at http://youtu.be/1nwFbeX8JWc

Satapathy, Dilip (8 October 2013). 'Niyamraja's Subjects Won't Bow to Vedanta'. *Business India.* Available at http://www.business-standard.com/article/companies/niyamraja-s-subjects-won-t-bow-to-vedanta–113100800014_1.html

Scahill, Jeremy (2008). *Blackwater: The Rise of the World's Most Powerful Mercenary Army.* New York: Nation Books.

——. (2013). *Dirty Wars: The World Is a Battlefield.* New York: Nation Books.

Shakil, Marya (2013). 'Manipur: Almost All Encounters in the State Are Fake, says NHRC'. *IBN* 13 November. Available at http://ibnlive.in.com/news//manipur-almost-all-encounters-in-the-state-are-fake-says-nhrc/433823-3.html

Steele, Johnathon (2012). *Ghosts of Afghanistan: The Haunted Battleground.* London: Portobello.

Thapar, Romila (1961). *Asoka and the Decline of the Mauryas.* Delhi: Oxford University Press.

UN (April 2011). Report of the Secretary General's panel of experts on accountability in Sri Lanka. Available at www.un.org/News/dh/infocus/Sri_Lanka/POE_Report_Full.pdf

Yang, Jushen (2012). *Tombstone: The Great Chinese Famine, 1958–1962.* Translated by Stacy Mosher and Guo Jian. New York: Farrar, Straus and Giroux.

3

Terrorism Interrogated

Naxalism to Maoism[1]

PARTHA NATH MUKHERJI

Creating panic through terror is an age-old practice that has always been condemned by those who are at the receiving end. Acts of terror abound in present times. Are all acts of terror, terrorism? Terrorists are invariably clandestine operators. It is important to distinguish the motive or purpose behind the practice of terror.

My talk today is in three parts. In the first part, I shall deal at the general abstract conceptual level of the phenomenon of terrorism, and its relationship with social movements. This will be followed by a more specific analysis of the Naxalite Maoist movement. Finally, I shall conclude by touching base with my field in West Bengal where I grazed for a time before the landmines were laid!

Terrorism and Social Movement

Ronald Reagan hailed the Afghan mujahideens as freedom fighters in their war against the presence of Soviet forces in Afghan territory in the eighties. Two decades down the line when these mujahideens were at war with a regime installed by Western powers, George W. Bush condemned them as terrorists.[2]

Guest of Honour lecture delivered at the National Seminar on "Youth, Naxalism and Terrorism: The Politics of Development in Indian Sub-continent" organized by the P.G. Department of Sociology, Isabella Thoburn College, Lucknow in February 2014.

Numerous acts of violence by *Irgun*, the underground terrorist group led by Israeli leader Menachem Begin, and those led by the African National Congress (ANC) under Nelson Mandela, during their respective liberation struggles, were dubbed as terrorism. Liberation struggles are over, and they emerged triumphant as iconic freedom fighters and statesmen worthy of the world's most coveted Nobel Prize. Close to home, Bhagat Singh, Surjya Sen, Khudiram Bose, and many others were declared terrorists deserving the noose round their necks by the colonial British masters; today they live in the collective memory of the Indian nation as *shaheeds* (martyrs). It is not difficult to imagine that in the eyes of these martyrs, the colonial masters were the perpetrators of state terrorism. Whether it is the *jehadi, mujahideen*, or the *fedayeen*, or the Maoists, they and their targets describe each other as terrorists.[3] Who practices terrorism depends on which side you are on.

The point being made is: it has been impossible to arrive at a universally accepted definition of terrorism because 'One man's terrorist is another man's freedom fighter'.[4] The phenomenon of terrorism is made extremely complex by the high moral ground that is invoked for its application for a 'just cause'. The term is heavily value loaded, consequently, emotionally surcharged.

Prime among the common denominators of terrorism is physical violence, actual, or threatened, sometimes brute and heinous, and pre-planned and premeditated, that is intended to send a chilling, pulverizing message of fear and panic to the target population, for achieving political ends, not to be confused with stray violence associated with public protests. It is not difficult to imagine that such terrorist violence by any social movement on citizens will invite *counter measures* by the state. Both parties can get locked in a spiral of violence until one is vanquished or they reach a negotiated settlement. If defeat/withdrawal from the 'war' is not in sight for any group, it enters a phase of 'protracted conflict or war'.

In the absence of any agreed definition, let us just examine the one provided by Bruce Hoffman one of the leading specialists in the field:

By distinguishing terrorists from other types of criminals and terrorism from other forms of crime, we come to appreciate that terrorism is the deliberate creation and exploitation of fear through violence or the threat of violence in the pursuit of political change. All terrorist acts involve violence or the threat of violence. Terrorism is specifically designed to have far-reaching psychological effects beyond the immediate victim(s) or object of the terrorist attack. It is meant to instil fear within, and thereby intimidate, a wider 'target audience' that might include a rival ethnic or religious group, an entire country, a national government or political party, or public opinion in general. Terrorism is designed to create power where there is none or to consolidate power where there is very little. Through the publicity generated by their violence, terrorists seek to obtain the leverage, influence, and power they otherwise lack to effect political change on either a local or an international scale (Hoffman, 2006: 41).

The definition assumes that terrorism is practiced as a strategy or tactic by non-state actors for bringing about political change. It is silent on the possibility of counterterrorism by the victim-non-state actors or the state. As social scientists, how do we steer ourselves with our subjectivities, in the absence of an intersubjective conceptual definition of terrorism for an objective analysis and understanding of this phenomenon?

The way forward, it seems to me, lies in distinguishing between *acts of terror* committed by any group, and *terrorism* that relates to ideologically driven social or transformatory movements. Acts of terror are committed also by groups *independent* of any political objectives, not guided by any ideological persuasion.[5]

When a social movement *ideologically* perfects terrorist violence as a *tactical* or *strategic instrument* of *social* conflict and intended *change*, it espouses terrorism. Charu Mazumdar, the founder of the Communist Party of India (Marxist-Leninist), pronounced the doctrine of *annihilation of class enemies*. Thereby, terrorism became an integral part of the party ideology. This doctrine, subsequently, led to the split in the party with politburo members such as Kanu Sanyal and Satya Narain Sinha, deserting the party to found their own political revolutionary groups, abjuring the doctrine of annihilation of class enemies, but not necessarily the well-deliberated selective use of violence when deemed fit. What they shunned was 'Left adventurism'. Nonetheless, the challenge of the Left extremist movement that the nation faces today is in tune with the annihilation doctrine.

Terrorism that concern us here *could* be associated with liberation struggles, or the capture of state power by an ideologically committed revolutionary/secessionist movement (Maoist, Naga insurrectionary), or sub-state level autonomy movements (Gorkhaland, Bodoland, Telengana), or extreme radical ethnic chauvinistic movements, and the like. Such movements seek to bring about social changes or transformation related to the social system.

Axiomatically, social conflict is a necessary, not a sufficient condition for violence. For, social conflict is also a necessary condition for *non-violent* action (*satyagraha)*. At the same time, not all acts of violence need be terrorist violence.[6]

Social conflict, it should be obvious, is inseparable from some concept or notion of social structure/system, *from* which it is manifested, and *for* which it has consequences. I have defined social system as:

> a *system of social interaction* being constituted of interrelated and interpenetrating 'parts' (or structures), such that changes in any one or more of these will/can have consequences for one or more or all of the others. (Mukherji, 2013; 110)

Since inequality in any society is ubiquitous (except in utopia), society could be conceived of being constituted of interrelated and interpenetrating *relations of asymmetries*, such as *social discrimination* (ethnic: caste, tribal, religious, racial, etc.), *exploitation* (economic: unequal life chances, right to livelihood, better wages, public goods, food security, etc.), *oppression* (political: suppression, coercion, intimidation, threat to life and property, etc.), *gender discrimination*, *eco-environmental* degradation and denudation of natural resources, and so on. These, I prefer to label, *counter-concepts*. Embedded in these asymmetries are *social contradictions*, defined as:

> actual or potential oppositions arising out of differences that are socially perceived, sooner or later, and/or ideologically/theoretically constructed, having change/transformation (or resistance to

change/transformation) consequences for the social system under reference. (Mukherji, 2013: 120)

At the level of society, when contradictions become sharp and antagonistic, in any one or more of these relations of asymmetries, they trigger social conflict that *could* culminate into social mobilizations or ideologically driven social movements seeking change. The changes sought by a social movement may range from changes *within* the system or change *of* the system: from grievance-redressal at one end of the spectrum, to capture of state power for transforming the system itself, or to seek secession from society, and so on.

Social movements resort to *institutional* (democratically accredited: protest rallies, fasts, sit-ins [*dharnas*], etc.) or *non-institutional* (illegal: violence, guerrilla warfare, civil war, etc.) means in their pursuit of intended changes. Probability is high that changes *of* the system will involve non-institutional means, whether violent or non-violent. It makes good sense to analyse social conflicts and social movements from the broader perspective of nation state building. We must not lose sight of the fact that social movements could either be *change-promoting* or *change-resisting*.

The politics of development can be viewed as the role of institutional structures or social movements in their efforts to bring about societal development by a *reduction* in the relations of asymmetry. Such reduction is most likely to bring about greater *inclusiveness* in the process of development. Social movements, in general, claim their struggle is for *justice* and *equity*, howsoever perceived.

From Naxalism to Maoism

Very briefly, and only to provide a link with past, we may recall that the Naxalite movement owed its origin to the peasant uprising in Naxalbari, Khoribari, and Phansidewa areas of Siliguri subdivision of the Darjeeling district of West Bengal under the leadership of Charu Mazumdar, Kanu Sanyal, Jangal Santhal, and several others belonging to the then newly formed Communist Party of India, Marxist (CPM), in 1964.

Soon differences surfaced within CPM between the ultra-radical pro-Chinese faction and the moderates. The North

Bengal group broke away and spearheaded the Naxalbari peasant movement, and later formed the Communist Party of India Marxist-Leninist (or the CPI-ML) in April 1969. By 1973, the movement was check-mated by an aggressive policy of land reforms by the CPM in power in West Bengal. Thereafter, CPI-ML splintered into several incarnations of CPI-ML, some disavowing the doctrine of annihilation of class enemies, and others holding steadfast to it.

The politics of Naxalism, as it was called, found ready soil elsewhere, more particularly, in Bihar and Andhra Pradesh. In Bihar, the Maoist Communist Centre of India (MCCI, founded in 1975 in West Bengal) appropriated the dominant role; and in Andhra Pradesh, it was the Peoples War Group (PWG, founded in 1980) upholding Charu Mazumdar's ideological line. Both merged to form the Communist party of India Maoist (CPI-Maoist) on 21 September 2004. This helped the new formation to claim a greater share in the 'political' market for the Left extremist radicals.

I find it useful to distinguish between phase of Naxalism and the current phase of Maoism post-2004 merger. Until the merger, the Charu Mazumdar's doctrine of annihilation of class enemies could not dig itself in. It now maintains an aggressive and expansive continuity.

The spread of the Maoist movement has been phenomenal, and it is really difficult to assess with exactitude its magnitude and its variations from one region to the other. It would be a mistake to think that the movement is inflexible. It is because of its capacity to adapt and innovate that it is resilient. The Ministry of Home Affairs in March 2004 admitted that Maoism had spread its tentacles in '55 districts in 9 states, namely, Andhra Pradesh, Bihar, Maharashtra, Orissa, Madhya Pradesh, Chhattisgarh, Jharkhand, West Bengal, and Uttar Pradesh (Annual Report 2003–2004, Ministry of Home Affairs, 3). By December 2009, government acknowledged their presence in 223 districts in 20 states across the country ('Communist Party of India Maoist (CPI-M)', 10 June 2011). The Bureau of Police Research and Development indicated marginal shrinkage, territorially, with their presence in 191 districts in 21 states in 2011 (Bureau of Police Research and Development, 2011). From the borders of Nepal to the depths of Andhra Pradesh, this is the so-called *Red Corridor* (Chakravarty, 2008: 9).

The impressive geographic spread is no less matched by its level of recruitment. According to Home Ministry sources, Maoist activists in 2004, the year PWG and MCCI merged, was around 93,000 (Ministry of Home Affairs, *Annual Report 2004–2005*, Government of India, New Delhi, 3). One source claims their strength currently to be anywhere between 10,000 and 25,000 activists, 10,000 armed cadres, and 45,000 to 50,000 workers (Gera, 2009: 369). Yet another source puts the strength at 14,000 regular soldiers, with an unestimated number of semi-trained permanent cadres ('India's Naxalite Insurgency: Not a Dinner Party', *The Economist*, 25 February 2010). That is not the end. A third source has reason to believe that they have 40,000 permanent armed cadres and 100,000 'militia members' ('Communist Party of India – Maoist (CPI-M)', *Jane's World Insurgency and Terrorism*, 10 June 2011). What is a good going for the Maoists is bad augury for the state.

A territorially expansive Maoist party with an expanding recruitment of cadre-based and cadre-supported militia, determined to continue the process of liberating more and more areas from the state, with the intent of ultimately capturing state power, inflict repeated injury, and defeat its class enemies in a 'protracted war'. The class enemies include the security forces, government officials, and political party leaders in direct confrontation, informers, and the like.

The PWG attack on the life of the Chief Minister of Andhra Pradesh Chandrababu Naidu in 2003 was the first sensational operation to drive a sense of fear in the establishment and the people. The seriousness of the problem of Maoism will be obvious from Table 1.

Table 1

Casualties in Maoist Violence 2004–2010

Year	*Civilians*	*Security Personnel*	*Maoists*	*Total*	*Remarks*
2004				500	Failed negotiations between PWG and government; merger of MCCI and PWG.

Cont'd ...

... Cont'd

2005	230			700	Low intensity guerrilla war.
2006	1/3rd		<50%	500–750	Chhattisgarh most affected.
2007	240	218	192	650	Chhattisgarh PS attacked, arms seized, dozens killed. Maoists join hands in Nandigram in West Bengal. Salwa Judum formed.
2008	394	221	174	794	Penetration in 16 states.
2009	392	312	294	998	Maoists active in 180 districts across 10 states. 56 attacks by June. PM: 'deprived and alienated sections of the population' provide the backbone of the movement.
2010	600+	277	277	1,000+	Eastern Frontier Rifles camp attacked in Sealdah, 24 killed (WB); 74 CRPF ambushed and killed in Chhattisgarh; 50 killed in attack on security convoy; landmine blows up bus in Chhattisgarh; derailment of Kolkata-Mumbai Mail, 150 dead; 26 policemen killed in Chhattisgarh; attacked Jt. BSF-Police team, 5 dead; ambushed Jt. paramilitary in Bihar, 10 killed, 10 wounded, 4 prisoners of which 3 released; Chhattisgarh: killed 3 police, 4 hostages – all 4 released; border of Chhattisgarh and Maharashtra: landmine, 3 ITBP soldiers killed, 2 wounded; Chhattisgarh: killed and dismembered 10 policemen and 1 Sr. Officer; Chhattisgarh, blew up bridge killing 4 and wounding 5, targeted Nand Kumar Patel, Congress leader.
2013					Chhattisgarh: Congress convoy ambushed, killing Mahendra Karma, V.C. Shukla

Source: Compiled from: Wikipedia, the free encyclopaedia, Naxalite–Maoist insurgency, http://en.wikipedia.org/wiki/Naxalite%E2%80%93Maoist_insurgency.

According to official sources, 6,800 were killed in 16,500 violent incidents, during the first decade of 21st century (Annual Report 2003–2011, MOHA). By now, the number killed may have reached 10,000.

Terrorism affecting citizens invites countermeasures from the law and order machinery of the state. If the state finds it difficult to establish supremacy over the insurgents, who do not constitute a regular army, instead, adept in guerrilla warfare, it tends to adopt counterterrorism. The state finds itself in a quandary as it cannot engage in a war against its own people. Terrorism of the Maoists and that of the state result in collateral deaths of harmless civilians caught in the crossfires. Hapless civilians become the targets of suspicion and torture and are left with only one choice – to be with the Maoists or against them, cooperating with the government forces. Unfortunately, in this game of winning over non-partisan people, who have only one of the two options, it is the government that keeps losing out badly. This exposes a general lack in our police and administration (barring honourable exceptions), the sensitivities and values that are so essential in the law and order machinery. They continue to remain in the clutches of a colonial–feudal hangover. The entire dynamic tends to gloss over the most important question: why is the population alienated? How have the Maoists been able to get a foothold?

When the Maoists started playing tribals against tribals along class divisions, after an initial period of tribal bonhomie, *Salwa Judum* (literally, Peace March or Purification Hunt, initially a genuine tribal outburst against Maoists) was formed by the affected tribals to counter the Maoist design to divide them. The state in 2005 embarked on a legally, ethically, morally opportunistic, stratagem to convert the *Salwa Judum* into an adivasi vigilante front. It was swiftly appropriated by the government to be made into a handmaiden of the security forces. From amongst them, a cadre of special police officers (SPOs) was created overnight with meagre arms training. Supported by the security forces, they operated as vigilante groups – raping, torturing, plundering, and destroying tribal life and property supposedly under the influence of the Maoists. (*The Adivasis of Chhattisgarh: Victims of the Naxalite Movement and Salwa Judum Campaign*, New Delhi, Asian Centre for Human Rights, 17 March 2006: 4).

The panic created by them drove out thousands of tribals from their village homes into predetermined refugee shelters provided by the government. An estimated 50,000 were accommodated in these camps (Motlagh, 2008: 104). Some questioned the motive behind this operation: Was it to get the areas vacated for mining purposes for the benefit of the industrial class?

As the crescendo of protests by human rights activists and concerned citizens rose against the brutalities of the *Salwa Judum*, the Supreme Court taking cognizance of the creation of this organization declared it illegal and ordered its disarming.[7]

It is little wonder that Prime Minister Manmohan Singh on 13 April 2006 betrayed a sense of desperation when he made his oft-quoted statement: *It would not be an exaggeration to say that the problem of Naxalism is the single biggest internal security challenge ever faced by our country.* He had noted that large parts of 160 out of 602 districts in the country were affected by the Maoist movement (Prime Minister's speech at the 2nd meeting of the Standing Committee of the Chief Ministers on Naxalism, 13 April 2006). According to an observer, Maoism is 'one of the biggest internal armed conflicts in the world (cited in Saboor, 2011: 33; Bendfeldt, 2010: 37).

To combat the mounting threat of Maoist terrorism, there evolved efforts to face the challenge. The special 'Greyhound' force mimicking guerrilla war came up in Andhra Pradesh, Central Paramilitary Forces (CPMFs), Commando Battalions for Resolute Action (COBRA), Indian Reserve (IR) battalions, and others got lined up to face the Maoist 'menace' (Annual Report 2010–2011, MOH: 24–25). Some states such as Bihar and West Bengal did not see eye to eye with the centre's perspective of predominant law and order solution. The party had been banned by the centre under the Unlawful Activities (Prevention) Act (UAPA) since 22 June 2009, declaring it a terrorist organization (Wikipedia, Communist Party of India [Maoist].

The situation, in fact, kept on worsening, and the writ was clear that mere law and order approach of establishing the superiority of white terror over red terror did not fit into the scheme of things. The incidents in 2010 sent the wake-up call. A whole contingent of CRPF was simply wiped off sending shivers in the spine of the security apparatus (6 April 2010). In a state of panic, the then Home Minster, Chidambaram, was contemplating unmanned aerial surveillance with drones, and air power support!

At this point, from within the Congress Party, senior leader Digvijay Singh, who belongs to that area, rubbished the Home Ministry move; 'He (Chidambaram) is treating (this) purely as a law and order problem without taking into consideration the issues that affect the tribals', Singh wrote in a newspaper column. 'We can't solve this problem by ignoring the hopes and aspirations of the people living in these areas' ('Massacre Pushes Maoists to Top of Indian Agenda', 16 April 2010). There are now a spate of development programmes that have either come up or are in the offing designed to bring development to Maoist-affected areas. They range from skill development initiatives for employment generation from the Ministry of Rural Development, to setting up of development authorities in affected areas in some states, to work out development projects according to the needs of the people. Prime Minister is keen that the panchayats are brought into the picture.[8]

In the *liberated* zones, the Maoists have established the trappings of a quasi-sovereign state. Revenue can be collected through taxes, extortions, and cultivation of herbs and plants (poppies, opium, and hemp) for production of contraband drugs; recruitment to the militia is by consent or coercion (demand on each family to contribute a family member); arms can be manufactured locally or procured or captured; educational and health needs are attended to at whatever level; justice, rough and ready, is provided by *kangaroo* courts, that follow no principles of jurisprudence.[9] According to a conservative estimate by the Institute for Defence Studies and Analyses in February 2014, their annual revenue was more than 140 crore. Their estimate and sources of revenue are described as follows:

> The Maoists have been collecting not less than ₹ 140 crore annually from a variety of sources: businesses – big and small – industry, contractors engaged in various trades, corrupt government officials, and political leaders. The largest and principal sources of income for the Maoists are mining industry, PWD works, and collection of tendu leaves. The Maoists have been able to put in place a well-organized mechanism to extort

> money on a regular basis. Besides, they have conceived ingenious ways to store money and ensure its safety. Even as they have issued guidelines for the collection of money, the Maoists have, similarly, also circulated guidelines on expenditure and maintaining fiscal discipline. (Ramana, 2014: 2–3)

Terrorism and its Justification

It will be obvious whether it is the Maoists driven by the fire of revolutionary zeal to bring about just social order or the state that is obliged to guarantee human security, good governance, and orderly and inclusive development. Although there may be justification for each other's position from their respective viewpoints, it is equally important that neither can be perfectly just. If the concept of development is premised on freedom and social justice, apart from equity and inclusiveness in the life chances, it is a moot question whether the Maoist movement fulfils some of the fundamental criteria of development. Likewise, if a democratic state lags behind in its obligation to provide distributive justice to large populations and fails in its role in providing equality of opportunity for access to quality education and health, thereby marginalizing large populations and making them a prey to exploitation, the blame, no less, should fall on the state for having provided space for ideologically driven terrorism by default.

How to View the Challenge

The sudden, rapid, and forceful recent surge in Maoist movement has come as shock to those who believe in a liberal democratic nation state, and as a surprise to those spearheading the movement, and even those who justify or rationalize or empathize with them. The movement seeks to *replace* the liberal bourgeois democratic nation state with a centralized Marxist-Leninist Communist party-directed 'people's democratic' nation state.[10] However far-fetched this dream may appear, it has forced the country to enter into a compulsive discourse and deliberative action on the paradigm of development and the grave shortcomings of governance. From the Prime Minister, the Home Minister all along the line, to almost all sections of the population, including NGOs are inescapably in an interrogative mode.

Such is the nature and gravity of the predicament that differences in views and opinions have cut across ruling party lines. The erstwhile Home Minister (P. Chidambaram) had articulated the government policy the essence of which was: (a) the Maoist objective is the armed seizure of power of the state by the Peoples Liberation Guerrilla Army which then would convert into the People's Liberation Army once the objective is achieved. This no state can accept much less the Indian state. The government had neither termed the Maoists as 'enemies', nor did it describe the situation as that of 'war' between them. The door for dialogues is open provided the Maoists abjure violence. (b) The strategic task of the security forces was to progressively clear one area after another under Maoist control creating an environment for development and follow it up by injecting resources for development of the people of the area. (c) The states have the primary responsibility of combating Maoists; and this has to be done by a policy of development and calibrated police action (*Hindustan Times*, 2010).[11]

I have already drawn attention to the cryptic criticism of the Home Minister by the Congress leader Digvijay Singh. The criticism within the Congress got further aired by the Congress leader K. Keshava Rao, Member of Rajya Sabha and AICC-in-charge Naxal-affected areas in Jharkhand and West Bengal. He stated that Naxals were not enemies but friends with whom talks were important to tackle the 'ugly face of our distributive justice'. The Minister of Minority Affairs Salman Khurshid expressed the strong apprehension that if socio-economic issues of the tribals were not given urgent priority then 'tomorrow we may have to face it in 400 districts'. The senior party leader Mani Shankar Aiyar was also reportedly not happy with the strategies of Home Ministry (outlookindia.com, 16 April 2010).[12]

Mamata Banerjee, the then Railway Minister, as a constituent coalition party in the central government (TMC) at that time had gone to the absurd extreme of vehemently denying the presence of any Maoist in West Bengal, consequently deploring the deployment of central forces in her state (*The Hindu*, 15 April 2010)![13] Nitish Kumar, Chief Minister of Bihar, was very much out of tune with the Home Minister, pressing for 'direct talks' with the Maoists (*Press Trust of India*, 16 April 2010).[14] Shibu Soren, the then Chief Minister of Jharkhand, appeared hardly enthusiastic about the armed intervention by the state on such a scale. Add to this the multitude of views from the NGOs and iconic activists. Clearly, the nation was confused in a fundamental sense, perhaps for the first time since independence, as the basic structure of our democracy crafted by our founding fathers of the nation was under serious trial. How then do we respond to the challenge of Maoist violence?

I have argued that social movements are conflicts that point to the contradictions within the society. It sets in motion a dialectical process that leads to its reasonable, if not complete, resolution. Social movements by the dalits, backward castes, women, environmentalists, peasants and farmers, and others have projected issues that otherwise would have, most likely, remained unattended with the seriousness they deserved. It is not possible for our democratic institutions to circumscribe and comprehend all the complexities of the world's most heterogeneous, plural society, and polity. Hence, social movements constitute an essential aspect of nation state building, which is a never-ending process.

The problem arises when a social movement seeks a change *of* the system and not just *in* the system. This amounts to a transformatory change involving *replacement* of the existing set of political and social institutions with alternative ones. A comprehensive replacement of major societal institutions constitutes a revolutionary agenda. In short, it would mean aiming to scrap the existing Constitution and replacing it with a different one. Obviously, the transformation envisaged is so far-reaching and radical that it questions the very existence of state in its present form. The confrontation takes the form of movement versus the state. This invokes the *legitimate* use of force by the state to protect its overthrow. It also raises the question of the *means* by which such a revolutionary transformation is envisaged. The means adopted could be non-violent (in the Gandhian mode) or violent (in the Maoist mode). Historically, both are accredited methods and have met with successes and failures, particularly in terms of sustainability if the movement succeeded. Hence, even if not constitutionally legitimate, the Maoist movement can claim a certain legitimacy from history.

Given this framework, it follows that the Maoist movement is a product of the large-scale disaffection and alienation among rural people, particularly among tribal communities, that lie embedded in the agrarian and other contradictions. It would, however, be simplistic to think that tribals form the wider base of the movement. If 220 districts covering 40 per cent of the land area are today under the complete or partial grip of the Maoists, with the tribals constituting only 8 per cent of the population, there is no mistaking that the movement has spilled over large areas of non-tribal populations as well. Whether the numerical support of the inhabitants in the Maoist-dominated areas is voluntary is a big empirical question.

The reasons for alienation of the people, especially the tribal population, in the movement-affected areas are well known and can be briefly recapitulated. For decades after independence, the tribal people have been a prey of rapacious, usurious landlord cum moneylenders. When that got under control, even if very late after much damage had been done, they became victims, of eviction from their own lands and forests in the 'cause' of economic development. Forests that were there from time immemorial became 'reserved'. Corrupt governance denied them a stake in the fair share in the distributive justice. They suffered the ignominy of being treated as cultural inferiors, as lesser humans. The cumulative effect of these and other factors have led to their disempowered condition in an unfriendly environment of structural violence.

These objective conditions by themselves do not provide sufficient reasons for an *insurrectionary* mobilization. This was provided by the organization and leadership of a radical Maoist party, predominantly non-tribal, that promised the emancipation of the masses from oppression through the capture of state power *after* the successful outcome of an indefinite violent protracted war with the state.

Whether we like it or not, no state will accept its own demolition in an insurrectionary war nor will it allow the coexistence of a sovereign space within its territory which allows insurrectionary strength to swell. Only after the state is vanquished can the rules of the game governing the new state be admitted. Alternatively, the state will be able to move to a new threshold after having overcome the insurrection through a satisfactory resolution of the contradictions that caused it.

The debate on which should command priority 'law and order' or 'development issues' is like a 'chicken and egg' argument. If ground realities are to be taken into account, there is no immanent law or principle that one should follow the other. In large areas of 'liberated zones' fully under military command of the insurgents, anyone can guess who will reap the political benefit of the state largesse to the people. It may amount to state support to insurgency. In the other situation, surely, all-round development of the region cannot but be of the highest priority.

Ground Realities in Lalgarh

In the concluding section, I will share my fieldwork experience in Lalgarh, known as the Junglemahal area of West Bengal to examine how policy pronouncements at the top relate to the ground realities. 'We are not fighting a war against an enemy' is our pronounced policy. Yet in Lalgarh, at that time the central security forces were sent to control the situation, the Santhal tribal could very well plead with the security personnel, 'I am a Santhal; I am not a terrorist'. In the eyes of the security forces, every Santhal *was* a real or potential terrorist, hence not to be trusted.

While this suspicion perhaps cannot be totally rooted out, what can happen is the manner in which this can be handled. I shall cite three empirical illustrations that were related to me by a knowledgeable person to make my point.[15]

1. Around 10/11 April 2010, in a place close to Sealdah, a marriage *barat* party of 35 persons were accosted by the security forces (*Jautha Bahini*, henceforward JB) when it was on its way to the venue of the marriage. They were not only physically thrashed (*dholai*) but rounded up and taken to the police lock-up, where they were again beaten up with *lathis*, not sparing women and children. One of the women succumbed to the injuries within a few days. The marriage was called off by the bride's party.

2. Around 17 April, in the Lalgarh (Bamal village) under Jhargram police station areas (Shirsi and Brindabanpur villages) the JB began lining up all the villagers outside their homes and then intimidating them with dire warnings if they did not come out with leads on Maoists. On one of these occasions, the local police was asked by the leader of the central forces to hit them painfully hard with lathis one after another. The local policeman finding the operation too harsh to follow was using the *danda/lathi* somewhat mildly on them. Impatient and dissatisfied, the security personnel wrenched the lathi from the local policeman and showered him (the local policeman) with a sample of hard blows to demonstrate how hard the hits should be.
3. On the 20 April, in Gamar village under Lalgarh police station the village folk had congregated for *haribasar kirtan*. The security forces came and beat them up to disband them.

On the one hand, civil administration was virtually taken over by the JB; on the other, Maoists found it fertile soil for recruitment. While Maoists promised to look after them, they would not brook any suspicion of betrayal and would not hesitate to kill, or destroy property with vengeance. It was said that day-long firing would be exchanged between Maoists and the 1,000 strong security, from safe havens with surprisingly no casualties on either side! It was openly rumoured that the CPM cadres were fighting side by side with the security forces.

The ground realities indicate that there was hardly any social, cultural, and democratic space remaining. Tribal people in the Maoist-affected parts could not participate in religious, cultural, and life cycle events. If they cooperated with the JB, they would pay with their lives as informers by the Maoists; if they wished to maintain a non-political, non-partisan existence, the space was closed. If the Maoists visited them at the dead of night demanding hospitality using arms, they had no choice. If the JB got the wind of the nocturnal visit, the family would be considered as an informer of Maoist and would be in trouble. The JB, it was said, ruled during the day, and the Maoists during the night. Children were losing out on education that could further retard their life chances in the market. How then were the adivasis surviving, suffocated and asphyxiated by circumstances beyond their control?

The prospect of Maoists overthrowing the Indian state seems unlikely. The obverse, the state overcoming the Maoists, in the long run, sounds more plausible. It is possible that a dialectical resolution may take place in the unforeseeable future. All said and done, checks and balances in the democratic polity has the capacity to restrain the excesses of the state from within. Further, the state is in a position to tackle the contradictions that gave space to the Maoist movement. For this the adivasis have to be given their rightful place in the development paradigm. In contrast, Maoists under a strict and ruthless authoritarian insecure regime can brook no opposition and must have to curtail freedom of speech and action of its people. This situation, in an environment in which the electorate has tasted the power to overthrow the most powerful politicians and their parties, is very likely to catch up with the adivasis under a dictatorial regime.

What we are witnessing is how the nation state is able to respond to a variety of social movements – gender-based, class-based, ethnic-based, against oppression, and so on for inclusive development – in its efforts to galvanize its democratic developmental frame. The critical question posed by Jean Dreze and Amartya Sen is: Are we basking in uncertain glory? Can we not expect the national and state governments in power to be able to pursue this contradiction with alacrity, firmness, empathy, and a mature policy towards an alienated tribal citizenry, who have far too long been subjected to exploitation and oppression?

Notes

1. Paper presented at the National Seminar on Youth, Naxalism and Terrorism: The Politics of Development, organized by the Department of Sociology, Isabella Thoburn College, Lucknow, 21 February 2014.
2. Speech of Ronald Reagan at the National Conservative Political Action Conference, 8 March 1985. On the Spartacus Educational web site. 'An unbiased look at terrorism in

Afghanistan (in 2009) reveals that many of these "terrorists" individuals or groups were once "freedom fighters" struggling against the Soviets during the 1980s'. [Chouvy, Pierre-Arnaud (2009), *Opium: Uncovering the Politics of the Poppy* (illustrated, reprint ed.) Harvard University Press, P. 119].

3. The types of terrorism listed in Wikipedia are: political, sub-state, social revolutionary, nationalist-separatist, religious-extremist, religious fundamentalist, Right-wing, Left-wing, single-issue, state-sponsored, regime or state, criminal, pathological terrorism (Terrorism: http://en.wikipedia.org/wiki/Terrorism).
4. Humphreys, Adrian (17 January 2006). 'One Official's "Refugee" Is Another's "Terrorist". *National Post.*
5. For example, terrorist acts are practiced by criminal organizations, such as the *mafias* who wish to carry on illicit mining (as in Karnataka) or illicit trade involving trafficking in women, or in smuggling of contrabands (across international borders), and the like. The purpose is to neutralize through fear any attempt at exposing their criminal activities and intents. These phenomena are not within our scope. This is primarily the concern of the criminal justice system.
6. For example, vandalism resulting in damage to public property during a protest demonstration.
7. The Supreme Court has declared as illegal and unconstitutional the deployment of tribal youths as special police officers – either as 'Koya Commandos', *Salwa Judum*, or any other force – in the fight against the Maoist insurgency and ordered their immediate disarming. Supreme Court judgment in *Salwa* Judum case, *The Hindu*, 6 July 2011. Available at: http://www.thehindu.com/news/resources/supreme-court-judgment-in-salwa-judum-case/article2185766.ece (Accessed on 27 February 2014).
8. See 'Special Skill Development Scheme for Maoist Areas'. Available at: http://www.sarkaritel.com/special-skill-development-scheme-for-maoist-areas/28471/ (Accessed on 18 February 2014).
9. Home Minister P. Chidambaram reported the execution of 21 people by Kangaroo Courts in 2010 (*Times of India*, 2 October 2010).

10. Planning Commissions Expert Group on Extremist Affected Areas in Central Belt of India in its report dated April 2008 recorded 125 districts in which political radicalism prevailed; *BBC News* dated 15 September 2009 stated, '[t]he rebels operate in 182 districts in India, mainly in the states of Jharkhand, Bihar, Andhra Pradesh, Chhattisgarh, Madhya Pradesh, Maharashtra and West Bengal'. Available at: http://news.bbc.co.uk/2/hi/south_asia/8256692.stm); Wikipedia gives the latest situation: '[a]s of 2009, Naxalites are active across approximately 220 districts in twenty states of India accounting for about 40 per cent of India's geographical area'. Available at: http://en.wikipedia.org/wiki/Naxalite-Maoist_insurgency.
11. The *TOI*. 15 April 2010. Available at: http://timesofindia.indiatimes.com/india/States-have-primary-role-in-fighting-Maoists-Chidambaram/articleshow/5811558.cms ?
12. Outlookindia.com. 16 April 2010. http://news.outlookindia.com/item.aspx?679588
13. *The Hindu*. 15 April 2010. http://www.thehindu.com/2010/04/15/stories/2010041561791300.htm
14. 16 April 2010. http://www.ptinews.com/news/612417_Centre-should-have-direct-talks-with-states—Nitish
15. No names have been recorded to keep the anonymity of individuals and groups, official or informal.

References

'The Adivasis of Chhattisgarh: Victims of the Naxalite movement and Salwa Judum campaign, New Delhi'. Asian Centre for Human Rights. 17 March 2006. 4.

'Annual Report 2003–2004'. Ministry of Home Affairs. New Delhi: Government of India.

'Annual Report 2003–2011'. Ministry of Home Affairs. New Delhi: Government of India.

'Annual Report 2010–2011'. Ministry of Home Affairs. New Delhi: Government of India.

Bendfeldt, Lennart (July 2010). Heinrich Boll Stiftung India. 1–40.

Bureau of Police Research and Development (2011). *Executive Summary: Genesis and Spread of Maoist Violence and Appropriate State Strategy to Handle It*. Ministry of Home Affairs. New Delhi: Government of India.

Chakravarty, Sudeep (2008). *Red Sun: Travels in Naxalite Country*. Delhi: Penguin Viking.

Chidambaram, P. (15 April 2010). *The Times of India*. Available at: http://timesofindia.indiatimes.com/india/States-have-primary-role-in-fighting-Maoists-Chidambaram/articleshow/5811558.cms

Communist Party of India–Maoist (CPI-M) (2011). *Jane's World Insurgency and Terrorism*. 10 June 2011.

Gera, Y.K. (July–September 2009). 'Naxalism: A Threat to India's Security'. *United Service Institution of India Journal*. 139(577): 365–377.

The Hindu, 15 April 2010, http://www.thehindu.com/2010/04/15/stories/2010041561791300.htm

Hoffman, Bruce (2006). *Inside Terrorism* (2nd ed.). Columbia University Press.

'India's Naxalite Insurgency: Not a Dinner Party', 25 February 2010, *The Economist*.

Motlagh, Jason (Summer 2008). 'The Maoists in the Forest: Tracking India's Separatist Rebels'. *The Virginia Quarterly Review*. 84(3): 102–129.

'Massacre Pushes Maoists to Top of Indian Agenda', *FT.COM UK*, 16 April 2010. Available at: http://www.ft.com/cms/s/0/447c4e8c–48ef–11df–8af4–00144feab49a.html (Accessed on 17 April 2010).

Mukherji, Partha N. (2013). 'Conceptual-Theoretical Re-orientation in Social Movement Discourse'. *Asian Journal of Social Science*. 41: 105–125.

outlookindia.com (16 April 2010). Available at: http://news.outlookindia.com/item.aspx?679588

Press Trust of India (16 April 2010). http://www.ptinews.com/news/612417_Centre-should-have-direct-talks-with-states—Nitish

Prime Minister's speech at the 2nd meeting of the Standing Committee of the Chief Ministers on Naxalism, Government of India Press Information Bureau, 13 April 2006.

Ramana, P.V. (2014). 'IDSA COMMENT: Maoist Finances: Sources, Methods of Collection and Utilization'. 17 February. Available at: http://www.idsa.in/idsacomments/MaoistFinances_pvramana_170214 (Accessed on 8 May 2014).

'Supreme Court Judgment in Salwa Judum Case'. *The Hindu* (6 July 2011). Available at: http://www.thehindu.com/news/resources/supreme-court-judgment-in-salwa-judum-case/article2185766.ece (Accessed on 27 February 2014).

Wikipedia. Communist Party of India (Maoist). http://en.wikipedia.org/wiki/Communist_Party_of_India_(Maoist) (Accessed on 8 May 2014).

Zaman, Saboor (Commodore Pakistan Navy) (2011). 'Naxalism: A Drag on India's Quest for Great Power Status'. Paper developed at the Defence and Strategic Studies Course at the Centre for Defence and Strategic Studies. 46. Australian Defence College. http://www.defence.gov.au/adc/publications/publications.html

4

Social Roots of Terrorism

A Critical Appraisal of Maoist Movement in India

BISWAJIT GHOSH

There has been rising trend of secessionist movements, terrorism, and armed conflicts across societies and countries in the contemporary world. This chapter, based on a review of relevant literature, seeks to explain the conditions that seem to promote terrorism particularly in the context of Maoist movement in India. Though the term 'terrorism' is defined differently in different contexts, for the purpose of this chapter, I would like to define it as a unlawful use of violence that seeks to kill people, destroy property and create fear for religious, political, or ideological purposes having far-reaching repercussions beyond the immediate victim or target. Those identified as 'terrorists' may also be called as separatist, freedom fighters, revolutionary, militant, guerrilla, or rebel by others depending on the context in which the person's role is analysed. But the essential differences among these groups should not evade out attention. Thus, both the Maoist and the secessionists take recourse to violence, spread terror; but while the Maoists are basically anti-capitalistic, the secessionists are anti-national. While individuals or group may rely on the tactic of terror, the state very often perpetuates reign of terror on the members of a community, group, or nation. Due to such contrasting yardsticks to judge an act of terror, terrorism is often labelled as justified means to seek an end. Hence, the decision to call or label someone including the Maoists as 'terrorist' becomes a subjective one.

It is therefore very difficult to define 'terrorism' as plenty of definitions exist and the word is also politically loaded and emotionally charged (Schmid and Albert, 1988). The only general characteristic of terrorism generally agreed upon is that terrorism involves violence and the threat of violence. Many of the terrorist outfits however have clearly defined political aims. The Maoists in India, for instance, want to challenge and replace the repressive state including annihilation of class enemies (Nigam, 2010). But, some of such outfits went for violent confrontation or use of terror tactics only at a later phase when the alternative line of action such as mass mobilization became redundant or when the Maoist became confident about challenging the state. For instance, the Maoist in Bihar depended on mass mobilization of dalits in the 1980s and the Mazdoor Kisan Sangram Samiti (MKSS), a Maoist mass front, carried out the task. But, in the 1990s, with shrinking space for such mobilization, the Maoist became increasingly reliant on armed actions (Shah and Pettigrew, 2009). Consequently, the Government of India has banned the Maoist as 'terrorists' only in May 2009. Also in the case of Nepal, the Maoists went for violent confrontation only after 2001, and later they also shunned such tactics and joined the democratic path. From such point of view, the production of 'red terror' appears to be a specific strategy that the Maoists use in a particular context (Lecomte-Tilouine, 2004). The major reasons for such a dynamic trajectory are (a) nature of leadership, (b) focus of the movement, (c) support base and strength, (d) opposition from private militia formed by higher caste, (e) success of armed struggle (in Nepal), and (f) state reaction or repression of democratic movements. If terrorism is only a means and not an end in itself, we also need to examine the reflexive character of the process in order to determine its true character.

Depending on the agenda and participants of any terrorist group, terrorism may be classified as political terrorism, nationalist-separatist terrorism, religious extremist terrorism, Right-wing terrorism, Left-wing terrorism, state-sponsored terrorism, and so on. There are however instances of Maoists changing their political colour by switching over to democratic processes. It therefore appears that 'terrorist acts are not committed in a social vacuum. Terrorists are emergent of the social processes' (Gondane, 2006: 3). It is influenced, encouraged, and caused by interaction between the individual, society, and the state. Social disintegration can alienate individuals and groups to such an extent that terrorism is seen as an available and expedient recourse to address their grievances. For this reason, 'terrorism cannot be addressed exclusively as a military or political problem, but rather must be confronted on a societal level as well' (Gondane, 2006: 26).

Growth and Spread of Maoism in India

The Maoist movement traces its origin to a place called Naxalbari in the Darjeeling district of West Bengal and thereby 'Naxalite movement' came into existence when a group of revolutionaries separated themselves from the then 'reformist' communist parties and launched an armed uprising of peasants against the landlords in May 1967. It spread quickly into parts of Bihar, Srikakulam District of Andhra Pradesh, Koraput in Orissa, and some other areas where guerrilla squad of poor and landless peasants drove the landlords away. In many cases, this movement degenerated into indiscriminate killing and violence (Harris, 2010: 8). It therefore met with matching violence from the state. Many Naxalite cadres then gave up their revolutionary dreams while others went underground to undertake grassroots mobilization. The Maoist subsequently got divided into several factions by 1971 on ideological, tactical, and regional grounds.

In the 1980s, which is argued to be the second phase of the movement (Banerjee, 2006), some survivors of the first phase started rethinking. Participation in parliamentary politics and trade union activity then became the possible path for them. Leaders such as Shankar Guha Niyogi and A.K. Roy build up a new tradition of social unionism within the political tradition of Maoism. Some, however, favoured a mixture of the line of armed struggle with mass mobilization through open fronts. These Maoists became successful in building a 'red corridor' over a huge geographical region that covers parts of states such as Andhra Pradesh, Bihar, Chhattisgarh, Jharkhand, Madhya Pradesh, Odisha, Uttar Pradesh, and West Bengal by the end of the decade.

In the third phase, in 2004, leaders of scattered and divided fractions of Maoist could create a single revolutionary party, the CPI (Maoist). The example of the Nepali Maoist could have influenced them towards such unification. Similarity in the objective situation, that is the negative consequences of the neo-liberal policy of the Indian state and displacement/marginalization of a large number of adivasis and dalits might also have been a factor. The movement then became able to make significant progress to be declared the 'single biggest security threat' the country has ever faced. Following such announcement, the country witnessed the beginning of a serious offensive in an unprecedented scale by armed forces and specially trained police to wipe out the Maoist. In the fourth phase, since 2009, the state's counterinsurgency initiatives have forced the Maoist movement to retreat and contract.

Though it is very difficult to suggest a clear cut genealogy of Maoism in India due to claims and counter claims, this brief depiction so far proves that the Maoist movement has taken several trajectories and shades over the years and despite certain declared uniformity they continue to differ on ideological and strategic issues. Retreat and disintegration have been a common story of the Maoists (Banaji, 2010: 138). Even during the early days, the Central Committee of the CPI (ML) expelled its founder Charu Mazumder from the party in 1971. Because it was thought that without mass struggle and mass organization, the peasants' armed struggle cannot be sustained. It is therefore hard to put the 'terrorist' tag on each and every Maoist. But at the same time, protest movement through mass mobilization as well as immediate socio-economic issues of the masses 'take a back seat' once the agenda of battle of supremacy with the state become central (Balagopal, 2006). We need to understand this dynamics to evaluate social-political movements such as Maoism in India.

Necessary and Sufficient Conditions

A review of relevant literature in the field suggests that the conditions that seem to promote conflictual group mobilization in the world today are diverse. It is true that questions regarding development remains at the centre point of any debate on anti-state movement. I call them 'necessary condition' that plays a critical role in explaining the origin of many social movements (Ghosh, 2003). The necessary conditions include several socio-economic factors such as demographic compulsions, cultural deprivation, poverty, land alienation and eviction, unemployment and underdevelopment, and so on. Despite being important, however, they alone cannot explain the rise and sustenance of armed conflict in many parts of South Asia. One, therefore, needs to go beyond the conventional models to explain the phenomenon and look for alternative conditions that I term as 'sufficient conditions'. These conditions include an acute sense of discrimination among the youth in particular, emergence of a strong elite leadership, political interest and manipulation, state policies and actions, easy accessibility to external support and geographical location.

So far as the question of Maoism is concerned, it is often argued that the movement has flourished due to a 'development gap' between the backward regions domesticated by the tribals and dalits and the developed regions of the country. The necessary postulate that results out of such argument is that Maoist will find it difficult to sustain if this 'gap' is bridged. Impressed by such logic, the Government of India and the affected state governments have announced a number of developmental projects. There is no doubt about the fact that backward regions of the country need special attention and there are also instances where Maoist movement has become considerably weak after positive intervention by the state. But, there are also contrary instance to prove that despite 'development', Maoism did not die a natural death in the area. The main reason for this lies in the fact that issues of public aggression are not only socio-economic or 'necessary conditions' but also 'sufficient conditions' such as quality of governance, state repression, political interests, geo-political constraints and outside support also determine the continuity and sustenance of a movement.

Let me cite some examples to explain the issue here. Thus, despite Maoist polemics, issues concerning the tribals of the Naxal-affected Malkangiri district of Odisha are not *jal, jungle, and zamin* (water, forests, and land). Rather it is decades of sheer administrative apathy that have offered an open space to the Maoist. Many key positions of the district administration have been lying vacant for several years resulting in poor implementation of the central government's fund and schemes of development. The case of Saranda forest of West Singhbhum district is another example. The area was 'freed' from the Maoist control in August 2011. But, subsequently the failure of Saranda Development Plan again led to the growth of discontent and antagonism (Nayak and Pradhan, 2014).

Research findings of many other scholars point out that we need to contextualize violent movement by regions as areas with better records of development also witness the growth of terrorist activities as compared to less developed districts. For instance, Bundelkhand is a backward district of Uttar Pradesh (UP) as compared to Chandauli. But, surprisingly, due to interplay of certain sufficient conditions, Chandauli is affected by extremism and not Bundelkhand. Again, the statistics in UP government suggest that eastern Uttar Pradesh is the most backward region in the state. But, it is mainly the southeast part of the state involving Mirzapur, Chandauli, and Sonebhadra that are affected by Maoism. Similarly, of the 24 districts in Jharkhand, 17 are affected by Maoist insurgency and the socio-economic indexes of these districts vary widely.

The fact that backwardness alone does not lead to joining the rank of Maoist is also supported by the caste affiliation of the supporters. Chandra (2013: 3) has shown that in south Bihar and northern Jharkhand, dalits have been instrumental in carving out a Maoist stronghold by aligning their interests with those of the party. During the caste conflicts of the past three decades, dalit castes such as Musahars and Dusadhs actively fought their landlords with the assistance of the Maoists. Yet other dalits such as Doms chose not to displease their landed patrons. Similarly, Chandra has shown that in the Bastar region of Chhattisgarh, Gond adivasis take prominence in the Maoist movement, even as local and regional party leaders, but extremely backward and smaller adivasi groups such as the Dhurwas and Murias have tended to keep the Maoists at arm's length. There is therefore no uniform and straight pattern of link between Maoism and socio-cultural backwardness. Let me now discus the necessary and sufficient conditions in some details.

Necessary Conditions

The significance of necessary conditions such as poverty, unemployment, backwardness, deprivation, land question, displacement, exploitation and marginalization have found prominence in any analysis of social movement in a country like India. The rise of Naxalite/Maoist (these terms are used alternately for the purpose of this chapter) movement also depicts the same story. Thus, the Naxalbari movement came into being as a result of prevailing social and economic issues. The West Bengal State Secretariat of the CPI(M) while conducting an enquiry into the uprising recognized that 'behind the peasant unrest in Naxalbari lies a deep social malady-malafide transfers, evictions, and other anti-people actions of tea gardeners and jotedars' (quoted in Dixit, 2010). All the regions in which the Naxal movement took place are ones with alarming levels of poverty. In the Karimnagar, Adilabad, and Warangal districts of Telangana, poverty was 95.8 per cent while in the rest of the state it was between 50 and 60 per cent. Alienation of tribal land was a major issue that crippled their economic welfare. This was evident in good measure in the Srikakulam Naxal movement. Andhra Pradesh accounted for the highest incidence of tribal land alienation in the country with non-tribals owning more than half the land in the scheduled areas (Banaji, 2010: 136). By the time of the uprising only one-third of the tribals owned land (Dixit, 2010). In the Kondeamodalu in East Godavari, the Maoist took up the demands of indebtedness of the tribals, their exploitation by moneylenders and farm wages (Sinha, 1989).

Currently, as many as 460 police stations spreading over 12 states and covering 125 districts in India are within the Naxal/Maoist-affected areas. The affected districts suffer, as observed by an expert group set up by the Planning Commission of Government of India (2008), from the lack of proper governance and appropriate implementation of poverty amelioration programmes. This results in discontent which has led to unrest, sometimes even of violent nature. The dispossession and oppression of tribals and dalits particularly in the context of large-scale displacement and impoverishments since economic globalization in India have been major sources of the firmness of Maoism.

The government started the Backward Districts Initiative in 2003–2004 and the Backward Regions Grant Fund (BRGF) under which 55 of the worst affected areas in 9 states were to be provided with funds of ₹ 2,475 crore to tackle the problem of Naxalism. Around 250 districts have been included in the BRGF scheme to accelerate socio-economic development in these districts, which is to be administered by the Ministry of Panchayati Raj.

Let me cite the example of Lalgarh in West Midnapur, West Bengal here, which became famous for Maoist activities in the recent past. Lalgarh is an undulated forest area within Junglemahal occupied mainly by the tribal communities belonging to the Santhal, Bhumij, and Sabar, along with the Mahatas who are recognized as an OBC community in West Bengal. The people here generally have little or no landholding, except a very few who enjoy political authority. The area virtually has no irrigation facility. The marginal economy is centred around collection of minor forest produces such as *sal* leaves (for making leaf-plates), forest tubers, *babui* grass (for making rope), and *kendu* leaves (for making *bidi*). The sale of these products is done through the middlemen at a much lower price than that in the market. Most of the young men and women are unemployed and engaged as occasional labourers with lower wage rate. People here are forced to go to *namaal* (low-land distant areas with rich agricultural prospects) as seasonal agricultural wage labourers at a cheap wage rate. Junglemahal being an underdeveloped area is marked by absolute poverty and dearth of proper healthcare and educational facilities. Furthermore, the distribution of food grains under the governmental Public Distribution System (PDS) was found to be in a very shabby state, and there were allegations of a corrupt nexus between local food grain shop owners with the CPI(M) party functionaries. The poor people were therefore deprived of their basic requirements for generations (Midya et al., 2012).

A survey by Midya and others (2012) revealed the social life of Lalgarh, which was characterized by early marriage of girls, high rate of illiteracy, and school drop-outs due to poverty, predominance of alcoholism, particularly among the males resulting in higher rate of widows, and a tradition of *dainee* (witchcraft) custom. Expecting safe drinking water is still far from reality. Nearly more than 85 per cent families among the communities studied depend on dug wells and approximately every one of four families has to walk down more than 500 metres for fetching water. Panchayats are, indeed, non-functioning entities and meeting of the *Gram Samsads* is non-existent. The disadvantaged people of the area have, thereby, become very frustrated, disappointed, alienated, and indifferent towards the functioning of government offices or agencies. They have a strong belief that the present administrative set-up as well as political order could neither ameliorate their poverty and misery, nor would protect their rights and culture anyway.

It is under this circumstance that the Maoists initially chose Banspahari, Jamboni, and Lalgarh for building up their organizational bases in the late 1990s. Their presence was felt during 1996–1997 when they were trying to achieve higher price for *babui* rope and *kendu* leaves in Banspahari area. They were then concentrating on establishing societal networks with the poor marginal people and trying to save the latter from political and police oppression. It is therefore argued that 'a symbiotic bond between the tribals and the Maoists seems to have evolved to address the genuine socio-economic grievances of those pushed out of their natural habitat because of an anti-people industrial agenda. Maoism is therefore 'an ideology of hope for those at the lower rung of rural society' (Chakrabarty and Kujur, 2010: 202).

Sufficient Conditions

An Acute Sense of Discrimination among the Youth

Studies on social movement have time and again stressed on the role of youth population in either perceiving prevailing discrimination or aspiring for a better system and thereby forming the core of any protest activity (Ghosh, 2003; Oommen, 2010). Studies on the Maoist movement in India and Nepal also reveal that the educated disenfranchised youth were the first to join it. Alpa Shah and Judith Pettigrew's research (2009) has also noted the importance of youth aspiration along with modernity and gender roles. The Maoist movement has enabled them to participate in a new type of modernity. The young cadres also started asserting their rights over the traditional authority of the village elders. Banerjee (2006) has also noted that the early activists of the Naxal movement were influenced by romantic ideals of revolution. These youths, who did not like working in the field and forests because of their education, liked the higher, masculine status of a 'terrorist' with gun or even the job of a special police (*Salwa Judum*) that entails a monthly salary (Guha, 2007). It is therefore argued that there is recognizable deterioration of the quality as the new cadres are 'more attracted to its weapons than its politics' (Balagopal, 2003: 515).

Elite Formation

Another interesting feature of social movement is the role of local and external elites in providing leadership. This is equally true about the Naxal/Maoist movement. The spread of modern education and the rise of middle class are found to be critical in developing a critique of the state and its policies. Thus, the Naxalist movement found enormous support among the educated youth (Banerjee, 2006). These young men and women belonged to the petty bourgeoisie class. Many of the young Naxalites who went off to the forests were medical and engineering graduates. For them, universities are hotbeds of radical ideology. Some went to rural areas to mobilize the people and some stayed back in Calcutta, perpetrating acts of violence in an attempt to overthrow the state. The sense of disillusionment and the fiery idealism of youth directed them to Naxalist ideology. The repression of Naxalism during the emergency also attracted a large number of youth to Naxalism as a rebellious reaction to the government's oppression (Dixit, 2010). Rabindra Ray (1988) has therefore argued that the Naxal movement is 'intellectually driven' as the doctrinal inputs of the movement came from middle-class ideologues who wanted to lead 'the people'.

In the subsequent phases of Maoist movement, the leadership, by and large, is also found to be from among the highly educated middle-class intellectuals who were often urban biased (Shah and Pettigrew, 2009; Banaji, 2010). The top Maoist leaders such as Koteswara Rao (alias Kishenji) and

Cherukuri Rajkumar (alias Azad) have almost invariably been men from upper- or middle-caste backgrounds. It is true that there is now an underlying layer of dalit and adivasi leadership within the movement, but it is equally true that men and women from subaltern backgrounds have yet to assume top leadership posts in the party (Chandra, 2013).

Maoists often believe that 'the adivasis cannot represent themselves; they must be represented, it would seem' (Nigam, 2010). Shah's work (2006) has found that the initial spread of movement of the Maoist Communist Centre in Jharkhand was not among the poorest tribal populations, but rather within an educated, often upper caste, rural elite, who intimately connected with the developmental state. The Maoist could trap the educated youth, who were no longer satisfied with tilling their land, by entering into the 'markets of protection' offered by locally powerful people. The Maoists in Lalgarh also roped in the educated as well as uneducated youths of the area, who were frustrated over employment opportunities.

Interestingly, tribals going to *Namaal* to work as agricultural labourer are also seen to come back with better knowledge about city life and its facilities. The development gap between the tribal and non-tribal areas in particular made them aggrieved about the role of state and its agencies (Saren, 2012). This feeling of deprivation is utilized by the Maoists to run their operation in the remote and hilly areas. Similarly, such parallels noted by scholars from different parts of the world prove that social movements take shape only after certain stages of development, and more importantly level of literacy, awareness and growth of middle class (Ghosh, 2003; Shah and Pettigrew, 2009; Oommen, 2010).

Political Interest and Manipulation

The Maoist motives to annihilate class enemies, create liberated zones and seize state powers through the barrel of the gun have strong political bearing and often these suit certain spurious interests. The critics of the Maoists, therefore, argue that they have vested interest to gain and retain control over a group of people and territory. Thus, Mukherji (2010: 16) reiterates,

> The state earlier did nothing for the Adivasis but, considering the time the Maoist have spent in the region, they themselves have achieved little by way of adivasi welfare, be it in wages, education, health or agriculture. This is because the Maoist's politics of waging guerrilla warfare on the road to seizure of state power has meant that they must focus on using the adivasis for their war.

There are more serious questions regarding the monetary interests of the Maoist as they collect huge amount as royalty/levy from the contractors, companies, and others. No one knows how much money is collected and how it is divided between military work and mass work (Mukherji, 2010: 19). Alpa Shah (2006) has shown that in Jharkhand, the Naxalites became much like the state, selling protection in return for support. The interconnections of politicians, private companies, and both Maoists and non-Maoists forces also lead to reproduction of conflict because so many powerful actors benefit from it (Harris, 2010: 22). It also cannot be denied that the Maoist allow the greedy contractor to cheat adivasis because they basically fund the armed war against the state. Hence, their arms deals lead them inevitably into shady transactions with rich and corrupt power brokers at different levels (Sarkar and Sarkar, 2009: 11). As a corollary, the Maoists do not allow the adivasis to prosper beyond subsistence as it will interfere with the plans for seizure of power. Additionally, recruiting minors for warfare, ban on employment generating public works, indiscriminate killing of common people, lack of broad-based mass movement, autocracy within party circle–all raises doubts about their commitment for the marginalized and a revolutionary ideology.

Interestingly, Kunnath's (2008) research show that the Maoists in Bihar have shifted their emphasis from mobilizing landless dalits to uniting the middle peasants (*Kurmis*) by addressing the latter's demand for government subsidies and remission of rents and more importantly protecting them from the classes below them. This led the dalits to suspect the Maoist's motive as dalits had basic contradiction with the landed *Kurmis*. The dalits therefore got alienated from the Maoist movement in the 1990s.

The armed strategy of the Maoists also has come under severe criticism. This is because the strategy of 'annihilation of class enemies' has ultimately led to killing of poor tribals in most cases (Nigam, 2010; Simeon, 2010). There are plenty of instances where the Maoists have liquidated common tribals, dalits, human rights workers, NREGA activists, and members of rival groups. Though scholars such as Gautam Navlakha have assessed this movement as people's rebellion to protect their traditional natural resources from the onslaught of the neo-liberal state, there are others who strongly believe that they are 'playing their "revolutionary fantasies" through the lives of the tribals' (Midya et al., 2012). Looking into the methodology of the Maoists, the people have rather realized that 'someone else' and not they were the liberators. For Dilip Simeon (2010), the Maoist movement is not a movement of landless tribals and peasants; it is rather designed to serve others' interests. He writes,

> The Naxalite movement is not a movement of landless peasants and tribals seeking to overthrow state power. It is a project defined as such by those who are neither peasants nor workers nor tribals, but who claim to represent their interests. (Simeon, 2010)

Similarly Aditya Nigam (2010) writes,

> So we have a Maoist-aligned intelligentsia vicariously playing out their revolutionary fantasies through the lives of adivasis, while the people actually dying in battle are almost all adivasis. Take the following killed in West Bengal in recent months: Rajaram Mandi, Lakhinder Mandi and Gopinath Soren on the side of the Maoists and Sadhan Mahato, Tapan Mahato, Barendranath Mahato and Gurucharan Mahato on the CPI(M) side. It will be hard to find a single Bhattacharya, Banerjee, Mukherjee, Basu or such like among the dead.

Interestingly, the active participation of the Maoists in popular social movement in urban and rural areas reveals their desire to mingle with even Right-wing opposition political parties. Thus, in the anti-land acquisition movement in Singur and Nandigram in West Bengal they participated in large numbers. Such participation provided them a political platform to raise voice against the ruling Left Front Government in association with other opposition parties including the Trinamool Congress (TMC). The TMC leaders were also seen taking up issues such as killing of a Maoist leader named Azad including underdevelopment of Junglemahal. Not only this, TMC also opposed any strong police action against the Maoist. Such overt political support for the Maoist in West Bengal allowed them an opportunity to use their trigger to test their hidden strategy at Junglemahal, a forested hill area in West Bengal, and to have some political mileage. Consequently, the Maoist helped the TMC to win the seats in the Junglemahal in the assembly election in 2011.

Here we will discuss the Lalgarh movement in details, in which the Maoists later gained entry, to explain the tendency of the Maoist to manipulate. The movement had begun at Dolilpur Chowk in Chhotopelia village on 5 November 2008 almost instantly to protest against police atrocities. Though such atrocities including those of forests officials were not uncommon to the tribals for several years, torture intensified after the explosion of landmine on 2 November 2011 near Kolaichandi canal, which was not far away from the Midnapur town but 30 kilometres away from Lalgarh. The Police, including CPI(M) armed cadres, then started looking for Maoist in the villages of Lalgarh tribals and arrested some of them. On 5 November, police injured Chhitamoni Hembram, a Santhal woman, *seriously*. She lost her left eye due to a deadly blow by the butt of a rifle. Immediately, the *Bharat Jakat Majhi Marwa*, a social organization of Santhals, decided to oppose the police entry into Lalgarh. Gradually the spontaneous and democratic movement spread across the entire Junglemahal area since the extent of police atrocities are almost similar everywhere. Along with the Lodha and the Bhumij, the non-tribal people of the region also got absorbed into the movement because they are also the disadvantaged people and had face similar oppressive treatment from administration.

When the Maoist extended support to this movement to resist and defeat the police, the people did not mind it. This is also because they appreciated the efforts of the Maoist to resolve certain issues such as (a) achieving higher price for *babui* rope and *kendu* leaves to be sold to middlemen/agents; (b) fighting for the causes of the tribal and other disadvantaged people; (c) resisting political interference; (d) empowering women to resist their drunken husbands; (e) eliminating gambling in rural fair or other social events, (f) protecting locals from harassment by police and forest officials; (g) confiscating and redistributing land of big landholders particularly who are political leaders and (h) targeting ration shops and owners appointed for PDS of food grains and accused of siphoning off these for sale in black market.

When the Maoist started forcing the tribals to adhere to their dictates and eliminating political rivals including women in the name of killing 'police informer', public stopped their support towards the Maoist activities. As soon as they began their terror operation in Lalgarh and its surrounding areas, the people started keeping distance from the Maoist. This is the phenomenal turning point for the villagers' movement that was initially against police atrocities. According to Abhijit Guha (2012), Lalgarh remained disconnected from the rest of the state for more than three months by the blockade put up by the Peoples' Committee against Police Atrocities (PCPA) led by Chhatradhar Mahato. But the Maoists have used this uprising for their own political benefit. The CPI(M) equally fell back on its vigilant groups and counterinsurgency forces to suppress the movement. The blame therefore should also be equally shared by the Communist Party of India (Marxist) and the state for suppressing the legitimate demands of the tribals from several decades. The poor tribals are caught between the CPI(M), the Maoists, and the state (*Economic and Political Weekly*, 2009).

Santosh Rana, one of the original participants in the Naxalite movement, has accused the Maoists that they had destroyed the people's unity by killing Sudhir Mandi in November 2008. Sudhir was a leader of Majhi Marwa. His only offence was that he refused to act according to orders of the Maoist squads (cited from Mukherji, 2012). During this last phase, the leadership of the PCPA also changed from the Santhals to the Mahatas, who were landholders. The Mahata leaders, often under pressure from the Maoists, were taking decisions on their own without always considering the views of the tribal people concerned. This has gradually been making the tribal people indifferent towards the movement, in which participation was once very spontaneous. An ethnic movement has, thus, lost its focus in the hands of the Maoists. A movement against dictates of political force has lost its relevance under the dictates of an ultra-violent force.

Maoist practices in Dandakaranya and elsewhere have also raised grave doubts as to whether the party is genuinely concerned with the welfare of the people. According to Mukherji (2010), the Maoist party has

- no history of struggle outside jungles
- no history of participation in broad resistance movements
- clear complicity with mafia and reactionary forces
- little concern about abject conditions of health and poverty in control areas
- enforced large-scale use of children for warfare

The cumulative evidence, argues Mukherji, are enough to conclude that, notwithstanding revolutionary proclamations, the Maoist party in practice is an undemocratic – perhaps even anti-people – force whose sole aim is to seize state power by hook or crook to bring the masses under the control of the leadership of the party.

State Policies and Action

While there is clear hiatus between Maoist policy and actions, the state is equally to be blamed for the rise of terrorism and conflictual group mobilization in India. In the context of ethnic movement in India, T.K. Oommen (1997: 158) has opined that the state does not even take the justified demands of ethnic minorities seriously unless the movement takes an anti-India or ethno-national character. Its approach to manage the tension is with force (Oommen, 1997: 158). Similarly, in case of protest movement by the tribals or dalits, the state and its agencies try to ignore the genuine issue until it becomes violent.

Let me discuss the case of Lalgarh once again. It was once a very peaceful area and the administrators of the districts could easily enter there, though it was squarely a backward area by any yardstick (read my discussion on Lalgarh under necessary condition). The tribals also did not launch any powerful protest movement, though they had serious complaints about forest officials, police, and contractors of the area. But a police action against the women forced the Maoist to join the peaceful movement. The tribals asked the police officials to just apologise for their action. But neither the Left Front Government nor the CPI(M) had shown any interest to resolve the matter. Over and above, one of the worst incidences of counterinsurgency measures has occurred at Netai village on 7 January 2011 where nine persons were gunned down and several others were injured by the assailants backed by the ruling political party. Obviously, the Maoist got the brilliant opportunity to exploit the situation.

It, therefore, appears that the Maoist movement arises, in Junglemahal and elsewhere, not out of the question of development alone. The issues of intolerance on the part of the state machinery to give redressal to people's demands and that of near-absence of governance and democratic principle have important bearing upon it. Economic and social backwardness has no doubt made the area breeding ground for the Maoist movement. But what has been the most contributive factor is the mal- or non-governance. The administration was running completely under specific political patronage. Democracy and governance were nowhere in the area for a long time. Rampant corruption, nepotism, and siphoning of funds allocated for development in other way were the rule of the area (Midya et al., 2012). It is an irony that the state starts confidence-building measures only after it was destroyed. Yet, government has already accepted that most Naxal-affected states have failed to spend allocated funds for development. There has also been very little progress to implement the Scheduled Tribe and Other Traditional Forest Dwellers (Recognition of forest Rights) Act 2006 or the Forest Rights Act properly. The Supreme Court has also termed as 'serious' the plight of tribal undertrials lodged in various central jails for several years in eight Naxal-affected states.

Let me analyse the issue from another angle. It is true that the use of arms by the Maoist ultimately results in huge casualties for the poor. The Maoist leaders themselves are concerned about great deal of undisciplined violence. But, if we look into the efforts of the government so far to contain forces such as Maoists, we would be surprised to note that these efforts also have put the tribals and scheduled castes into troubles. Whether through operation

'Greyhounds' in Andhra Pradesh, or through 'Operation Green Hunt' in the Dandakaranya forests and again through *Salwa Judum* in Chhattisgarh, the state has in fact launched a 'white terror' to repress brutally the common man along with some hard-core Maoists. Interestingly, these 'cleansing operations' have rather allowed the Maoists intellectuals and activists to gain fresh support and followers (Shah and Pettigrew, 2009; Harris, 2010; Chandra, 2013). This is because when the state attacks and the economic lives of adivasis and dalits are further disrupted, enrolment for the militia increases sharply. In other words, 'more the repression by the state, the bigger the "people's army" of starving children' (Mukherji, 2010: 20).

Outside Support

The involvement of outside leaders/agencies has been found to be instrumental in aggravating the issues of the tribals and dalits. In case of tribal movements in Northeast India (also in many other cases), tacit support of outside agencies such as Christian Missionaries and foreign governments played a major role to sustain the aggression. Similarly, the Maoist movement did not emerge from within. Instead, it was brought to the forest highlands by committed cadres seeking to expand their revolutionary ambit. In case of Singur and Nandigram movement, the Maoist took advantage of anger of the peasants to show their presence. Maoists in certain parts of Bihar and Uttar Pradesh have also taken advantage of Nepal border to organize their guerrilla activities. Additionally, the Maoist entry into tribal homelands has coincided with the growing presence of NGOs (Chandra, 2013: 3). In Jharkhand, for example, tribal youth with the appropriate language and technical skills can join the Maoists, NGOs, and sometimes, even both.

Geographical Location

The fact that the Maoist movement is concentrated in a specific geo-political space for more than four decades raises serious questions about close connection between Maoism and hilly terrain or jungle that are inaccessible (Banerjee, 2006). It is also a coincidence that marginalized population live in these hilly terrains where there are semblance of any government. But the continuous forest terrain of the states such as Jharkhand, Chhattisgarh, Madhya Pradesh, Uttar Pradesh, Bihar, Orissa, Andhra Pradesh, Telangana, and West Bengal have allowed the Maoists/Naxals a free space to conduct arms training, hide themselves, and conduct guerrilla warfare. The remote areas of Sonebhadra, Chandauli, and Mirzapur districts of UP are all considered the hotbed of Maoist activity. Again, the Maoist chose as their base the Junglemahal area of Burdwan in West Bengal, an inaccessible terrain covered with forests from where they launched guerrilla warfare in 1974 (Banerjee, 2006). But when their original base in Burdwan dwindled by the end of the 1970s, they moved over to the neighbouring forest areas of Bihar over the next decade. Harris (2010: 26) therefore argues that 'the essential reason for the strength of the Maoists in the hilly, forested tracts of eastern and central India is that this terrain, in India and elsewhere in the world, most favours guerrilla insurgency'. It is equally a major challenge for the police force during combing operations. Instead of immediately planning to spread the armed struggle all over India, the Maoist leadership therefore thought that 'the forests and mountainous areas quite naturally get priority as these are the strategic areas where base areas can be set up' (Banerjee, 2006: 3162).

Conclusion

The issue of Maoism or any other variety of terrorism should be studied from the perspective of social movement. Such a perspective would allow reasonable space to study the growth of anti-state movements and insurgent activities from a longitudinal and holistic point of view. I have tried to argue that Maoism and similar other insurgent (as well as ethnic) movements that the country has witnessed since independence are a result of developmental (necessary) and sociological (sufficient) issues. Rise and fall in the number of Maoist-affected areas in the country over the years can also be explained from this point of view. The fact that the Maoist movement has passed through four distinct phases and has surfaced again and again despite retreating to subterranean levels speaks about its adaptive capacity. In a country like India, terrorism of one kind would continue to get replaced by the other if the context that gives rise to such unlawful activities is not mitigated. The state should therefore just not treat terrorism or insurgency merely as a law and order problem but it should introspect seriously into the conditions that promote such movements. Similarly, the support of the impoverished tribals and dalits for the Maoist should not be treated as support for their ideology and method. It is high time that we recognize the basic human rights of the tribals, dalits, and other marginalized groups and communities in India and allow them to take decision and implement appropriate schemes of development.

Acknowledgements

I am grateful to Professor Partha Nath Mukherjee, Professor Felix Padel, and other participants of the seminar for providing me certain valuable inputs.

References

Balagopal, K. (2003). 'People's War and the Government: Did the Police Have the Last Laugh?'. *Economic and Political Weekly*. 38(6): 513–519.

——. (2006). 'Maoist Movement in Andhra Pradesh'. *Economic and Political Weekly*. 41(29): 3183–3187.

Banaji, Jairus (2010). 'The Ironies of Indian Maoism'. *International Socialism: A Quarterly Journal of Socialist Theory*. (128). October: 129–148.

Banerjee, S. (1980). *In the Wake of Naxalbari: a History of the Naxalite Movement in India*. Kolkata: Subarnarekha.

——. (2006). 'Beyond Naxalism'. *Economic and Political Weekly*. 41(29): 3159–3163.

——. (2006). 'Tortuous Odyssey of Indian Naxalites'. Available at: naxalrevolution.blogspot.com/2006/08/beyond-naxalbari.html

Chakrabarty, B. and Kujur, R.K. (2010). *Maoism in India: Reincarnation of Ultra-left Wing Extremism in the Twenty-first Century*. London: Routledge.

Chandra, Uday (2013). 'The Maoist Movement in Contemporary India'. *Social Movement Studies: Journal of Social, Cultural and Political Protest.* Available at: http://dx.doi.org/10.1080/14742837.2013.845730.

Dixit, Raman (2010). 'Naxalite Movement in India: The State's Response'. *Journal of Defence Studies.* April 4(2). http://www.idsa.in/jds/4_2_2010_NaxaliteMovementinIndia_rdixit'?

Economic and Political Weekly (Editorial) (2009). 'Lalgarh: Question to the Left'. 44(26–27): 5.

Ghosh, Biswajit (2003). 'Ethnicity and Insurgency in Tripura'. *Sociological Bulletin.* 52(2): 221–243.

Ghosh, S. (1974). *The Naxalite Movement: A Maoist Experience.* Calcutta: Mukhopadhyay.

Gondane, Ajay (2006). 'Lessons from India: Confronting the Sociological Causes of Terrorism'. Available at: www.stimson.org (Accessed on 19 May 2014).

Government of India (2008). 'Development Challenges in Extremist Affected Areas'. Report of Expert Group. New Delhi.

Guha, Abhijit (2012). 'The Bankruptcy of the Ideology of Violence'. In Abhijit Guha (ed.) *Maoism in India: Ideology and Ground Reality.* 90–99. Jhargram: Indian National Confederation and Academy of Anthropologists.

Guha, Ramachandra (2007). 'Adivasis, Naxalites and Indian Democracy', *Economic and Political Weekly.* 42(32): 3305–3312.

Gupta, Tilak D. (2006). 'Maoism in India: Ideology, Programme and Armed Struggle'. *Economic and Political Weekly.* 41(29): 3172–3176.

Harris, John (2010). 'The Naxalite/Maoist Movement in India: A Review of Recent Literature'. ISAS Working Paper No. 109. Available at: www.isas.nus.edu.sg.

Kunnath, G. (2008). *From the Mud House of Magadh: Dalits, Naxalites and the Making of a Revolution in Bihar, India,* Ph.D. Thesis, SOAS, London: University of London.

Lecomte-Tilouine, M. (2004). 'Regicide and Maoist Revolutionary Warfare in Nepal: Modern Incarnations of a Warrior King'. *Anthropology Today.* 20(1): 13–20.

Midya, Dipak K., Bej, Chandan, and Shit, Siddhartha (2012). 'Assessing the Dying Life: The Lalgarh Context'. In Abhijit Guha (ed.) *Maoism in India: Ideology and Ground Reality*. 63–89. Jhargram: Indian National Confederation and Academy of Anthropologists.

Mukherji, Nirmalangshu (2010). 'Arms Over the People: What Have the Maoists Achieved in Dandakaranya?'. *Economic and Political Weekly*. 45(25): 16–20.

——. (2012). 'Resistance and Democracy'. In Abhijit Guha (ed.) *Maoism in India: Ideology and Ground Reality*. 21–39. Jhargram: Indian National Confederation and Academy of Anthropologists.

Nayak, Deepak Kumar and Fakir Mohan Pradhan (2014). 'Naxalism in India: Debating the Developmental Synergy between Centre and State Development: A Panacea for Naxalism', Paper presented in a National Seminar on *Youth, Naxalism and Terrorism* at IT College, Lucknow in between 21 and 22 February.

Nigam, Aditya (2010). 'The Rumour of Maoism'. *Seminar*. 607. (March). Available at: www.india-seminar.com

Oommen, T.K. (1997). 'Social Movements and the State Response: The Indian Situation'. In A.M. Shah, B.S. Baviskar, and E.R. Ramaswamy (eds.) *Social Structure and Change*. Vol. 4. 134–162. New Delhi: Sage Publications.

——. (ed.) (2010). *Social Movements I: Issues of Identity*. New Delhi: Oxford University Press.

Rana, Santosh (2010). Interview. *Seminar*. March. 607. Available at: www.india-seminar.com

Ray, Rabindra (1988). *The Naxalites and Their Ideology*. Delhi: Oxford University Press.

Saren, Gurupada (2010). *A Study on Santal Migration: Its Context and Ramifications in Relation to Tribal Identity*, Ph.D. Thesis, Department of Sociology, The University of Burdwan, West Bengal.

Sarkar, Sumit and Tanika Sarkar (2009). 'Notes on a Dying People'. *Economic and Political Weekly*. 44(26–27): 10–14.

Schmid, Alex, and Jongman, Albert (1988). *Political Terrorism: A New Guide to Actors, Authors, Concepts, Data bases, Theories and Literature*. Amsterdam: Transaction Books.

Shah, Alpa (2006). 'Markets of Protection: The "Terrorists" Maoist Movement and the State in Jharkhand, India'. *Critique of Anthropology*. 26(3): 297–314.

Shah, Alpa and Judith Pettigrew (2009). 'Windows into a Revolution: Ethnographies of Maoism in South Asia'. *Dialectical Anthropology*. 33(3–4): 225–251.

Simeon, Dilip (2010). 'Permanent Spring'. *Seminar*. 607 (March). Available at: www.india-seminar.com.

Sinha, Santha (1989). *Maoist in Andhra Pradesh*. New Delhi: Gyan Publishing House.

Singh, S.B. (2005). 'Limits to Power: Naxalism and Caste Relations in a South Bihar Village'. *Economic and Political Weekly*. XL(29): 3167–3175.

5

Development Paradigms and Naxalism

Resource, Development, and Indigenous People

BIKRAMADITYA KUMAR CHOUDHARY

Development is said to bring opportunities to the people and new possibilities that were not available before the humanity. It is seen and defined in terms of technological advancements, increased mobility both horizontal and vertical, enhanced skills and means of communication, and so on. It is now accepted that single Eurocentric definition of development does not address the aspiration of all because more than one meaning of development exists amongst societies across globe. Consequently, people have different expectations and aspirations depending upon their exposure to the larger world and known level of technological advancements. However, one thing remains common and is that everyone expects to be better of himself or herself compared to the past. The notion of betterment is not in contrast with the most basic and widespread propagated notion. If this is put as a concept, this refers to 'upward mobility'. In other words, development ensures upward mobility of everyone in all societies across the globe. The major question that comes to mind is 'if it is true', and if not, then how the very basic assurance of developmentalism is unreal. The question does not end here but has multiple dimensions and inherent contradiction that arises out of the existing development paradigm, such as if everyone is not ensure of upward mobility, then does it mean failure of the concept of development? If so, why even today the leading economists and developmentalists are arguing for development even when the fruit of development is not reaching to the masses? Does this notion of development bring something else other than upward mobility? These are difficult questions and often may be termed as absurd on the ground that development has brought many changes to different regions and continue to bring latest comfort, new technological superiority and new adventures. One cannot deny this reality; however, it does not ensure absurdity of the question that why development does not ensure upward mobility of everyone? The gap between the propagated notion and the lived reality often gets manifested as violent conflicts, and at times remains suppressed like a boil and burst with pain and anger. The question gets further complicated, and if the propagator of development is known to this contestation and conflicts, then what alternative development model is available to ensure upward movement for all. Answer to these questions is not easy and probably not at all known to us at this point of time. Time is the best healer and will bring answer through movements and discontents, as has always been in human history.

It is in this context that the present chapter attempts to analyse the contestations, conflicts, and discourses of upward movement of individual and communities based on resources. The chapter will also try to put a critique of the existing essentialist paradigm of 'development-displacement-disparity'. For this political ecology, perspective would be adopted. Political ecology approach is a critique of 'order of existing things' but remains largely rooted in political economy. It combines the concerns of ecology (resources) and a broadly defined political economy. Together this encompasses the constantly shifting dialectic between society and land-based resources and also within classes and groups within society itself that shape the structure of society, the extent of subtractability and exclusion within and between community.

Changing Conception and the Changing Resource: Putting Political Ecology in Perspective

Resources refer to all kind of endowments that form the basis of human survival and can also be appropriated by dominant section of society at any given point of time. These refer to stock and flow of natural endowments. Fixity of resources is supposed to be a boon for people since the dawn of civilization. As in different ages of history, it has attracted human agglomeration and civilization. Nevertheless, such fixity of resource has also been a reason for conflict and consequent displacement of certain communities including human societies, periodically owing to appropriation of such resources as needed at particular point in history. Fixity of resource has also been questioned in the context of power and knowledge for a long time; yet localization and fixity of resources and differentiation of spatial characteristics has been central to the explanation of concentrated development (Choudhary, 2009). Such existing explanations make relationship between developmental process and geographical space a universal factor since the conceptualization of development and actual as well as expected upward movement of communities in the modern sense.

As per the history, the development started since human learned about accumulation of resources and it traces back to the beginning of agriculture when people started storing the agricultural output for using later on. The sense of space, initially as a physical entity and later as cultural landscape, remained attached with the process of development. Initiation of industrialization and its reliance on fund resources made the case for space more distinctive, and dogmatic theorization about the space began. Such development also led to dislocation and relocation of human population world-wide as the space got transformed to a new industrial landscape. This also results in alienation, marginalization, and exclusion of communities, groups, and individuals and often leads to conflict at different levels in society. There have been critiques of concentrated development and also about the nightmare of developmentalism that often results in the 'anti-politics machine' or leads to violence as well as excessive prosperity (Escobar, 1994). Partha Chatterjee (2004) talks of unscrupulous invitations, and Jean-Philippe Platteau (2000) has drawn our attention to the generalized and limited moralities. However, these great economists miss the intricate relationship between ecology, resource, and the processes that results in differentiated development over space. Each region of the globe has different resources, and their utility in each geographical setting for ages has been different, hence giving rise to different spaces in other world of different cultures. The on-going process of generalization has also brought a uniform way of using resources and hence discomfort to many and in other way making majority of work and inherent knowledge irrelevant. It is here the political ecologists argue that nothing on the planet is irrelevant, and definitely the sills that have fed millions for years and that have ensured their survival amongst all odds cannot be irrelevant in whatever age we live in. Political ecology approach on one hand is a critique of 'order of existing things' but remains largely rooted in political economy.

Nature of Development in India

India like other developing countries has encountered with the colonial model of development wherein resource-rich peripheries and market-rich cores still exist after 60 years of independence. Since independence, regional development was started as a strategy to reduce accentuated regional disparity, but situation under structural adjustment programme has worsen rather than improving in the last decade. Since 1990, there is growth-oriented development and has resulted in the marginalization of various kinds such as economic marginalization, social and political marginalization, and so on. All kinds of marginalization can be broadly put into two categories: spatial marginalization and non-spatial marginalization. There are several ways to understand development, and spatial dimension has been more commonly known as regional development. The various paradigms of development depend upon the researcher's own theoretical position and the locale that they represent. One of the common concerns in the arena of developmental debate remained the analysis of existing economic structure and different spatial expression of such structure. Structuralist interpretations of the economy are often put under the purview of neo-Marxism as the concerns in this paradigm have been on the analysis of the impact of capital on labour. The dominant literature on regional development have generally been put under two broader categories: one that analyses spatial division of labour depending upon the product cycle model and the second that is concerned with profit cycle model (Rees, 1992). Regional development remains a widely debated and loosely implemented concept in the developmental discourse across the world with India not being an exception. Several reasons are cited for this state of affair. The weakness of the implementing agencies, bureaucratic character of the executive organ/s of the state, lack of active participation of the people, and so on have been the dominant reasons for not fulfilling the aspirations of the people of the poor regions. The backwardness or relative underdevelopment of the forested region, tribal region border regions, hilly terrain, and desert region is a well-known fact. Further, with the concentrated development, glaring examples of various kinds of disparities at international, interstate, and interregional levels continue to emerge. Even in the most developed countries such as the United States the same scenario has been observed a few decades ago (Ullman, 1958: 179–200),

> ... notable is the disparity within United States, where, in the northeast, about 7 per cent of the US area has about 70 per cent of the nation's industrial employment; the rest of the country fights for the remainder in a manner not unlike dogs fighting over a dry bone.

It is also true that in the poor countries or poor regions such disparities are larger, and in the beginning of developmental process these inequalities are supposed to be larger (Myrdal, 1957). India is a country with wide natural variations that include lofty Himalayan Mountains, great Gangetic Plain, vast Thar Desert, and deep black soil of the Deccan. These natural diversities often provide a shield for the states that are not being able to eliminate existing or rather increasing regional disparities. It is most common to relate non-development to lack of resources. However, resources available in the nature cannot be used as without the use of modern technology. A gaze on noted historical developments tarnishes such notion. The example from China will strengthen this point clearly. The current 'inaccessible regions' of China used to be the centre of economic activities till 11th century, and the current thriving regions of China used to be the areas where offenders were sent to exile. The change in the technology from land route trade (silk route) to trade via sea route changed the landscape of the country. The concentration of development in few parts of the worlds or in few parts of the nation seems to be the law of economics at least for some point of time. The same law of economics also proposes that there are no alternative to development, and if a country or a nation or a region aspires to be developed it has to go the way 'developed regions' have ferried over time. In a way, it implies that all parts of the world have to feel the negativity of development process in terms of interregional disparity and interpersonal disparity. The inevitability of deprivation of some is to be interpreted in this chapter with special focus on those who lives on the margin as Subba Rao (1968) calls in the area of relative isolation.

India started her economic development with a vision document of National Planning Commission chaired by Jawaharlal Nehru, who later became the first prime minister of the country. In the independent India, it started with Nehru on the Bhakra-Nangal Dam declaring that as modern temple of India. It was not only an expression of secular statehood but also an indication of the coming future of India that would be dependent on large projects: large dams, big factories, heavy engineering, and so on. The beginning continued unabated with many such new additions such as Hirakud, Sardar Sarovar, Ukai, and so on. Along with the irrigation cum power projects came new mineral-based industrial complexes such as IISCO spreading over Burnpur, Hirapur, Kulti; Rourkela, NALCO, Damodar Valley Corporation, and many more. The projects of the first two to three decades infused high hopes amongst different communities across the country. People including the displaced thought that these projects will bring betterment to their lives in near or distant future. There was no story of failure or cheating in the nation state as it was in the process of becoming. However, with the passage of time the cruel truth of the development processes unfolded and so started the protests, followed which the constitution of committee started looking into the grievances of the displaced communities. The discontent amongst different sections of displaced people and the voices of their incapability compared to those who displaced them to deal with the larger and more powerful became louder by the late 1980 especially when the World Bank withdraw itself from Sardar Sarovar Project citing the unsettled rehabilitation claims. This can be taken as a blatant slap on the face of democratic socialist state that vows to ensure welfare to all its citizens. Moreover, this was not a sporadic incident; there has been systematic and continuous deprivation of the people who got displaced against their will from the land that goes to different development project (Fernandes, 1994, 2004; Oommen, 2006). With liberalization, globalization, and privatization (LPG Model), a new dimension was added to this when private entrepreneurs started setting mining and other projects purely for profit generation rather than the earlier held notion of national development. This also meant running out of patience of those getting displaced and evaporation of hopes whatever they had from the nation state. The outcome of this change in the perception and conception of people has been violent protest and brutal state response in many parts of the country like that of Kalinganagar of Orissa where 13 tribals were gunned down by the state agencies for protesting against the setting up of a plant (Meher, 2009: 466).

Outcomes

The violent protest and brutal state responses are not the only result and neither the prime outcome; these are rather natural fallout of an unjust economic order that is being allowed to continue, operate, and proliferate across mineral-rich regions of the country despite two policy documents by the state agencies, one in 1998 and the other in 2004 (Fernandes, 2007). The contemporary development literature seems to be depending on the slogan of 'large, more and quick'. The outfall of such slogan does not always bring fruits to all and for sure not the fruit that will have nourishment for all. Some does get wealthy with such endeavour at the cost of majority who gets marginalized economically, and consequently socially and politically. Resource is localized in India as any other part of the world and has been declared as national asset under the British Empire so that they can be exploited by the British Empire unhindered. Independent India continued with the same definition of the natural resources and used the resources for 'national goals'. This pattern though tried towards dispersal of industries during 4th to 7th plan remained concentrated within pockets of the so-called backward state. After globalization, centrality of economic activities increased as all incentives for decentralized development seize to exist. These widening disparities and continuous marginalization often can be manifested in violent conflicts. One such example is of civil unrest in different parts of the word owing to various reasons. I take example of Naxalism from India. Genesis of the problem is related to the development that is further linked with geography to the region. Large area that is affected by conflict is the backward region of the country. In Myrdal's term 'they are poor because they are poor'. The reason is because these are dry parts of the country with undulating terrain and low water table. There is scarcity of fertile agricultural land. Forest resource was earlier excessively used in the name of local by corporate taking patta in some of the regions. Mining-based industries do not consider the residents of the areas as skilled. There is hardly any effort to enhance the skill or improve the human resources of the region. Further, few parts of the country have grown too fast and now under the electronic media, and the extravagant use of different kinds of resources by few is vividly visible. I think this is sufficient cause for conflict. The complexity of human–environment relationship of the region, the changes that were brought to the region, the failure or success of such interventions, and the current possible relation need to be studied to understand the complexity of the conflict in these regions. Further, the nature of political intervention in each of the affected areas has been different and has got different responses depending upon the level of political awareness of the people of the areas.

Further, since 1990, the country allowed private operators to mine the national wealth and accrue profit at the unmatched level. This is contradictory to the basic economic principles on two counts and beyond the understanding for anyone knowing A B C of economics. First is that with increasing level of development, the country, the nation, and the region start higher level of production and export more complex product, and production technology is liable to be better. India after 60 years of independence and much cried 'shining India campaign' started selling unprocessed minerals, that is, the raw material. Second is the definition of nation asset. How a private firm or individual within the territorial boundary or an MNC is allowed to sell of the national wealth? And if this national wealth is to be sold in the open market how they continue to remain national asset for which indigenous community should continue to sacrifice their local interest? These two sets of question do not have an answer because they are contradictory to the same economic principles that argue for initial disparity between persons and regions in the beginning of development.

These sets of economic premises are open to debate; nevertheless the millions are displaced from their home and their environment every day and contribute to the accumulation of wealth by the global billionaires. The process is aptly articulated as accumulation by dispossession by Swapna Banerjee-Guha (2010), though in a completely different context, while she was deliberating the global accumulation of wealth across city regions of the world. The process, that is, accumulation by the 'haves' based on dispossession of the 'have-nots' and their complete marginalization and delegitimization (most react violently with no option remaining for peaceful airing of discontent) remains same in the dark jungles and in deep mines far from the glitters of global metropolis. The people who have been living in the forested areas of central India and elsewhere in similar areas have been categorized as areas of relative isolation by Rao (1968) and as backward inaccessible area needing special assistance by the Planning Commission. The Constitution of India recognizing the special character of the region including that of the inhabitants has also put them under special category, that is, Schedule V. The contemporary pattern of development in India has been such that majority of new economic activities are getting located in these areas as they house all the major minerals in the states of Orissa, Chhattisgarh, Jharkhand, and the major source of hydroelectricity in the seven sister states of Northeast India. The outcome of the adopted lopsided elite-focused development has been such that power is generated not for those whose water is used; minerals are extracted and exported by those who have nothing to do with the nation building. The statement is liable to be contested by the state loyal elitist development economists saying that it is from that taxation and levy that the major social welfare schemes such as MGNREGA, and Midday meal and others are running. There has been deconstruction of these myths at more than one place and here attempt would only be focused to analyse the outcome of these development in terms of displacement of millions in India

Forced Outward Mobility and Indigenous Community and Naxalism

Development based on available resources and optimal utilization of resources by indigenous community is said to be the best remedy for the empowerment of people. However, in the contemporary dominant development paradigm, this option remained confined to the pages of radical journals and books authored by critical scholars. The current paradigm of development is dependent on the model based on three words: more, more, and more. The economy promote more consumption to battle the slowdown, hence it is required to produce more to match the demand and consequently required more raw material and more power to match the level of consumption and production. We do find international submits from Copenhagen to Rio rhetorically aiming at the earth sustainability; though often these places get invaded by the corporate who are concerned only with the sustainability of their firms (*Hindu*, 24 June 2012).

In such a scenario, development-induced displacement remained an unavoidable outcome that results in pauperization of masses especially the indigenous community with no fault of their own. Concentration of resource is said to be the prime mover of development even in the not so people-friendly model of Export Substituted Industrialization. It is understood that export of resources would bring the required wealth and will lead to capital formation at regional level and will finally lead to economic and social development of the region. The reality of mineral-rich region of India does not support this model. There has been different estimation about the magnitude of displaced people. Fernandes and Thukral (1989) estimated the total number of displace people between 1951 and 1990 as something between 11 million and 18.5 million; Fernandes (1994) in another study put the figure of displaced by different projects at 21.3 million. The latest estimate available on displacement places the total number displaced in India owing to different kinds of development projects as about 60 million (Mathur, 2008).

One can argue that these numbers are exaggerated, however, but none can deny that some people have been displaced and there is no official statistics or any effort to collect data on displaced people beyond the individual and records. It is well known fact that when displacement of entire settlement village or town or hamlet takes place, it is in all likelihood not possible to displace those who do not possess land in their name; as there are more agricultural labourer than cultivators, more landless than land owning people, and so on. Fernandes (2007) has put forward similar argument on the basis of more than about 10 studies which he along with his team has conducted across different parts of India. This is an indication about the official sensitivity towards the displaced. In general it is understood that no one has moved voluntarily from their own home leaving land and all asset. However, there is another argument that all of the 60 million or 21 million are not displaced using force. This is an interesting argument that I tried to establish when I was in the district of Keonjhar. It is true that in the initial phase, the displacement was not voluntary but they were not forced. They moved from their own abode with the hope that there will be betterment in their economic condition over time. In recent time, it is noticed that all major or even minor projects site has also been the sites of protest. The reason for such protest is the past experience of the displaced in the surrounding that remained unsettled and uncompensated displaced and in certain cases they even lost their mere existence. The rampant fear of repetition of past and ruthless brutal state response against any protest has left the indigenous community in fragile social, political, and psychological condition. Different studies such as Mandal (2009), Meher (2009), and Mishra (2002) have also indicated towards the state responses and in certain cases such as in Meher (2009) outlined the details of protests and the loss of life of indigenous community during that the displacement. They are losing land, common property resources (CPRs), home, water source, and all their means of livelihood and are also subjected to various traumatic experiences including physical torturer in majority of cases.

Before I get back to the questions on development model, it is pertinent to briefly discuss about the state response, policy document, and legal and constitutional safeguards. The large area facing displacement especially mining-induced displacement and recent hydrological projects of northeastern India are covered under the Schedule V of Indian Constitution. Further, three-fourth of the land that belong to the state in these regions are as either a forested land diverted for mining as in the districts of Sundargarh, Keonjhar, Kalahandi and Koraput (all in Orissa) or compensatory forest land. This compensatory forest land is another means of dispossession for the tribals in the state of Orissa, Chhattisgarh, Jharkhand, and others. These lands were under cultivation by the tribals without having individual patta in their names, when the forest land got allocated to mining purpose. Under the environmental protection act, these lands were ought to be brought under forest. In this process, the land under cultivation including land under shifting cultivation got diverted to compensatory forest land, depriving the tribals of their means of livelihood.

In the wake of large-scale displacement and internationalization of the issue in 1993 by the World Bank in case of Sardar Sarovar Project, the state under the aegis of Ministry of Rural Development came up with a policy paper in 1994 and again in 1998. The policy was intended to apply to projects displacing about 500 or more families in plains and 250 or more families in hills. This limitation of number is manipulated every day in more than one way especially in plain areas where roads and other linear infrastructure projects are sanctioned in sub-units to avoid the total number of displaced crossing over 500 families. Let's take an example of Mumbai Pune Expressway, where project authorities continue to deny the compensation to the displaced till the High Court intervened and order the disbursement of compensation. The irony of the situation is that the corporate developers were not ready to pay even minimum compensation under the law, though law is not encompassing and not for the poor at least in 1994 at the time of the project implementation. National Advisory Council itself modified the 1998 draft in 2003 which was published in 2004 for the rehabilitation of the displaced, and this was passed in 2007 in the parliament as National Policy for Rehabilitation and Resettlement Bill. The provisions of the bill would be a matter of separate discussion on each of the point and scholars have studies and analysed the same elsewhere (Madumdar, 2010). The most important aspect of the bill that I would discuss here is that of 'defining public purpose' and 'informed prior consent' for any land acquisition. There is acceptance that no democratic society can accept a decision without the participation of affected persons. But the bill came into existence without the participation of those who are ought to be affected. Further, the proposal of the project and the sanction of the project do not include consultation with those who would be displaced by that project. It is after the finalization of the project that their view on land would be asked. The question remained whether this can be called an informed consent or a participatory decision-making process. The other aspect, public purpose, is more problematic. The question is who is public and what is public purpose; here the statement of Crush (1995) is relevant when he says it depends on 'who defines for whom'. The definition of public purpose is always guided by the time we live in the power we are ruled by. If the world is ruled by corporate power, the profit extraction by the corporate is only public purpose. Moreover, the question remains that what would the development theorist suggest to those who are displaced and what premise the elites who displace them would provide as justification for such forced displacement of millions belonging to indigenous community and others. The theory of development starts with the basic premise that everyone is to be better compared to pre-development era; here most tribals are not at all better off not even same as the pre-project period. The best of the resettlement and rehabilitation options only argue for a condition for all displaced to that of pre-project scenario.

Is There a Way Forward?

Resource is one of the prime sources on which development is based at least after industrial development at international as well as local level. Pattern of conflict, discontent, and consequent marginalization over space is as varied as that of pattern of development and concentration of a particular kind of resource. When we take broader perspective of resource, everything around us including physical and social environment constitute part of the resource.

References

Banerjee-Guha, S. (2010). *Accumulation by Dispossession: Transformative Cities in the New Global Order*. New Delhi: Sage.

Chatterjee, P. (2004). *The Politics of the Governed: Reflections from Popular Politics in Most of the World*, New York: Columbia University Press.

Choudhary, B.K. (2009). 'Rethinking Regional Development: Challenges and Possibilities for Geography'. In R.S. Singh (ed.) *Indian Geography in the 21st Century: The Young Geographers Agenda*. 333–351, UK: Cambridge Scholars Press.

Crush. J. (1995). *Power of Development*, Taylor and Francis.

Escobar, A. (1994). *Encountering Development: The Making and Unmaking of the Third World*. Princeton, NJ: Princeton University Press.

Fernandes, W. (1994). 'An Active Process around the Draft National Rehabilitation Policy'. *Social Action*. 45: 277–298.

——. (2004). 'Rehabilitation Policy for the Displaced'. *Economic and Political Weekly*. 39(12): 1191–1193.

——. (2007). 'Singur and the Displacement Scenario'. *Economic and Political Weekly*. 42(3): 203–206.

——. and Thukral, E.G. (1989). *Development, Displacement and Resettlement*. New Delhi: ISI.

Madumdar, B. (2010). 'Land Acquisition for Industrialization in India: Displacement of People and the Role of the State'. In O.F.V. Feigenblatt (ed.) *Development and Conflict in the 21st Century*. 27–42. Bangkok: JAPSS Press.

Mandal, M. (2009). 'Internal Displacement in India: Status, Condition and Prospects of Return'. *Refugee Watch*. 33: 33–47.

Mathur, H.M. (2008). 'Introduction and Overview'. In H.M. Mathur (ed.) *India Social Development Report 2008: Development and Displacement*. 3–13. New Delhi: Council for Social Development and OUP.

Meher, R. (2009). 'Globalization, Displacement and the Livelihood Issues of Tribal and Agriculture Dependent People: The case of Mineral-based Industries in India'. *Journal of developing Societies*. 25(4): 457–480.

Mishra, S.K. (2002). 'Development, Displacement and Rehabilitation of Tribal People: A Case of Orissa'. *Journal of Social Science*. 6(3): 197–208.

Myrdal, G. (1957). *Economic Theory and Underdevelopment Regions*. London: Duckworth.

Ota, A.B. (2010). *Development Projects and Displaced Tribals: An Empirical Study*. Bhubaneswar: SCs and STs Research and Training Institute.

Rao, S. (1968). *The Personality of India*. Mysore: University of Mysore.

Rees, J. (1992). 'Regional Development and Policy under Turbulence'. *Progress in Human Geography*. 16(2): 223–231.

6

Maoists' Tactical United Front (TUF) and Urban Movement

P.V. RAMANA

The arrest of J. Appa Rao, Head of the Department of Telugu, Andhra University, Visakhapatnam, on 6 November 2014, 'for allegedly facilitating procurement of explosives, including 300 kg of ammonium nitrate for the East Visakha Division of CPI (Maoists)'[1] has, once again brought into focus the urban movement and network of Naxalites of the Communist Party of India (Maoist), or Maoists in short.

Earlier, G.N. Saibaba, an Assistant Professor in Delhi University, was arrested by Maharashtra Police for allegedly abetting the Maoists. These incidents bring into relief the urban network of the Maoists.

A Communist Party, according to classical understanding, requires 'three magic weapons' to achieve its goal of capturing political power. These are (a) Party, that is, a strong organization; (b) Army, that is, a body of fighters – the People's Liberation Army (PLA); and (c) United Front, that is, alliances or linkages with groups that would facilitate its ultimate goal.

A United Front is of two types: 'tactical' and 'strategic'. The Strategic United Front is formed with various underground organizations of the CPI (Maoist), which are engaged in waging a new democratic revolution (NDR).

In the Tactical United Front (TUF), through the formation of coalitions with persons and groups that are opposed to the state and its policies, on one issue or the other, the Maoists seek to fight the state through 'peaceful', political means, as well as broaden their support base.

This chapter seeks to understand the United Front tactics of the CPI (Maoist) and describes how it has been put into operation. The activities of the TUF can best be noticed in urban areas because these are the 'centres of struggle by various classes, under the leadership of several organizations representing them'.[2] Hence, according to the CPI (Maoist), 'it is essential that we unite with such struggling organizations and build up broad struggles against the ruling classes'.[3] In this light, this chapter also seeks to examine the 'urban activities' of the CPI (Maoist).

At the outset, it needs to be borne in mind that urban activities are not only limited to TUF activities alone, but also encompass military tasks, organizing the industrial/working class, mobilizing the educated and or unemployed youth, as well as organizing logistics support to the armed struggle. At the same time, it also needs to be noted that TUF activity is a 'very important' component of the work of the Maoists in urban areas, that is, cities and towns.

Tactical United Front

The TUF is a secret committee. It functions directly under the guidance of the Sub-Committee on Mass Organizations (SUCOMO), which itself is a sub-set of the all-powerful and apex Central Committee of the CPI (Maoist). In fact, the then Communist Party of India (Marxist)-Leninist (People's War) (CPI-ML [PW]) considered forming the United Front in 1995.[4] However, these efforts did not take a concrete shape.

Meanwhile, the PW merged with the then Communist Party of India Marxist-Leninist (Party Unity) in 1998, and a process of consolidating the organization engaged much of the PW's attention. In 2002, the TUF activity took a firm shape with the formation of an outfit known as Forum against Imperialism and Globalization (FAIG), which is a conglomerate of various revolutionary and mass organizations. This paved the way for the then PW jointly hosting with the Maoist Communist Centre of India (MCCI) a huge congregation known as Mumbai Resistance 2004, or MR 2004.[5] MR 2004 was the Maoists' answer to the World Social Forum (WSF).

The success of MR 2004 persuaded the CPI (Maoist) to give a fillip to TUF activity. At that time, Narayan Sanyal alias Naveen Prasad alias Bijoy Da – the general secretary of the erstwhile Party Unity – proposed the formation of a TUF Committee to oversee the United Front; this was carried through.[6] The committee was given the mandate to supervise all the broad front activities across the country.

At the January 2007 Unity Congress, the Maoists passed resolutions on a number of issues, which points to the kind of TUFs they would have already formed or form in the days ahead. The issues included atrocities on dalits, formation of special economic zones (SEZs), agrarian crisis and farmers' suicides, secessionist movements which they claim are nationality struggles, minority rights and so on. Thus, calls given by the front organizations or affiliates[7] of the CPI (Maoist) from 2007 against the massacre of dalits in Khairlanji, their vocal, and reported/alleged physical support to displacement struggles[8] of Singur, Nandigram and POSCO, the incidents in Lalgarh, and so on should be seen through the prism of TUF.

In a nutshell, the TUF serves the agenda of the Maoists in the following ways:

- To consolidate various 'anti-imperialist' struggles and bring them on to one platform on the basis of a common working understanding;
- To expand the reach of the Maoists to various sections of the society by building contacts with them;
- To expand over-ground cadre strength, thoroughly indoctrinate them and then completely incorporate them into organizational work, especially in urban areas;
- Poach partners for potential leaders and ideologues;
- Serve as a good cover from the long arm of the state;
- Essentially being a political activity, it reinforces the military activities, that is, armed struggle.[9]

Presently, the organizations with which the Maoists have formed the TUF include the Revolutionary Democratic Front

(RDF), the People's Democratic Front of India (PDFI), the Committee against Violence on Women (CAVOW), and the Committee for the Release of Political Prisoners (CRPP), among others.

Besides, the RDF, a front organization of the CPI (Maoist), which is proscribed by the union government under the Unlawful Activities Prevention Act, is a key component of the TUF. Among its various activities, besides issuing calls and statements on various issues, including one on 16 December 2007 calling the people to 'Lend Support to the ongoing revolutionary movement in Dandakaranya, India!', an RDF representative presented a paper entitled 'Nandigram: The Road to Sovereignty of India', at the conference against SEZs and other industrial projects displacing people, on 2–3 June 2007, in Kolkata. In December 2007, all-India leader of RDF, G.N. Saibaba, gave an interview[10] to a Norwegian journalist, Lars Akerhaug, which was subsequently published and also posted on the RDF blog. In 2007, it also launched its own blog, http://rdfindia.blogspot.com.

Moreover, the RDF is a key mover[11] behind the formation of a broad front known as the PDFI, which was founded in July 2006. Its members include Medha Patkar, Nandita Haksar, S.A.R. Geelani, B.D. Sharma, President, Bharat Jan Andolan, Maoist ideologue P. Varavara Rao, and RDF leader Darshan Pal. Some of its constituent organizations include Samyukta Sangram Committee (West Bengal), Indian Federation of Trade Unions, All India Federation of Trade Unions, Chhattisgarh Mukti Morcha, Daman Virodhi Manch (Orissa), Jharkhand Progressive Students Union – an affiliate of the All India Radical Students Federation (AIRSF) – and others. While the various constituent organizations of the PDFI organized their activities in their respective areas of operation, the PDFI hosted a meeting on 12 May 2007, in Delhi, to commemorate the First War of Independence of 1857 and a conference to debate on the 'need to initiate third wave of independence struggle'.

The CRPP released the first volume of its bulletin, 'The Arrested', at gathering in Chennai, on 6 July 2008.[12] The first volume was received by Amit Bhattacharyya, Secretary-General, CRPP, from S.A.R. Geelani, vice-president, CRPP.

Earlier, on 31 March and 1 April 2008, the committee held a similar meeting at the LTG Auditorium in New Delhi.

It has long been the contention of the Maoists that their cadres and leaders detained in various prisons across the country should be treated as political prisoners. In fact, on many occasions these arrested activists staged protests and sat on hunger strikes inside the jails demanding that they be given the status of, and privileges accorded to, political prisoners.

The Maoists have made attempts to form a TUF with the Muslims. This effort has been on since the past few years. In the wake of the proscription imposed on the Students Islamic Movement of India (SIMI), which has been involved in a series of bomb blasts in different cities and towns of India. According to media reports of 23 August 2008, Azad, spokesperson of the Central Committee of the CPI (Maoist), said 'it was a reiteration of the (government's) policy to continue its brutal war on Muslims'.[13]

Further, in another statement Azad also condemned what he called 'double standards of the Indian ruling classes in Kashmir'. He called upon Kashmiri Muslims to 'fight back Hindu fascist forces and Indian expansionists'. All along, the CPI (Maoist) held the secessionist insurgencies in Kashmir and India's Northeast, as well as the LTTE's war against the Sri Lankan government as 'nationality struggles'.

In fact, at its Unity Congress (also known as 9th Congress) that concluded towards the end of January 2007, the CPI (Maoist), among other things, passed a resolution on 'Nationality Struggles', another resolution on 'nationalities', and yet another resolution on 'Hindu fascism'. While it extended support to the secessionist-terrorist movement in Jammu and Kashmir terming it a nationality struggle, in the last resolution it held that: 'The Indian state too has targeted Muslims, branding them "terrorist". After the 9/11 incident and the Parliament Attack Case Muslims were targeted once again … . Indian state forces are even capturing and annihilating innocent Muslims now and then, in the name of nabbing terrorists'. The resolution further declared: 'Our party is willing to unite in a broad front with all the genuine democratic forces which would be willing to fight back the Hindu fascist offensive'.

In the past, too, with a view to winning the support of the Muslim community, the Maoists sought to convey that they empathize with them. For instance, in 2005, the then Andhra Pradesh State Committee Secretary of the CPI (Maoist) issued a statement extending moral support and condemning the arrest in Hyderabad of one of the accused in the Hiren Pandya murder case.

The statement relating to the proscription of SIMI could be understood by considering the following. One, it is an attempt to win over the support of the Muslim community and thus broaden their base. Two, the Maoists are making common cause with SIMI by condemning its proscription, as they, too, are a proscribed organization in some of the affected states; they are also banned by the central government under the Unlawful Activities Prevention Act.

Three, and more importantly, this should be seen in the context of the Maoist tactic of making common cause with any organization or body that opposes the Indian state either through peaceful means or violently. This is part of the United Front tactics of the Maoists

Besides, according to a media report from Kolkata, 'Lower rung leaders of the CPI (Maoist) have been monitoring the functions of these mass organizations (which they have founded). Those who had put up Maoist posters at the Writers' Building last month have been identified …'.[14]

Urban Movement

Nature, Scope, and Objectives

The activities of the CPI (Maoist) in urban areas – cities and towns – need to be understood because of the implications they hold. These activities should be understood together with TUF activities because urban presence would give a fillip to TUF activities.

For reasons such as merger, consolidation, and survival from what the Maoists term as state repression, the Maoists in their earlier *avatar* did not pay much attention to building their movement in urban areas. However, they always had a presence in towns and cities to cater to logistics needs and stay in safe houses during medical treatment or in transit. 'Because of the anonymity it accords, it becomes easy for the Maoists to stay and operate in urban centres'.[15]

The Maoists have also prepared an *Urban Perspective Plan*,[16] which is a roadmap to the type of activities they would undertake in towns in order to enhance their support base.

In January 2007, the Central Committee of the CPI (Maoist), at its meeting, is believed to have constituted an Urban Sub-Committee (USCO) to implement the plan.[17] USCO is believed to be comprising five very senior Central Committee members and has been tasked with the building of the working class movement.[18]

Surely, the Maoists envisage penetrating the trade union movement in industrial centres of the country. Besides, essentially, the rebels would seek to work among the youth and un-employed sections of the society, as well as the student community to increase their support base and possibly draw cadres from these sections.

The urban movement has a defined role in the political strategy and military strategy of the CPI (Maoist). According to the CPI (Maoist), 'being the centres of concentration of the industrial proletariat, urban areas play an important part within the political strategy of the new Democratic Revolution'.[19] The Maoists envisage that they would mobilize and organize the industrial workers and channelize them towards playing 'leadership role in organizing the agrarian revolution by sending ... advanced detachment to the rural areas'.[20] The role of the urban movement within the military strategy of the Maoists has been best explained by Mao Tse Tung thus: 'the final objective of the revolution is the capture of the cities, the enemy's main bases and this objective cannot be achieved without adequate work in the cities'.[21] The CPI (Maoist) holds that '(they) should, by building up a strong urban movement, ensure that the urban masses contribute to creating the conditions that will obtain success for the armed struggle in the countryside'.[22]

In the Maoist scheme of things, the objectives/tasks of the urban movement could be classified under three broad heads or categories[23]: (a) mobilize and organize the basic masses and build the party on that basis;[24] (b) build the United Front;[25] and (c) military tasks.[26]

The Maoists contend that the urban movement should be conducted through various types of mass organizations; the wider the organizations, the better. These organizations are of different types: secret revolutionary mass organizations,[27] open and semi-open revolutionary mass organizations, and open legal mass organizations which are not directly linked to the CPI (Maoist).[28] The last of these would include Maoist-inspired cover organizations and legal, democratic organizations.

Logistics Support

The utility of having a presence in urban centres and operate there was best illustrated in recent times when police seized empty rocket shells and rocket launchers on 8 September 2006, in Mahabubnagar district, Andhra Pradesh. The kingpin, 'Tech Madhu', later surrendered to the police on 17 October 2006, in the district headquarters town of Warangal, Andhra Pradesh. The seizures and surrender led to the detection of an elaborate network the Maoists had built to manufacture rocket parts and transport them to different parts of the country. The network originated in the industrial centre of Ambattur, a suburb of Chennai where these were fabricated in separate foundries and stealthily transported in private commercial carriers to different parts of the country. The network spread across five states: Tamil Nadu, Andhra Pradesh, Madhya Pradesh, Chhattisgarh, and Orissa.[29]

In fact, on 10 January 2007, police in Bhopal, Madhya Pradesh, unearthed an R&D-cum-arms making unit of the Maoists. The interrogation of the arrested persons brought to light that the rebels earlier ran similar units in other towns in Madhya Pradesh such as Jabalpur and Indore.[30] Barely a few days later, police in Rourkela, Orissa, unearthed another similar unit.

Rest and Recuperation

On many occasions important top-level leaders of the CPI (Maoist) have been arrested from cities and towns. Malla Raji Reddy alias Sattenna was arrested on 17 December 2007, in Angamaly town, Ernakulam district, Kerala. He is a member of the Central Military Commission that guides all military activities, member of the all-powerful and apex Central Committee, and the core politburo. Earlier, Sridhar Krishan Srinivasan alias Vishnu was arrested on 19 August 2007, in Mumbai. He is a member of the politburo and Maharashtra State Committee Secretary of the CPI (Maoist). A subsequent media report had this to say: 'They are using Mumbai as a place of rest, planning and recruitment. The guerrillas who get injured in encounters with the police are sent to Naxal dens in Mumbai for treatment, education and relaxation'.[31]

Separately on the same day, Vernin Gonsalves alias Vikram, member of the Maharashtra State Committee, was arrested in Mumbai. In December 2007, Somen alas Suman da, the West Bengal State Committee Secretary was arrested from Kolkata. He was trying in the process of building the urban movement and mobilizing youth and students and was, therefore, frequently visiting Kolkata, at the time of his arrest.

Tapping Industrial Workers

The detection of Maoist activities in towns such as Surat, in Gujarat, earlier in 2006, clearly indicates that the Maoists are attempting to penetrate the urban-based working class movement in the country. Besides, there have been reports since September 2006 of the detection of Maoist activities in Haryana – in Jhind, Kurukshetra, Panipat, and Sonepat. A closer look at these areas reveals that are these industrial hubs. In Delhi, the Maoists have reportedly infiltrated the Delhi Safai Karmachari Sangathan (DSKS). In fact, according to a media report quoting unnamed intelligence officials: 'The rebels, the sources add, have plans to strike in the industrial belts of Bhilai-Ranchi-Dhanbad-Calcutta and Mumbai-Pune-Surat-Ahmedabad to take their battle into the heart of India.

In Maharashtra, too, the Maoists apparently devised a plan to operate in urban areas in a big way. Some Maoist documents, reportedly, contained encrypted writings and code names for various cities and towns in Maharashtra.[32] The documents referred to Mumbai as mango, while tamarind and date could have been used to refer Nashik and Nagpur. Similarly, code names were used to refer to Thane, Pune, Aurangabad, and Malegaon. The top brass of Maharashtra police have asked the Mumbai police to be alert and 'stressed on the Naxalite strategy of tapping into "urban discontent" by involving themselves in controversies over SEZs and other development issues'.[33] In fact, in Kolkata the Maoists had attempted to set a tram on fire.[34]

As one journalist noted: (these) 'efforts are part of a grand strategy to mobilise a section of the discontented population, especially industry workers ... by aiming at heightened "mobilisations" around industrial establishments and simultaneously indulging in disruption strategies'.[35]

Thus, the Maoists seem to be acting on a long-term perspective plan. In their scheme of things, they hope to gain control over the working class movement and use it appropriately at a later stage when their so-called NDR advances and furthers. In the immediate to short-term the objective is to gain control over key (strategic) industries with a view to inflicting 'damage' on the state's capacity to fight the Maoists, either through organizing sabotage activities or bringing production to a halt. According to an internal document of the CPI (Maoist), they envisage penetrating the working class movement in industries such as communication, oil and natural gas, coal, transport, power, defence production, and so on.[36]

For instance, if the DSKS were to go on a flash strike, say, for three days, sanitation in Delhi is likely to be seriously affected. In May 2007, the Maoists blasted and brought down three High Tension (HT) towers in Narayanpur district, in the Bastar region of Chhattisgarh, thus plunging into darkness five districts for two days and two districts for 10 days. There was a blackout and life literally came to a standstill in Narayanpur and Dantewada districts.[37] Also, there have been infrequent reports of ammunition with markings of Ordnance Factories being seized from Maoist dumps. Clearly, some employees of those factories connived with Maoist contacts and have helped smuggle the ammunition out. Besides, in 2006, the then Union Home Minister, Shivraj Patil, reportedly said in the Lok Sabha that the Maoists were 'planning to target important installations in major cities, including Mumbai'.[38]

In their earlier *avatar* as the People's War Group (PWG), the Maoists had gained good experience in penetrating and spearheading the working class movement. The Singareni Karmika Samakhya (SIKASA), a Maoist front and trade union of miners in the Singareni Collieries in Andhra Pradesh, had near total control over mine labourers and had successfully fought for better wages to miners. At that time, its influence was such that all mining activity came to a grinding halt when SIKASA issued a strike call for better wages and implemented it for 58 days at a stretch.

Besides, reports from different states indicate the CPI (Maoist) is making attempts to penetrate educational institutions with a view to recruiting sympathizers and cadres.

Students and Youth

The urban movement has attracted students towards the Maoist fold in various parts of the country. In the 1980s, hordes of students from Kakatiya University and Regional Engineering College (now National Institute of Technology), Warangal, and Osmania University, Hyderabad, joined the then PW cadres. In fact, Nambala Kesava Rao, the lynchpin of the Central Military Commission of the CPI (Maoist) holds a masters' degree in technology (MTech).

According to an activist-college teacher, Shoma Sen 'as far as some of my friends in the student movement (are concerned), they did continue their revolutionary lives and make these sacrifices. Some of the people I knew, Vernon (Vernon Gonsalves, Central Committee member of the CPI [Maoist]), Sridhar (Maharashtra State Committee member) and others seem to have gone underground'.[39] After the arrest of Vernon Gonsalves and Sridhar, it became known that they were reportedly 'trying to indoctrinate and recruit people, and collecting funds'.[40] Quoting an unnamed police official a media report said, 'There is no armed activity in Mumbai at the moment and the Maoists have kept their activities limited to propagating their ideology, setting up secret cells for frontal organisations and recruiting people'.[41]

Besides, according to one media report,

> ... security agencies believe that the front organisations have started vigorous movement in the education sector, to rope in students from several reputed colleges for their cause ... (they) warned the (Nagpur) city police about these student-oriented revolutionary organisations. People working under banners with hints of revolution, like 'sangharsh' and 'kranti' are under the scanner.[42]

Following the arrest of Himadri Sen Roy, a very senior Maoist leader, and Somen alias Sumanand, West Bengal State Committee Secretary, near Kolkata, police claimed that '[t]he CPI (Maoist) has initiated a drive to spread its network in the city (Kolkata) and its outskirts and the outfit has brought some youths and students from premier educational institutions like Presidency College under its fold in the last two years'.[43] In fact, reportedly, it was Somen who insisted at the 9th Congress of the CPI (Maoist) that the focus of attention should now turn towards urban areas. According to a media report, 'In the last CPI (Maoist) Congress (9th Congress), Somen had emphasized that the party needed to focus on urban areas, particularly the industrial belts and educational institutes'.[44]

In this wake, he frequently visited Kolkata trying to mobilize students and industrial workers. During his visits, he was reportedly staying in colonies close to jute mills in Howrah's Shibpur and Dasnagar and had also been to Nadia. Besides mobilizations, he was actively involved in raising funds for the West Bengal unit of the CPI (Maoist), to make it financially less dependent on the all-India funds.

In Bangalore, too, Maoist activities in colleges have been noticed. According to a media report, the police suspected that a group known as the Karnataka Communal Harmony Group (KCHG), a congregation of intellectuals and activists, is a Maoist-front. Apparently, top police officials visited the famous Jesuit College – St Joseph's – to investigate the involvement of students with the KCHG and the Maoists. In fact, in Karnataka, it was the urban movement that was stronger than the rural movement.

The then Karnataka State Committee Secretary, Sundararajan insisted that the focus of the Maoists should be on urban areas and, owing to differences with the other members of the State Committee, he split the outfit vertically, walking away with nearly two-thirds of the total strength of the state unit.[45] Earlier, sometime in 2002, Malik, the West Bengal State Committee secretary, resigned from the then PW following sharp differences over the area-wise seizure of power strategy of the PW. He, too, argued in favour of a strong urban movement. It is, thus, interesting to note the shift in the line of thinking of the

Central Committee, which is now emphasizing on enhanced urban activity and building a strong working class movement. A crucial question that has no immediate answer is: A quite strong urban movement in Andhra Pradesh faded away in the decade of the 2000s. How did this happen, and what lessons have the Maoists learnt to now sustain and heighten the urban movement?

Conclusion

The TUF and urban movement are extremely important elements of the activities of the Communist Party of India (Maoist). These are just about taking shape over the past three to four years. Being political and peaceful in nature, it is not surprising that TUF activities have not received adequate attention in the media. At the same time, because they are legitimate, over-ground, democratic activities, the state's hands are tied-down. At best, it can keep a close watch on these organizations but cannot halt their activities.

However, if it was possible on the part of the state to prove that outfits that are part of the Maoist-led TUF are, indeed, Maoist fronts or have direct linkages with them, it is then feasible to proscribe such organizations. Since these organizations mobilize, organize, propagate, and indoctrinate the people to attract them towards the over-ground activities (i.e. create a sympathizer base), and, perhaps, subsequently as part of the underground, the state should make every effort to expose these organizations and ban them.

Moreover, if and when the urban movement catches on among the industrial workers, the state will have to deal with possible sabotage activities and industrial unrest. When the urban movement becomes strong, the state will then have to deal with urban terrorism. It is a different matter for places that have not been Maoist strongholds, as well as for those places that were once strongholds but had subsequently been weakened since Maoists have committed violence. In other words, the occurrence of violence, or the lack of it, cannot be a true indicator of the strength and influence of the Maoists in a town or city.

Andhra Pradesh is replete with such examples. Towns in the North Telengana Special Zone Committee area in Andhra

Pradesh had experienced this kind of urban violence by the Maoists, as well as their TUF activities. Even as late as December 2001, the Maoists set-off an explosion targeting the Hanamkonda police station and it's station house officer, Ghulam Samdani, in the heart of the district headquarters town of Warangal, barely a stone's throw away from the office of the district police chief. There were many other instances of killings, including killings of political leaders and Indian Police Service (IPS) officers, in broad daylight in Hyderabad and other towns. Also, if the state is vigilant enough it can disrupt the logistics support activities of the Maoists in urban areas.

Urbanization itself has some fault lines and the Maoists could well exploit these to their advantage. Also, the stronger the movement becomes in the urban areas the more it is likely to contribute to the agrarian revolution – in terms of providing leaders and men and material to the people's war. Besides, the Maoists enjoy some degree of sympathy and support among the urban intellectuals and middle class, including students and teachers in schools, colleges, and universities.

It is, thus, essential to keep a close watch on Maoist activities in towns and cities.

Notes

1. See http://indianexpress.com/article/india/india-others/ andhra-university-assistant-professor-arrested-for-suspected-links-with-maoists/
2. An internal document of the CPI (Maoist) read during a field visit to Andhra Pradesh, November 2008.
3. Ibid.
4. Interview with an Inspector General of Police, Andhra Pradesh, 25 November 2008.
5. MR 2004 was attended by over 250 organizations – 24 of them international fraternal groups, besides the PW and MCCI, among others. MR functioned as a platform for expressing opposition to imperialism and globalization. It was an event organized by several front organizations of Maoist outfits following a call given by the International League of People's Solidarities (ILPS).

6. Interview with an Inspector General of Police, Hyderabad, 25 November 2008.
7. The CPI (Maoist) has front organizations or affiliates among various sections of the society in different states. The list mentioned here has been collated from the author's databases on the Maoist movement in India. These include: *Andhra Pradesh*: Rythu Coolie Sangham (Agricultural Labourers Association), Singareni Karmika Samakhya (Singareni Collieries Workers Federation), Viplava Karmika Samakhya (Revolutionary Workers Federation), Radical Students Union, Radical Youth League, All India Revolutionary Students Federation, Viplava Rachayitala Sangham (Revolutionary Writers Association); *Bihar*: Lok Sangram Morcha (People's Struggle Front), Mazdoor Kisam Mukti Morcha (Workers-Peasants Liberation Front), Jan Mukti Parishad (People's Liberation Council), Mazdoor Kisan Ekta Morcha (Workers-Peasants Unity Front), Bharat Navjawan Sabha (Indian Youth Association), Mazdoor Kisan Sangrami Parishad (Workers-Peasants Struggle Council), Shramik Sangram Manch (Workers Struggle Platform), Nari Mukti Sangharsh Samiti (Women's Liberation Struggle Association), Sangharsh Janamukti Morcha (People's Liberation Struggle Front), Democratic Students Union, All India People's Resistance Forum; *Madhya Pradesh*: Adivasi Kisan Mazdoor Sangh (Tribal Peasants-Workers Association), Krantikari Kisan Mazdoor Sangh (Revolutionary Peasants-Workers Association), Krantikari Balak Sangh (Revolutionary Children's Association), Gram Raksha Dal (Village Defence Force), Gram Rajya Samiti (Village Governance Council), *Karnataka*: Karnataka Vimochana Ranga, Mahila Jagruthi, Karnataka Rythu Cooliee Sangam, Progressive Democratic Front, Karnataka People's Resistance Forum, Samrajyashahi Virodhi Okkoota, Progressive Youth Centre, Bababudangiri Solidarity Forum, Adivasi Solidarity Group, *Tamil Nadu:* Makkal Jananayaga Ilaingnar Kazhagam (People's Democratic Youth Association), *Chhattisgarh*: Dandakaranya Adivasi Kisan Mazdoor Sangh, Krantikari Adivasi Balak Sangh, Krantikari Adivasi Mahila Sangh, Krantikari Kisan Committee, Mahila Mukti Manch, *Orissa*: Daman Pratirodh Manch, Revolutionary Democratic Front, Chasi Mulia Samiti, Kui Labanga Sangha, Jana Natya

Mandali, Krantikari Kisan Samiti, Bal Sangham, *Maharashtra*: Deshbhakti Yuva Sangathan; and *Kerala:* Revolutionary People's Front.

8. The struggles/agitations were launched by people who are opposed to the government acquiring their lands for giving them away to industrial houses for setting-up factories. Largely, these are the tribal population.
9. Participants in political struggles could eventually be drafted as armed cadre. Besides, the success of political struggles would also give an impetus to the protracted people's war (PPW), that is, military struggle. On the other, successes in the military struggle would lead to a greater number of people joining the political struggles carried out by front organizations. The underlying assumption is that the general public are, essentially, fence-sitters and would lean towards the winning side – the state or the rebels – depending upon successes and set-backs.
10. Among other things, the interview touches upon increasing poverty, opposes setting-up SEZs, holds that India is still a feudal economy, highlights underdevelopment, criticizes the rise of Right-wing fundamentalism, expresses solidarity with the Muslim community, and, understandably, sings praise for Maoist ideology.
11. See the September 2006 issue of *Liberation*, the mouth piece of the Communist Party of India (Marxist-Leninist). Available at http://www.cpiml.org/liberation/year_2006/September/nepal_uprising.htm (Accessed on 20 December 2007).
12. See *The Hindu*, Chennai, 7 July 2008.
13. *The Hindu*, 23 August 2008.
14. *Statesman*, Kolkata, 26 February 2008.
15. Interview with K. Srinivas Reddy, Deputy Editor, *The Hindu*, Hyderabad, 26 November 2008.
16. An internal document of the CPI (Maoist) read in Hyderabad during a field visit to Andhra Pradesh, September 2007.
17. Ibid.
18. Ibid.
19. Ibid.
20. Ibid.
21. Selected Works of Mao Tse-tung, Vol. 2, 237.

22. An internal document of the CPI (Maoist) read during a field visit to Andhra Pradesh, November 2008.
23. Ibid.
24. The Maoists consider this as the 'basic and primary' task. They hold that no progress could be made on the other tasks unless this is achieved.
25. This involved the task of unifying the working class, building worker–peasant solidarity and alliance, uniting with the other classes in the cities, building fronts against globalization, Hindu fascism, repression, and so on.
26. These include sending cadres to the rural areas to fight in the people's war, infiltration of all government structures, especially the armed forces, organizing in important industries, conducting sabotage, and, lastly, extending logistical support.
27. For instance, All India Revolutionary Students Federation (AIRSF), Dandakaranya Adivasi Kisam Mazdoor Sangh (DAKMS), and so on.
28. For instance, People's Democratic Front of India, All India Coordination Team of Workers, People's Movement against Imperialism, and so on.
29. See *The Hindu*, 13 September 2006. (The report filed from Nalgonda is entitled 'Arms Haul Probe: Five States Join Hands').
30. Interview with S.K. Raut, Director General of Police, Madhya Pradesh, 12 January 2007. At that time ha was the Additional Director General of Police (Intelligence).
31. 'Maoist Menace Spreads to Urban Areas', *Times of India*, New Delhi, 17 February 2008.
32. See Anupam Dasgupta, 'Maoists Target Industry Units', *Daily News and Analyses*, Mumbai, Available at http://www.dnaindia.com/report.asp?NewsID=1123803 (Accessed on 28 September 2008).
33. 'Top Cop Wants Protest Rallies to Be Monitored', *Daily News and Analyses*, Mumbai, 5 November 2007.
34. *Statesman*, 26 February 2008.
35. Ibid.
36. An internal document of the CPI (Maoist) read in Hyderabad during a field visit to Andhra Pradesh, September 2007.

37. P.V. Ramana, 'Maoists Designs: Target Infrastructure, Paralyse Economy', *Tribune*, Chandigarh, 2 July 2007; also see, P.V. Ramana. 'The Growing Maoist Menace', *Deccan Herald*, Bangalore, 25 June 2007.
38. 'Maoist Menace Spreads to Urban Areas', *Times of India*, New Delhi, 17 February 2008.
39. See www.ndtv.com, 28 August 2007. According to this report, students from Mumbai with revolutionary leanings went and worked with the Naxalites in the Vidarbha region of Maharashtra.
40. 'Maoist Menace Spreads to Urban Areas'. *Times of India*, 17 February 2008.
41. Ibid.
42. *Times of India*. http://timesofindia.indiatimes.com/city/Nagpur/Naxals-eye-urban-students-as-recruits/articleshow/2777733.cms? (Accessed on 14 February 2008).
43. *Statesman*. Kolkata, 26 February 2008.
44. Ibid.
45. The split occurred sometime during 2006. See, K. Srinivas Reddy, 'Karnataka Naxal Movement Splits'. *The Hindu*, 14 February 2007.

7

Women and the Naxal Movement

Retrospect and Prospect

RAJAT KUMAR KUJUR

Sexual and gender-based violence is one of the most insidious violations of women rights during armed conflict. Sexual assault and exploitation are frequently employed by different actors in an armed conflict situation; victimization leads to isolation, alienation, prolonged emotional trauma, and unwanted pregnancies that often result in abandoned children. Sexual violence against women during conflict is a tactic of war that has reached epidemic proportions. For example, up to 500,000 women were raped, many at gunpoint, in Rwanda in 1994.[1] Amidst a number of armed conflicts going on in different parts of the country, in India women are also at great risk of sexual and gender-based violence. Of course India's decade-old experience of handling insurgencies have resulted in the development of law and policy on addressing sexual and gender-based violence in armed conflict, yet individual cases as well as patterns of abuse against women still continue to be reported. In a country like India where women are still looked down with inequality, women experience greater violations being caught between different violators and in view of the fact that in such situations, patriarchal values are strongly reinforced. On the one hand, the state targets women and uses violence against them as a means of suppression and on the other hand the community is apathetic to the special problems faced by women.

Naxal movement[2] is one such case of armed conflict in India where the role of women or the position of the women is one of the most talked about topic. While CPI (Maoist) has come out with volumes of writings on women liberalization through the Naxal movement, there have been instances when former women Maoist cadres have alleged sexual harassment by their fellow male counterparts. Recently in 2014 Minister of State for Home Affairs Kiren Rijju stated in Lok Sabha that several surrendered women CPI (Maoist) cadres of Odisha, Maharashtra, Bihar, Jharkhand, and other states have alleged sexual exploitation of tribal women cadres in the Maoist camps. He added 'this has been widely reported in the media also from time to time. Such instances of sexual exploitation include rape, forced marriage and molestation by senior male CPI (Maoist) cadres'.[3] On the other hand, allegations of sexual harassment by the security personnel against the arrested women Naxal cadres and also against civilian women living in the Maoist-infested areas are another emerging trend of the decade-old Naxal movement. In the year 2012, Soni Sori, a tribal teacher in a government school in Dantewada, Chhattisgarh, who was arrested in October 2011 on charges of being a courier between the Maoists and Essar Group, which has mining interests in the region, alleged that she had been sexually assaulted by the Chhattisgarh police and a Kolkata hospital that examined her had found stones in her private parts and rectum.[4]

Over the years, Naxal movement has been able to attract a number of women cadres. Recently, we have witnessed the number of women combatants outnumber their male counterparts in some of the deadliest Naxal operations. According to various reports of CPI (Maoist) which is also supported by Home Ministry reports, women constitute 60 per cent of active Maoists in most of the states affected by Left-wing extremism. It's a recent development. Till 2010, women formed 40 per cent of the Naxalite fighting force; it was under 25 per cent in 2008. On the other hand, Naxal organizational set-up at the leadership level has a very few women representation. This contradiction in the Naxal modus operandi has given rise to several critical questions. Does the gender issue play a role in the issue of women joining the Naxal movement? Why is there no significant representation of women in the upper echelons of the political structure and leadership? If there is a parity of membership among women and men, why is it that women are unable to rise to the position of intellectual and political leaders of the movement? This chapter will revolve around these questions and by doing so we will highlight the depth and different dimensions of violations/discriminations suffered by women in the Naxalite conflict and get government/nongovernment organizations to address the specific needs of women in such situations.

Feminist Currents within the Naxal Movement: The Reality Bites

The Naxalbari movement of 1967 was short lived but it was successful enough to generate plenty of euphoria among the minds of academicians. During 1970s and 1980s, Naxal movement remained one of the most popular social movements to be studied by Indian academics. There has been thorough studies on the cause, nature, and impact of the movement, some of which recorded considerable women's participation.[5] Surprisingly, however, most studies on the movement fail to concentrate on the gender dimension. The silence about gender issues, including women's role and contribution to the movement, continues even in the modern day writings of Naxalism.[6] I have no hesitation in admitting that even my own book falls short in explaining the gender equation in the Naxal movement.[7] However, the problem lies not with the academician but somewhere else. Even the worst critic of Naxalism would admit that women played a crucial role in the Naxalbari uprising and to be more specific seven peasant women were killed during a mass meeting of the armed peasants in Naxalbari in 1967.[8] Ironically but the party documents, leaflets, and essays written by the Naxal ideologues are conspicuously silent about the 'presence' of these women activists, sympathizers, and supporters. 'This failure to acknowledge women activists carries an interconnected double meaning – it did not only erase from the official documents the physical presence of women in organizing and leading the movement, but, equally important, it obfuscated the ideological possibility of redefining women's role and status in the larger social context'.[9]

The chief architect of the Naxal movement in India Charu Mazumdar was instrumental in shaping the mind of thousands of revolutionaries. Through his speeches and writings, he designed a road map for the Naxal movement in India. In order to reach out to the cross sections of the society, Mazumdar wrote a number of essays addressing different sections and classes, that is, 'To the Youth and Student', 'To Those Comrades Who Are Working in the Rural Areas', 'To the Working-Class', and 'To the Revolutionary Peasants' – however he never wrote a piece addressed as 'To the Women'. It's quite surprising that while Mazumdar examined power relationships between classes, castes, and the state, the more fundamental and ubiquitous power relationship between men and women never entered his mind. Thus, one can argue that women were taken for granted, even by the highest leadership, to unquestioningly follow men in the revolution and their physical presence did not initiate any radical thinking about their role in the movement. Probably this is the reason for which women are completely absent from any accounts of intellectual creativity or agency in the struggle and consequently in the leadership as is evident from the composition of the front face of the Naxal groups.

It is in this context I want to reproduce what Ajitha had said way back in 1999:

> The women were always in an inferior position in the movement. I was highly disturbed by the loss of opportunities on account of being a woman. The men either showed a protective approach towards women or treated them as a sexual commodity. They considered the support the revolutionaries got from their wives and mothers as their duty. They did not realize that these innocent women had to suffer a lot because of their actions. The police and the authorities constantly harassed them. They also failed to appreciate our intellectual capacities and human feelings. Marriage was prohibited for revolutionaries as the party felt it hinders freedom. Later, however, the party allowed marriages approved by it. If anybody fell in love with those who did not like the party, it acted like a feudal lord.[10]

Ajitha was no ordinary woman, in the late 1960s she was active in the Naxalite movement and was the only female member in the group that organized and executed the Thalassery–Pulpally Naxalite 'actions', which consequently led to her arrest and imprisonment in 1968. This statement of Ajitha depicts the condition of women Naxal cadres during the first phase of Naxal movement in 1967–1968.

From 1967 to 2014, Naxal movement has seen many ups and downs in all these years. From CPI (ML) to CPI (Maoist), the movement has also witnessed several changes in its strategies and leadership structure. However, one thing does not seem to have changed that is the failure of the Naxal movement to give a definite shape to the question of feminism in the movement. Ganapathy, after getting elected as the first secretary of the CPI (Maoist), gave an interview to the media where he spoke at length about the official position of his party on crucial issues. He spoke on the unity congress of CPI (Maoist), on the losses in Andhra Pradesh, on SEZs, Nandigram, and role of CPI(M), on the annihilation of Sunil Mahto, on the biggest ever attack by the Maoists in Chhattisgarh, on the party's plans to win over the middle class, in defence of armed struggle, on the fight against the 'mighty' Indian state, on the question of parliament and party's stand, on the mass base of the Maoists, on people's war, on the Islamic upsurge, on the developments in Nepal, and on the role of the party in the contemporary world.[11] CPI (Maoist) so far has prepared several plans of actions for the empowerment of tribes, dalits, peasants, and displaced persons, however till date I have not come across any specific document prepared by CPI (Maoist) which draws an outline for women empowerment. Of course in recent past the CPI (Maoist) has come out with numerous publications glorifying the martyrdom of its women cadres but that does not serve any purpose.[12] In all major party documents of CPI (Maoist), women's liberation is thought to be a necessary follow-up to people's revolution, though the party still fail to notice the intricacies of gender discrimination.

> Women hold half the sky. Without unleashing the pent-up fury of women as a mighty force of revolution, victory in revolution is impossible. It is a matter of pride that the women masses, particularly from among the poor and landless peasants are increasingly coming forward to take an active and sometime front-ranking role in advancing the armed agrarian revolution … . Real equality between men and women can be realized only in the course of the new democratic revolution and further in the process of socialist transformation of society as a whole.[13]

This glorification only masks the active denial of entitlements and equal citizenship in practice, while idealizing sacrifice, service, and unquestioning surrender to sons. This glorification is a mirror image of the simultaneous worship of the mother goddess and the debasement of women in reality. The collapsing of all issues of women's rights into liquor and prohibition reflects blindness to the much larger, much more pervasive violence against women. Finally this trend of translating the history of women's participation in the Naxal movement into either narratives of 'loss and pain' or a celebration of women's 'astounding heroism' in periods of crisis reinforces the question of women's political agency into two polar opposite images of women – either as victims or as agents, which certainly is an insufficient explanation.

The Impact of Naxal Movement on Women: Oppression or Liberation

A closer look in to the Naxal map of the country would reveal the fact that over the years Naxals have been successful in creating their liberated zone around the inaccessible habitats of tribal people. People in those areas have been witnessing armed conflict for more than forty years, and that means in those areas many children have grown into adulthood without any experience of peace. Everyone lives in an atmosphere of fear, suspicion, and terror, an atmosphere conducive to further conflict and instability. Though everyone else suffer, the pain and agony of a tribal woman is unbearable because of her economic roles and vulnerability to sexual, mental, and physical violence. In this protracted low intensity war (a title endorsed by the government agencies) or People's War (as proclaimed by the Naxals), the daily life of a women is at constant struggle.

In a tribal society, feeding the family has always been the responsibility of the women. Tribal women whether from Bastar (Chhattisgarh), Gumla (Jharkhand), or from Malkangiri (Orissa), or from Gadchiroli (Maharashtra) or from any other Naxal-affected area have traditionally worked in the field but this work has been affected by the existing chaotic atmosphere. In a village inside Rairakhol of Sambalpur district in Orissa, for instance, women worked late in the afternoon. However, during the last one decade or so fear of rape and molestation by armed actors has forced change. Women must stop working early and lose income, which they can ill afford or they can ask men to accompany them for protection. By asking men for protection, they lose both power and autonomy. Forced migration of male workforce has emerged as another related livelihood problem for women in the Naxal-infested areas. Initially men made significant percentage of agricultural workforce particularly in the tribal districts of Chhattisgarh, Orissa, Jharkhand, Bihar, and Andhra Pradesh, but their numbers are declining as they flee the conflict, join the militancy, or take up nonagricultural work outside their village. This again has resulted in the decrease of their contribution to the family which adds more to the agony of women in the family.

Another dimension of the decade-old Maoist conflict is the health hazards faced by women in the Naxal-infested areas. In almost all the areas, the health services have completely broken down or are disrupted. The health personnel are reluctant to enter and work in the Naxal-infested areas for security reasons. While this affects both men and women, Women in need of reproductive health support services are especially affected. They have to either travel long distances for such services or do without any medical help. They are often unwilling or physically or financially unable to travel. When services are not available, the tendency of the women or by male family members to underplay women's health needs is further accentuated. Furthermore, there is a high prevalence of malnutrition especially among women and children. And of course there are the largely hidden but long-term problems of fear, pain, loss, guilt, anxiety, hatred, and depression.

Growth of militancy in the Naxal-infested areas has resulted in relentless violence against tribal communities, especially against tribal women. Going by reports, rape is a part of everyday life for the adivasi women of the red territory. Imagine the condition of women in a Naxalite zone; on the one hand security personnel are alleged of committing rape while on the other hand surrendered women Naxal cadres too allege sexual harassment by their male cadres in the Maoist camps.

Following are two media clippings to substantiate the fact that rape has been consistently used as a weapon of war by varied armed actors in the Naxal zone.

> On 22 May 2010, three Adivasi women of Mukram village near Chintalnar, Chhattisgarh, said they were raped by members of the security forces. Four women claim to have been raped in Samsetti, Dantewada by Special Police Officers in 2006. Five women from Potenar said they were raped in the Jangla camp in 2005. Two women were raped by the Salwa Judum and SPOs in Lingagiri in 2006. Three women claimed to have been gang-raped at Tatemargu in November 2009 during a combing operation. The list is endless. And not even once were FIRs registered by police. Five girls from Potenar testified to the NHRC's enquiry team in 10 June 2008, but the team (comprising 15 police officials out of 16) inferred that the allegations could not be substantiated.[14]

> Instances of rape and sexual torture in Naxalite camps are coming to the fore with more and more disillusioned members deserting the CPI (Maoist). The Maoists have also been jolted by the arrest of senior leaders in Orissa. Two women extremists, who recently surrendered in Keonjhar, said they were repeatedly raped by male colleagues in jungle camps. 'After getting drunk, they would sexually assault me', Dipti Munda (name changed) said. She had joined the extremists at 16. Anita Munda (name changed), 18, who surrendered last month also said she was subjected to sexual torture in the forests. Women members were reportedly forced to spend nights with men. 'It was tough and disgusting', another former Maoist said. She hoped the government would help her live a better life. Last year, at least 29 Maoists, including 12 women, gave up arms. They accused the leadership of deviating from the movement's core ideology of protecting and empowering Dalits. The women invariably alleged sexual abuse by male colleagues.[15]

While the consequences of sexual violence is physically, emotionally, and psychologically devastating for the women victims, the survivors of such violations have the burden of silently coping with post-trauma stress almost without any kind of support. This is so because any kind of sexual violation is looked upon by society as an act of 'dishonour' rather than as a violation of the fundamental human right of every woman. While the Naxals are never tired of claiming of liberating the women in the red territory, the reality speaks that the Naxal brand of armed conflict has brought in more miseries to the life of women. Unfortunately but at the government level, policy makers are yet to focus on this crucial area which could play a decisive role in the process of conflict resolution as far as Naxal movement is concerned.

Conclusion

Over the years women in the Naxal-infested regions have been forced to get into one of the following roles, that is,

- *Women relatives of armed activists:* Mothers, wives, sisters, daughters, and partners of armed activist who are in the *struggle* by choice or without choice but impacted upon in the same way and also especially targeted by the state.
- *Women relatives of state armed forces:* Mothers, wives, sisters, daughters, and partners of the police, armed personnel and targeted state officials, and others who have no choice in being part of the conflict and who often remain the forgotten and invisible 'other' category.
- *Women militants or combatants*: Women who are actively involved in the struggle (a) by choice, (b) through coercion, or (c) who have become part of the struggle because of circumstances.
- *Women as shelter providers*: Women who provide food, shelter, and labour (as porters) to the combatants either as sympathizers or through coercion but either way, extremely vulnerable.
- *Women as victims of sexual and physical abuse*: Mostly uninvolved, innocent civilians but also any of the other categories, belonging to any age group and targeted by both state and non-state abusers.

However, regardless of the role women play, all women are uniformly discriminated against, although the dimensions of violation may differ. Unfortunately but the number of women joining the Maoist movement is on rise now. The numbers of women cadre among the rebels began to increase in the late 1990s and some of them are highly educated, urban ideologues, and leaders. For instance, Anuradha Ghandy, a sociology lecturer, best illustrates this category. At the time of her demise due to cerebral malaria, she was leading the all-India women's movement and was the lone member of the Central Committee. Her husband Kobad Ghandy was heading the Central Propaganda Bureau of the Maoists until he was arrested in the national capital New Delhi, on 20 September 2009. Women have been joining the rebel-fold for various reasons. Some have joined the underground due to desperation. Exploitation at the hands of the high and powerful in the village is another reason. It is important to pay attention to each of these factors and surface the depth and dimension of the violations and the causes underpinning these. Furthermore, Naxal movement as a whole has emerged as a conflict where women are at the receiving end from multiple actors. As far as feminism is concerned, Naxalism has proved to be grossly inadequate an ideology to address the issue of gender power equation. On the other hand, the state cannot escape the blame of lacking political will on the account of women empowerment. The level of awareness about the impact of conflict on women has steadily risen over the past decade, though much remains to be explored about the complex issues surrounding this subject. As far as the Naxal movement is concerned, both long-term and short-term measures are required to prevent the victimization of women. Programmatic responses aimed at improving the lives of conflict-affected women may involve overlapping and complementary approaches. In order to be effective, all development programming must incorporate an understanding of the myriad of ways that gender shapes various determinants and dimensions of conflict. Protection, women's participation indecision making, involvement of women in conflict resolution and peace, specially designed programmes of livelihood for women, special surrender, and rehabilitation package for women Naxals are some of the areas which if worked out properly will save women from the curse of the Naxal armed conflict. It's high time to move out of all the glorification and rhetoric of feminism. Rather it will be the greatest contribution of Naxal movement (including the state actors) if it can make people act to restore women to history, and also to restore history to women.

The writer teaches Political Science at the Post Graduate Department of Political Science and Public administration,

Sambalpur University, Odisha. He may be reached at rajatkujur@gmail.com

Notes

1. Organisation of African Unity (2000) Rwanda the Preventable Genocide, Report of the International Panel of Eminent Personalities to Investigate the 1994 Genocide in Rwanda and the Surrounding Events.
2. 'Naxal movement' refers to the Left-wing extremist movement that traces its origin to the May 1967 peasant uprising at Naxalbari in the Darjeeling district of West Bengal. Its prominent ideologues and leaders in the first phase included Charu Mazumdar, Kanu Sanyal, and Janghal Santhal. The movement was launched under the banner of the Communist Party of Indian (Marxist) (CPI-M), but, in April 1969, a split occurred in the party and the radical platform was adopted by the new formation, the Communist Party of India (Marxist-Leninist) (CPI-ML) whose programmes and activities were 'based on the thought of Mao-Zedong', broadly translated by Mazumdar to its fundamentals as 'the physical annihilation of class enemies'. The movement immediately and completely dominated West Bengal and had some impact on a number of other states, including Andhra Pradesh. Since the death of Charu Mazumdar in July 1972, the movement has witnessed innumerable of splits and mergers. Today, even where no historical links exist between the original parties, leadership, and often even ideology or programme, of contemporary Left-wing extremist movements, each of these continues to be referred to as a 'Naxalite' organization.
3. http://zeenews.india.com/news/nation/women-naxal-cadres-sexually-exploited-govt_952740.html (Accessed on 10 September 2014).
4. *Times of India*, 29 December 2012.
5. Banerjee (1980), Mohanty (1977), Ghosh (1974), Dasgupta (1974), Ram, Mohan (1971), Johari (1972), and Roy (1975).
6. Singh (1995) and Gupta (2004).
7. Chakrabarty and Kujur (2010).

8. Chhatopadhyay, Suhrid Sankar (10–23 April 2010). 'End of Revolution'. *Frontline*. (27).
9. Roy (2006).
10. http://www.rediff.com/news/1999/jan/12keral1.htm
11. I got the interview via an e-mail in 2007.
12. *Women Martyrs of Dandakaranyam*, Radical Publications, Kolkata, 2005.
13. CPI (Maoist) Party Programme, http://www.satp.org/satporgtp/countries/india/maoist/documents/papers/partyprogram.htm
14. *Expressbuzz*, 11 June 2010.
15. http://indiatoday.intoday.in/site/story?sId=87571&secid=4

References

Banerjee, Sumanta (1980). *In the Wake of Naxalbari: A History of the Naxalites Movement in India*. Calcutta: Subarnarekha.

Chakrabarty, Bidyut and Kujur, Rajat Kumar (2010). *Maoism in India: Reincarnation of Ultra Left Wing Extremism in Twenty First Century*. London: Routledge.

Dasgupta, Biplab (1974). *The Naxalite Movement*. Calcutta: Allied Publishers.

Ghosh, Sankar (1974). *The Naxalite Movement: A Maoist Experiment*. Calcutta: Firma K.L. Mukhopadhyay.

Gupta, Ranjit Kumar (2004). *The Crimson Agenda: Maoist Protest and Terror*. Delhi: Wordsmiths.

Johari, J.C. (1972). *Naxalite Politics in India*. Delhi: Institute of Constitutional and Parliamentary Studies/Research Publications.

Mohanty, Manoranjan (1977). *Revolutionary Violence: A Study of Maoist Movement in India*. New Delhi: Sterling Publishers.

Ram, Mohan (1971). *Maoism in India*. New York: Barnes and Nobles.

Roy, Asish Kumar (1975). *The Spring Thunder and After: A Survey of Maoist and Ultra-Leftist Movements in India (1962–75)*. Calcutta: Minerva Associates.

Roy, Mallarika Sinha (2006). 'Speaking Silence: Narrative of Gender in the Historiography of the Naxalbari Movement in West Bengal (1967 –75)'. *Journal of South Asian Development*. 1: 207.

Singh, Prakash (1995). *The Naxal Movement in India.* New Delhi: Rupa and Co.

Violence against Women in situations of Armed Conflict and Displacement. World Health Organization. July 1997.

War in the Heart of India: An Enquiry into the Ground Situation in Dantewada District, Chhattisgarh. Independent Citizens' Initiative. 20 July 2006.

Where State Makes War on Its Own People, A Report on Violation of Peoples Rights during the Salwa Judum Campaign in Dantewada. Chhattisgarh. April 2006.

Women and Armed Conflict. International Network on Small Arms. 2003.

Women and Conflict. USAID.

8

Contemporary Social Movements in Tribal Regions of Central India

S.N. CHAUDHARY

About 80 per cent tribes of the country live in the states of central India such as Jharkhand, Odisha, Chhattisgarh, Madhya Pradesh, and Rajasthan. These tribes are from different linguistic, racial, economic, and social categories. Some are numerically inferior but others are numerically superior. Some are highly vulnerable but some are relatively in a better position. In spite of these variations on certain issues, they are similar in different ways. Most of them live in villages. They depend on primary sources for livelihood. The rate and magnitude of backwardness is very high among them, and most of them are historically found in the natural resource-rich areas. Most of them have enjoyed symbiotic relations with nature, and today all of them are experiencing negative consequences of the breakdown of symbiotic relations with nature. Further, whether these tribes are the original inhabitants of the places where they are settled today or they are the in-migrant population it may be controversial but it is beyond doubt that during the last several centuries gradual intensity of their interaction with non-tribal cultures and traditions have significantly increased. There are certain gains of this process. There is an emergence of tribal elites. There is direct impact on mortality rate. There is improvement in enrolment and literacy rate. There is class formation among them, although the process is slow in comparison to the scheduled castes. The number of tribal representatives in formal political institutions have increased. The number of tribal welfare and development projects and schemes have also increased. But the intensity of pain and miseries is more widespread. There is massive degeneration of their identity. The support base, both material and non-material, have experienced serious degeneration. Coping mechanism of different types are largely failed to arrest the degeneration process. Even the constitutional provisions and state initiatives are not able to arrest the ongoing pauperization in a successful manner. Civil society initiatives, including social and environmental movements, are also badly failed to arrest pauperization.

However, there are a section of scholars (Atal, 2012) who are of the view that such criticism gives the impression that development has done nothing positive and, in the fact, development efforts have further worsened the life of tribals. Implicit in it seems to be the plea that the process needs to be halted almost instantly. Such a position not only makes an interesting copy for a political statement, but also misguides the common man. But the highest number of illiterates, malnourished, and poor; their massive dependence on primary sources of livelihood; day by day diminishing status of their sources of livelihood; and so on support the counter argument.

The chapter is an attempt to underline history of dispossession, emergence of protest movements, and institutional mechanisms to question the degeneration as well as to repair the fractured state of affair with reference to tribal masses of central India. This chapter is divided into four parts. Opening part describes richness of tribal culture and their cordial relationship with local ecology and environment. It also covers environmental degradation and their gradual move towards insecurity and deprivation zone. Second part examines process and consequences of the establishment of mega development projects on tribal economy, livelihood, and their culture. The third part briefly examines some of the social and ecological movements going on in tribal regions that have emerged to address plights and miseries of tribes and regions resided by tribes. Towards the end, some of the institutional steps taken during the era of globalization, particularly for the restoration of human rights and dignity of tribes have been examined.

I

It is very difficult to locate zero point in the history of social change and social transformation because the process of continuity and change in society and its different elements and traits is an ongoing phenomenon. But for logistic purpose a benchmark in history needs to be identified to regulate academic discourse in a proper perspective so that a comprehensive understanding of social change is made possible and some reliable conclusions may be drawn for further investigation. Therefore, when we use the word 'contemporary' in the tribal context in order to analyse social movements, we are primarily concerned with those social movements that have obviously occurred since independence. Therefore, in principle, scope of the chapter is primarily not to discuss social movements that have taken place during the British or pre-British days. This does not mean underestimation of historical conditions and circumstances that may be held responsible for the origin and perpetuation of movements either as a necessary or sufficient condition, during the post-independence period. Of course, ongoing social movements (including unrest) needs to be understood in relation to the past but it is not essential that every present movement may have its roots in the past. Hence, to devote more on nature and dynamics of contemporary movements only passing references of movements before independence have been made and more focus is on movements that have taken place after independence.

If we restrict to the cases of social movements in the tribal areas, it seems that its history is very old. It goes back to the pre-British days. For example, the rise of the Marathas from the mid-17th century onwards for the first time led to serious inroads into the Bhil homelands. In order to develop trade and settled agriculture so as to boost their revenue, they carried out sustained campaigns against the Bhils[1] who refused to agree to this incursion into their lifestyle. Peasants and traders from Gujarat and Maharashtra were encouraged to settle in the Bhil regions, and forests were cleared to bring land under the plough. Thousands of Bhils were massacred when they rose in revolt against this policy (Manohar, 2001). Kol revolt (1832–1833), Bhumij revolt (1832), Santhal revolt (1855), Birsa Munda movement (1895–1900), Tana Bhagat movement (1915), Jharkhand movement (1950) in present Jharkhand state, Juang movement (1837–1856) and Kaujhar movement (1891–1893) in Orissa state, Naga revolt in 1940s and Gond revolt against British Raj (1911) and movement for separate Gond state (1940) in Madhya Pradesh may be taken as few examples (Chaudhary, 2013: 21). Many more examples of similar movements from different tribal belts of central India may be quoted. Most of these social movements were against high handedness of the local and non-local administration and vested interests.

During the British period, these social movements largely aimed to social reform, eradication of different evil practices that were perceived as dysfunctional by local tribal and non-tribal social reformers. These movements were also against different types of exploitations by the British Raj and local non-tribals, who were subsequently termed as *Diku* (enemy) in certain pockets of the country in the 19th century. Actually Kol revolt and Birsa Munda movement, mentioned above, were against the imposition of the concept of private property in the land of present Jharkhand state. These movements led to introduction of Chhotanagpur Tenancy Act, 1908, Wilkinson Rule of 1833 in Kolhan area, and the recognition of *Manjhi* system of the Santhals in the Santhal Pargana Settlement (Amendment) Regulations of 1908. These legislations not only provided legitimacy to the tribal land tenure system but also recognized the communal land ownership system such as *Mundari Khuntkhatti Dari* system (Areeparampil, 2002: 39). This does not mean that movements directed to ecological and environmental issues were completely absent from the scene during the British period (Chaudhary, 2013: 21).

But after independence there is a trend of departure from the earlier genesis of social movements. During post-independence period, because of number of external forces the amount of acculturation between tribal society and non-tribal society has massively increased and it is further increasing. Tribal areas have been perceived as a heaven of natural resources by the industrial houses, nation-state, and other investors. This thinking with having its roots in the past has gradually become dominant in the development discourse today. As a result, hundreds and thousands of development projects have been either established in tribal areas itself or even if they are established outside the tribal area, these projects are directly or indirectly dependent on tribal locations for raw material. Ever increasing number of industries and projects in tribal areas from 1950s onwards have already led to massive exploitation of natural resources even without critical examination of its cultural, economic, and environmental consequences on the society in general and locals in particular. In the ongoing model of development, which is capitalistic in nature, with having strong faith in the top-down approach of development with its roots in the British period, there is no scope and space for cultural, social, ethical, environmental, and botanical issues. Nadkarni (1987) rightly said that economic planning in India has paid little attention to the ecological constraints to economic expansion or to the impact of environmental degradation on livelihood and work. Only economic issues are provided the front seat in the development debate and decision. The idea of either 'industrialize or perish' given by Visveswaraiyya[2] (1920) became the buzzword in the development discourse since the beginning of the second Five Year Plan for which underdevelopment was essentially perceived as a consequence of insufficient technological progress (Government of India, 1956: 6).

This model of development was followed by Government of India for modernization and development in different sectors. It was also followed in the field of science and technology. Industrial policy was formulated keeping this objective into consideration. These steps subsequently increased number of industries of various types in the country in general and in the tribal areas in particular. Thousands of jobs were created in these industries. Skilled personnel from across the country joined these industries. Most of them were non-tribals. The door of employment for tribals is virtually closed for want of required skills and qualification. Besides easy availability of raw materials, there are other factors which have historically enabled industrial houses to establish their projects in tribal areas. Because of mining and industries, thousands of tribes have lost their land. It was said that they have lost land in favour of 'national development'. According to Barik (2013), 'a little more than five lakh cases of tribal land alienation were registered, covering an area of 9.02 lakh acres in 12 states. And of this 2.25 lakhs cases went in favour of tribals where 5 lakh acres of land was involved. Also, two lakhs cases covering 4.18 lakh acres of land area were restored to the tribal petitioners. Tribals had to go to the court of law for restoring their land (p. 85).

The concept of national development was defined primarily in economic term. Per capita income, GDP, GNP, percentage of industrialization, urbanization and so on were perceived as indices of development. No emphasis was given on the issues of equity and justice, ecological stability, and environmental sustainability. As a result, traditional sources of livelihood of tribals such as water, forest, and land (*jal*, *jungle*, and *zamin*); their culture, tradition, or what may be called 'Identity'; and so on were forced to reach to the critical stage. Needless to mention that tribal identity was formed in the light of their natural surroundings and if condition of natural resources decreases identity is also like to disintegrate. Tribals at large are the involuntary victims of degeneration.

Indigenous knowledge practiced by tribals since long in their day-to-day activities are either about to die or lose its utility (Chaudhary, 2008). Even if it is found, it is massively misappropriated by the vested interests without any benefit to the locals who have retained and preserved these knowledge since long.

Revisiting identity with the help of modern education, cultural organizations, and vote bank politics is not at all mass based and, therefore, largely ineffective. It appears that tribals have become an outsider, unwanted, or uncalled for in their own homeland. Increasing number of non-tribals in tribal-dominated areas, where development projects have been established, and near exclusion of tribals from the new opportunity of livelihood created by these initiatives is an example of tribal exclusion and marginalization in their own homeland. It also appears that gradually tribals have lost their access to century-old natural and autonomous control over land and water-based natural resources. Because of poor bargaining power of tribal masses, poor bargaining power of tribal representatives, or tribal elites and apathy on the part of state and its functionaries working at the grassroots level, tribals at large have been forced to reach to the stage of insecurity, deprivation, marginalization, and dependence in different walks of life during the last decades in spite of the presence of number of constitutional provisions,[3] tribal development projects, presence of NGOs in tribal areas, seasonal outmigration by tribal themselves as a coping mechanism, rehabilitation policies of the government, promises made by investors through attractive phrases such as 'corporate social responsibilities' and expansion of market forces, and so on in major parts of the tribal world. Only small number of tribals have been able to reap benefits of development promised under different schemes. Only few tribals, particularly those who are educated, depend on salary, and live in urban areas with having some amount of modern network, have been benefited. But more than 90 per cent tribals live in villages with having poor safety net and bargaining power. They are at the bottom of the development process. Those few who have been benefited by the development process have been made dependent prone. In the absence of most of the Human Development Index (HDI), tribals at large have been further forced to become like a marginal man (Desai et al., 2010). Their socio-economic condition is inferior in comparison to scheduled castes (Chaudhary, 2010). Their human rights are violated every now and then primarily by the state and the industrial houses (Dungdung, 2013). They have become what Cernea (1988) called the victim of landlessness, joblessness, homelessness, marginalization, food insecurity, increased morbidity and mortality, loss of access to common property, social disintegration, loss of access to community resources, and violation of human rights. In short, only few of them have been able to improve their quality of life by availing fruits of development in a tenable manner but majority of them have failed to avail benefits mainly due to problems at the delivery level and a section of them have been pushed to the insecurity zone.

II

Instead of needful correction in the ongoing development projects keeping in view tribal interest the entire tribal locations were opened for investors and industrial houses during globalization period. Globalization was formally introduced in India in the middle of July 1991. Both in principle and in practice it has further added fuel to the fire to the ongoing development or what Padel (2013) called 'investment-induced displacement', degeneration, and marginalization of tribes by increasing the number of various types of industries and development projects in tribal areas. States who are rich from natural resources point of view have fearlessly signed countless number of MoUs with investors and industrial houses. According to Dungdung (2013), in Odisha state alone, for example, more than 90 memorandum of understandings (MoUs) have been signed with corporate houses. These initiatives are likely to industrialize and strengthen the state but on the other hand locals are also likely to suffer and become deprived. Chairperson of National Human Rights Commission K.G. Balakrishnan apprehended, 'As Odisha is emerging as an industrialized state, we apprehend more cases of human rights violation' (p. 162).

According to Iyer (2013) in a span of less than a decade, the government of Jharkhand for example has signed well over hundred MoUs. Notable among these are ArcellorMittal, Jindal, Essar, Tata Hindalco, Abhijit Group, and so on. According to a human rights report published by Jharkhand Human Rights Movement (JHRM), the state government of Jharkhand has so far signed 102 MoUs that go against the Fifth Schedule of the Constitution that guarantee tribals their right over the land they live in. The Jharkhand Industrial Policy 2001 and the Jharkhand Vision Document 2010 strongly wish to exploit its natural resources by making it investor friendly by providing various concessions and government help to industrial houses by acquiring land for private industrial estates and making it available at acquisition cost.

The same process of industrialization and signing of MoUs with investors and subsequently displacement is going on in the neighbouring states of Chhattisgarh,[4] Odisha, Madhya Pradesh, Andhra Pradesh, and Maharashtra. According to the Annual Report 2007–2008 of the Ministry of Rural Development, a total of 105,491 cases alleging alienation of 104,742 acres of land have been filed in the court in Orissa. An estimated 104,644 cases were disposed of by the court. Out of these 61,431 cases were disposed of in favour of tribals and 56,854 acres of land was restored to tribals. What will happen to the human rights of the locals, mostly tribals, in these states? Who will ensure the future of forests, water, land, climate, biodiversity, and so on which are immediately and directly responsible for the survival of tribal masses? How to ensure survival of tribal masses, their culture, and tradition and their geographical space under the given economic and political scenario? Padhi and Panigrahi (2011) documented consequences of deforestation and displacement in Orissa. More or less similar is the situation in other parts of central India. They said,

> The impact of massive deforestation has been observed in the life-way processes of tribal people and can be categorized as environmental effects, social effects and economic effects. The social effects of deforestation restrict tribal people's access to the forest and affect their religious activities, life-cycle rituals, customs, practices and habits. Similarly, the economic effects of deforestation have drastically influenced the traditional livelihood resource of tribal people, which were providing them with food and economic security. (p. 16)

These are some of the critical issues which needs to be examined and resolved in the interest of tribals in particular and country in general.

Of course there are some areas where the amount of forests as well as non-timber forest products (NTFPs) are found in plenty but poor tribals are today far away from these resources. It seems that during globalization period maximum parts of these resources are grabbed by the agents and representatives of market forces. Tribals have now no access to these resources. It is claimed that rehabilitation policy was adopted for the welfare of the displaced. But it appears that functioning of rehabilitation measures is not up to the mark (Chaudhary et al., 2013). There is wide gap between what is promised and what is performed. It appears that the implementing agencies are not serious on these issues. But the theoretical question is, even if implemented honestly, can any scheme rehabilitate social, psychological and cultural displacement? In many cases, tribals are either forced to displace themselves or they are terrorized to out-migrate so that land encroachment drive is not opposed strongly (Dungdung, 2013: 162).

It seems that injustice of all types generated by globalization and related forces and schemes have individually and collectively frustrated tribal masses. Institutional initiatives taken during the last decades are by and large failed to arrest the amount of frustration of tribes, particularly tribal youths. There is no ray of hope from any corner to restore their environment and human rights. Sometimes it appears that either tribals or their non-tribal advocates fight a lost battle. The amount of frustration is high in those areas where the so-called alternatives of traditional livelihood are totally missing and coping mechanism to adjust with the adverse situation is either ineffective or beyond the reach of tribal masses.

III

Hence, in reaction to these frustration and anxieties there is a crowd of social movements[5] in the tribal areas today. These social movements are basically collective response to injustice, both historical and contemporary, committed on tribes and their socio-environmental heritage and life-supporting resources by external forces. And over the time, the number of these external forces and atrocities committed by them on tribes have increased manifold. Tribal social movements are today broadly of two types, namely secessionist movements and reformist movement. The former is not found in the central India. There is no movement in favour of separate state in tribal belt. But there are movements against the functioning of the state and corporate houses working in tribal areas.

Some of these social movements are highly local and some are working at the macro level. Some are exclusively headed and run by tribals and some are run by non-tribals. There are several social movements jointly organized by local tribals and the non-local and non-tribals. While some of these movements are highly organized, systematic, and structured, others are highly temporal, local, and focused. Some movements are highly emotion ridden. Some have historical roots and some are recent in terms of its origin. Some of these movements are independent and autonomous and some have linkages with other social movements working in other parts of the country. Hence, in spite of some structural and compositional differences, these movements are socio-economic, political, and civilizational. Case studies of some clearly reveal that these movements are correctional in nature. They do not put question mark on the existence of the state rather they do not agree with the functioning of the state. They perceive functioning of the state in favour of alien interest, that is, in the interest of the market forces or DIKUS of different varieties. Hence, they are in favour of change in the system and not change of the system. These movements may also be perceived as advocates of human rights and dignity of tribal masses. On the basis of objectives, these protest movements are also of different types. And, whether it is primarily addressed to social and economic exploitation or ecological and environmental degradation, development, displacement, rehabilitation, and deforestation, these movements have become very popular these days. These movements have now drawn some attention of both print and electronic media. However, there is a serious criticism that the modern media is pro-elite and it is not sensitive to the concerns of tribal areas and tribal masses (Dungdung, 2013).[6]

Precisely, most of these local-level social movements are against the exploitation of natural resources, land encroachment, establishment of mega development projects, and atrocities on tribals by different interest groups including the state and implementation of the so-called rehabilitation policy in dishonest manner and so on. It is reported that in many cases if voice of protest is raised by tribals and their supporters, instead of having respectful dialogue with them, attempts are being made to suppress these voices ruthlessly. Many times participants and sympathizers of these movements are termed as extremists. Many among them are made victims of state violence. Many of them are put behind the bar for indefinite period. And such incidences contribute to prolonged protest movement by tribals and others in the tribal world. The net result of this process is further perpetuation of rural unrest and violence. For instance, from 2001 to 2012 total 4,759 Naxal incidents took place in the state of Jharkhand alone in which 424 policemen, 602 citizens, and 1,019 Naxals (total 2,055 people) were killed (JHRR, 2007–2012). More or less similar is the situation in Chhattisgarh state. Large number of innocent tribals, police personnels, paramilitary force personnels, the so-called Naxalites and their supporters, and others have been killed in Chhattisgarh during the last two decades. It raises some ethical questions that instead of engaging in the meaningful dialogue in a peaceful manner both the state and the extremist groups are constantly engaged in violence, how they may be termed as legitimate and pro-people?

The Naxalite movement most often follow undemocratic means to establish their hegemony. If they kill innocent tribals, it cannot be justified in a legitimate manner. There is a point of view that even poor policemen, poor tribal informers, and those locals who do not submit before them are perceived as agents of the state. Since they are perceived negatively therefore, it doesn't matter if they are rich or poor, tribal or non-tribal, and local or outsider they become victim of Naxalite violence. More or less similar is the situation with the state. Even if dialogue is initiated by the state, they seldom obey the agreement.

There is a preconceived notion among change agents, particularly the state that tribal society is relatively static, their needs and demands are limited, and the local resources are capable enough to meet their limited needs. Their ecological and environmental base is still sound and therefore movement launched by them in favour of their human rights are not seriously taken. Their voice is grossly unheard.[7]

But the pertinent question is that through violent means are both the state and extremists successful in storing/restoring human rights of tribal masses? There are views, observations, and descriptions available to show their failure in restoring dignified life of tribals. Rather there are number of studies and narratives to prove that both of them are miserably failed on this front, many areas in the states of central India are declared as disturbed areas. State is almost invisible in these areas. However, it claims that welfare measures are not effectively functioning in these areas due to disturbance created by Naxalites. To what extent this claim is valid and acceptable? To search answer of this question, one can go to the history of the movement. History reveals that after its birth in 1967 in the West Bengal, the movement did not directly reached to the tribal belts of central India, For couple of decades it was confined to the non-tribal areas and in the due course of time due to push and pull factors it moved to the areas which are tribal, forest, and mountain dominated. One of the pull factors available in the tribal areas since the British days was ever decreasing quality of life of tribal masses. Pauperization increased over the time as the process of acculturation with non-tribal traditions increased. It encouraged Naxalites to enter and expand their support base in tribal areas. According to a report *Tribal: Victims of Development Projects*,

> The naxal violence in the tribal areas of the country is not because they invited or harbored the naxal groups. It flourished mainly because the political class and the administrations left them utterly neglected. The armed naxals occupied the vacuum and started ruling through terror and extortion of money from everyone who had something to offer them. Hence, they became rulers of the areas where police or government officials did not dare to go. (p. 19)

Naxalites also made promises to enhance tribal's quality of life which enabled them to trust each other. Already several years have gone but to what extent these promises have been translated into action? What benefits tribals at large have received from Naxalite movement? Studies on this issue provide rather negative picture. Most of the studies conclude that instead of improvement there is constant decay in the quality of life of tribal masses. In most of the cases, the movement has contributed to violence at the local level. Normal life of tribals are badly affected. In the areas where Naxalites dominate, innocent villagers are perceived as sympathizers and supporters of these movements. As a result, in many cases they become the victim of police atrocities. Actually tribes are forced to remain confined on a thin line between the Maoists and the state administration. They are exploited by both of them. Many tribals have been killed by Naxalites for not obeying their order. Any meeting called by Naxalites is an unsaid compulsion for villagers. They have no option but to attend the meeting. And if they attend the meeting, state administration brand them as Naxalites or their supporters and the security forces go after them. For instance, in an anti-Naxal operations in Saranda forest of Jharkhand state, which is inhabited by tribes, the deployed central and state forces devastated several homes, killed innocent people, and did not even spare food that was in possession of tribals. They arrested 33 villagers but the police failed to provide any evidence against them. Every now and then search operation is conducted by the police. Edible and non-edible items are destroyed. Tribals are beaten, abused, and in several cases their women are humiliated. In certain cases, tribals are forced to out-migrate permanently in order to reduce amount of resistance created by them at the time of displacement and land acquisition drive launched by the state and corporate houses.[8] Because of fear psychosis created due to insecurity, tribals are pushed to move and remain in the insecurity zone from social, psychological, and economic point of view.

Naxalite movement is not the only movement which is going on in tribal areas. There are host of environmental movements. Some are against land encroachment, the others are for respectful rehabilitation package; some are for dignity and respect, the others are against mega development projects. This is clear from brief case studies of following movements:

Narmada Bachao Andolan (Save Narmada Agitation)

This movement was started in 1970s in favour of human rights of common people including tribals in the affected areas of Madhya Pradesh and Gujarat. The movement was not only against the increase in the height of the *Bandh* on the Narmada River, which will displace thousands of villagers but it was also in favour of proper rehabilitation of beneficiaries. The movement received support from well-known environmentalists of the country as well as abroad. In fact the main reason behind the World Bank's withdrawal of funding to the project was due to international pressure. The Japanese environmentalists convinced their government to discontinue the release of grant to the project. In America, environmental groups also suggested the government to discontinue the grant. Similar voice of protest came from other countries of the world. As a result, the World Bank discontinued its further aid to Sardar Sarovar. The entire Narmada Valley Project is dislinked from the World Bank. Hence, this movement may be perceived as a success story which was created because of pressure from different corners on the donor agencies.

Kalinganagar Movement (Odisha)

Kalinganagar is a small town in Jajpur district of Odisha. The area has been declared as Industrial Development Corporation of Odisha. It acquired land from public for setting up of steel plants. Needless to mention that minerals such as iron ore and chromite are located closer to this area. Tata signed MoU to set up a six MMTPA steel plant in this town with an investment of approximately ₹ 154,000 million. There are number of other industries located in and around this small town. In two blocks of the district namely Sukinda and Danagadi, there are significant number of tribal population. Huge amount of land have been acquired by the government both from villagers and different government departments. Locals do not like the factory because of number of cultural, environmental, and economic reasons. They apprehend that the company will disown the promises which they will make for rehabilitation. About thousands of people have agitated on different occasions against this project. The conflict between locals and TATA along with police is going on. Police is strictly following the dictation of higher authorities which are in favour of TATA and against the legitimate interest of locals. In between, the government of Odisha is trying its best to earn crores of rupees out of this deal. Villagers also apprehend that those tribals and others who are cultivating the land but who do not have *patta* cannot get any rehabilitation package and therefore they are agitating and the movement is going on.

Lanjigarh, Niyamgiri Movement against Vedanta Aluminia Ltd.

Vedanta is an England-based investment company. It is working in different sectors in certain parts of India. It has planned to establish a refinery plant in Lanjigarh, Odisha. The area is inhabited by number of tribes such as Dongria, Kondh, Kutia Kondh, and Desia Kondh. These tribals are since long dependent on forest and ecology of Niyamgiri hill for their cultural and economic requirements. Except the forest and forest produce, they do not have other sources of livelihood. Once the hill is permitted for digging, the tribals have to move from this place and in this way they have to die. Hence, they are strongly opposing their displacement. The area is under Schedule V, and the government is playing all politics to organize meeting of gram sabha and take their permission to allot the hill to the concerned company. The area is also dominated by Maoist, and they are supporting tribals in their class war. The company is promising number of package to the people. Number of committees constituted to look into the matter have also rejected the idea to allot the hill and forest to the Vedanta. And the conflict is going on between tribals, their supporters, free thinkers, and Maoist on the one side and the Vedanta and the state on the other side. In the meantime, the Supreme Court of India has strongly directed the state government to produce complete facts before the gram sabha, and it has said that the final decision will be taken by concerned gram sabha only and the battle is still going on.

Movement Against GMR Energies

Power producer GMR Energies plans to build a 1,200 MW Thermal Power Project in Raipur district of Chhattisgarh. They have decided to invest about ₹ 5,500 crores in this project. For this purpose, the power company needs more than 1,100 acres of land but this effort is strongly opposed by farmers on health ground. For this purpose, a public hearing meeting was organized on 15 January 2009 but it was strongly opposed by the locals. Villagers said that they are already facing serious health problem due to pollution caused by industrial units in the neighbouring Siltara Industrial Area but government officials and GMR Energy officials are trying to convince people in favour of the project. They are quoting the features of Chhattisgarh industrial policy which says that those who will give land for industries will be given job and attractive compensation. But villagers do not trust them and tug of war is going on between them since 2009.

There are number of consequences of these movements. These consequences are both functional and dysfunctional as well as intended and unintended from environment, culture, and human rights perspective. Sometimes mega development projects are either delayed or withdrawn due to protest as it has happened in the case of Sardar Sarovar Project, or the catchment area of the movement becomes conflict prone or number of welfare schemes are introduced by the state. Sometimes welfare schemes are halted. For instance, Narmada Bachao Andolan (Save Narmada Agitation) was for complete stopping of the dam, resettlement, and rehabilitation benefits to the ousters and so on (Wood, 1993). These demands were supported by many environmentalists and reputed social workers. It was because of international pressure created particularly by the environmentalists of Japan and United States that the World Bank was forced to withdraw its financial aid to the Sardar Sarovar Project on Narmada river. In the year 2000, the Andhra Pradesh government passed a G.O. (No. 112) to transfer forest lands to industries such as Reliance and ITC, Bhadrachalam, through the village institutions of *Van Sanrakshan Samitis*. Strong protests from NGOs and opposition parties who highlighted the government's back door approaches to privatization of forest resources led to hasty withdrawal of the proposals. Similarly in Jharkhand, ArcelorMittal had to face challenge created by tribals against their effort to acquire about 11,000 acres of land, of which 8,800 acres is required to set up a 12 million-tonne steel plant and 2,400 acres for establishing a township. The tribals claimed that the land identified by ArcelorMittal for the steel project is agricultural land and tribal lands are not transferable to non-tribals. And tug of war is going on between these two stakeholders, and the project has been halted.

But in spite of sustained protest by tribals against displacement and mega development projects, it appears that the movement is forced to largely remain ineffective. It happens that in several cases the so-called development process is halted or delayed but in exceptional cases such projects are withdrawn. According to Annual Report (2007–2008) of Ministry of Rural Development, GoI, more than five lakh cases of tribal land alienation were registered, covering an area of 9.02 lakh acres in 12 states. And of this, 2.25 lakh cases went in favour of tribals where five lakh acres of land was involved. Also two lakh cases covering 4.18 lakh acres of land area were restored to the tribal petitioners. Tribals had to go to the court of law for restoration of their land. As a result, the establishment cost of these ongoing projects substantially increases which encourages change agents to compromise on the rehabilitation package. Also in such cases, ultimately it is the locals who are made victims of the development process. Further, if we look into the history of mega development projects in tribal locations, it appears that from 1991 onwards, there is massive increase in its number. This clearly shows that in spite of continuous protest there is an increase in the number of development projects in tribal areas and in most of the cases because of logistic reasons doors of these projects are virtually closed for local tribals who are poor and in most of the cases illiterate. Even if educated, they lack technical skills and therefore doors of these industries and mines are practically closed for them. Also, as stated earlier, these development projects have massively eroded local ecological and environmental bases which have forced local tribals to become alien and marginalized in their own homeland.

In response to social and ecological movements in tribal areas and increasing cases of violence by Naxalites, in order to provide safe passage to the investors and in order to correct historical injustices to the tribes popular steps have been taken by the state during globalization period. Important among these are (1) Panchayat (Extension to Scheduled Areas) Act (PESA) and (2) Scheduled Tribes and Other Traditional Forest Dwellers (Recognition of Forest Rights) Act 2006. Theoretically these two initiatives are pro-tribal and pro-tribal areas but the grass-root experience is not praise worthy. Rather the picture is alarming. This is evident from the following observations:

Panchayat (Extension to Scheduled Area) Act, 1996

This is popularly known as PESA. This act came into force on 24 December 1996. It empowers gram sabha in the designated areas to safeguard and preserve the traditions and customs of the people, their cultural identity, community resources, and the customary mode of dispute management. Features of this act are as follows:

1. The village councils (panchayats) and gram sabhas have ownership of the minor forest produce.
2. Gram sabhas approve beneficiaries under poverty alleviation programmes.
3. Before any land is acquired for development purposes, it is mandatory to have consultation with the gram sabhas and panchayats.
4. Recommendation of the gram sabha or the panchayat at the appropriate level is mandatory for granting any prospective license or mining lease for minor minerals.
5. Requirement that the state governments change their existing laws wherever these are inconsistent with the central legislation.

This act is applicable in the districts and development blocks declared as Schedule V areas in the states of Andhra Pradesh, Gujarat, Himachal Pradesh, Madhya Pradesh, Chhattisgarh, Maharashtra, Odisha, and Rajasthan. With some modification, it is also working in Jharkhand state.

But to what extent the act fulfilled the purposes for which it was enacted? There are number of studies. However, in most of these studies it has been underlined that it was a near failure intervention. The act could not become 'mainstream' policy (Sinha, 2011), some states had misinterpreted the concept of gram sabha and equated it with the meeting of the gram panchayat (*The Telegraph*, Guwahati edition, 9 April 2012). In the case of Pachwara coal mines project of Jharkhand state at no point of time, starting with the survey and the recent exercise of acquisition, any consultation in any form with the affected Santhal and Paharia households, the villagers, and the gram sabha was made (Iyer, 2013). The purpose of PESA has not been understood either by the politicians or by the bureaucracy. People at large are also not aware of the provisions of PESA except in those areas where the NGOs are seriously working (Tripathy, 2013). PESA is supposed to protect against any arbitrary, discriminatory, and motivated action of the state relating to land acquisition, resettlement, and rehabilitation in tribal region but it has been observed that the local administration in league with the company officials was indulged in deliberate falsehood. In the consultation of gram sabha, the method adopted is dubious as the consent was obtained through coercion and brutal force (Das, 2005). According to Sisodia (2009) at the grass-root level, the situation is not as per the assumed goal of this endeavour. The level of participation of people has been very low, meetings of gram sabha is rarely held and even if hailed it was mere a formality without fulfilling the quorum. The grass-root experience suggests that majority of the panchayat representatives and villagers are not aware of the quorum required for gram sabha meetings. The reasons behind the low attendance of people are engagements of the people in agriculture and labour, migration, groupism, scattered habitation, and so on. Gram sabha has been empowered to safeguard and preserve the traditions and customs of the people, cultural identity, and customary mode of dispute resolution. But it is not done. Also, in the name of traditions and customs, social evils such as use of liquor and dowry are getting place in society.

The Scheduled Tribes and Other Traditional Forest Dwellers (Recognition of Forest Rights) Act, 2006

This act was passed on 18 December 2006 and notified on 31 December 2007. Some of the specific features of the act are as follows:

1. Right to hold and live in the forest land under the individual or common occupation for habitation or for self-cultivation for livelihood by a member or members of a forest-dwelling scheduled tribe or other traditional forest dwellers;
2. Community rights such as *nistar*, by whatever name called, including those used in erstwhile princely states, zamindari, or such intermediary regimes;

3. Right of ownership, access to collect, use, and dispose of minor forest produce (includes all non-timber forest produce of plant origin) which has been traditionally collected within or outside village boundaries;
4. Other community rights of uses or entitlements such as fish and other products of water bodies, grazing (both settled or transhumant) and traditional seasonal resource access of nomadic or pastoralist communities;
5. Rights including community tenures of habitat and habitation for primitive tribal groups and pre-agriculture communities;
6. Rights in or over disputed lands under any nomenclature in any state where claims are disputed;
7. Rights for conversion of pattas or leases or grants issued by any local council or any state government on forest lands to titles;
8. Rights of settlement and conversion of all forest villages, old habitation, unsurveyed villages, and other villages in forest, whether recorded, notified, or not into revenue villages;
9. Right to protect, regenerate, or conserve or manage any community forest resource which they have been traditionally protecting and conserving for sustainable use;
10. Rights that are recognized under any state law or laws of any autonomous district council or autonomous regional council or that are accepted as rights of tribals under any traditional or customary law of the concerned tribes of any state;
11. Right of access to biodiversity and community, right to intellectual property, and traditional knowledge related to biodiversity and cultural diversity;
12. Any other traditional right customarily enjoyed by the forest-dwelling scheduled tribes or other traditional forest dwellers.
13. (a) *Title rights:* that is, ownership to land that is being framed by tribals or forest dwellers as on 13 December 2005, subject to a maximum of 4 hectares; ownership is only for land that is actually being cultivated by the concerned family as on that date, meaning that no new lands are granted

(b) *Use rights*: to minor forest produce (also including ownership), to grazing areas, to pastoralist routes, and so on.

(c) *Relief and development rights:* to rehabilitation in case of illegal eviction or forced displacement; and to basic amenities, subject to restrictions for forest protection

(d) *Forest management rights:* to protect forests and wildlife.

Number of studies are now available to show impact of this act on distribution of lands to tribals and other forest dwellers. According to Chaudhary (2014) in Madhya Pradesh, for example, till March 2010, altogether 404,591 claims were received from both individuals and community, but only 109,000 (about 25%) claims were cleared. Altogether 359,502.09 acres of land were allotted under 89,035 titles. It is also claimed that the pattas distributed are not accepted as negotiable instruments for receiving subsidies or accessing bank loans.

Hence, it can be said that in spite of continuous social movements of different types in tribal regions of central India in favour of human rights of tribes and protection of ecology and environment, the outcome is not praiseworthy. Institutional initiatives also failed to restore human rights and dignity of tribes. It seems that social movements of all types, environmental degradation, pauperization of tribal masses, and establishment of mega development projects, which are antagonistically related to each other, are going on side by side and the state which is theoretically democratic and welfarestic is either silent or it is with the industrial houses, growth process, and so on. It has either joined hands with the corporate houses or it has decided to be indifferent. Hence, under the given socio-political regime they along with their ecological base have to move towards insecurity and deprivation.

Notes

1. According to Padel (1998), the Bhils, Hos, and Konds were forced to submit to British rule in the early 19th century in

similar wars of conquest or 'pacification'. The Munda (Kol) uprising of 1831–1832 and the santhal *bul* (rebellion) in the 1850s point to the great increase in exploitation that took place after British rule was imposed in tribal areas: *diku* (foreigner, non-tribal) landlords, merchants, and money-lenders had established a hold over Mundas and Santhals that made them work on the land that had been theirs virtually as serfs to create a profit and to pay the revenue demanded by the East India Company. This was the period when the company, in the face of much opposition, forced farmers in the Gangetic plain to grow opium for the lucrative trade with China.

2. He (Visvesvaraya, 1920, 'Biomass for Business' in 'This Fissured Land: An Ecological History of India', Madhav Gadgil, Ramchandra Guha (pp. 183) said:

   'Indians will have to choose whether they will be educated or ignorant whether they will come into closer contact with the outer world and become responsive to its influences; whether they will be organized or disunited, bold or timid, enterprising or passive, an industrial or an agricultural nation; rich or poor; strong and respected or weak and dominated by forward nations.

3. All the major articles can be classified into four broad categories. These are protective provisions (Articles, 15, 16, 19, 23, 29, 46, 164, 330, 332, 335, 338, 339, 342, and 371), development-related provisions (Articles, 15, 16, 19, 46, 275, and 399), administrative provisions in the 6th Schedule (Northeast states) areas (Articles, 344, 338, and 339) and reservation facility (Articles, 330, 332, 334, 335, and 340). In order to actualize the spirit of these provisions, from time to time hundreds of development schemes have been formulated and implemented.

4. In Chhattisgarh since the beginning of globalization 121 MoUs have been signed. The total proposed budget of all these MoUs was ₹ 192,126 crores. About half of them have already started functioning. In Madhya Pradesh, 324 MoUs were signed of which 12 MoUs have been implemented and 18 are in process. The areas where MoUs have been signed are agriculture and food processing, forest and herbal, industries, infrastructure, minerals, power, textiles, and tourism. In Odisha, 235 MoUs were signed during the above period.

These were in the following sectors: air products (04), alumina and aluminium (12), aviation (01), cement (26), ferro products (09), food processing (08), mining (03), others (13), paper (05), pelletization (14), petroleum (05), power (63), and steel (72) (Source: Different web site sources of the concerned state governments dated 24 June 2014).

5. Many Indian scholars have conceptualized and classified social movement. Important among them are Ghanshyam Shah (2004), P.N. Mukherji (1988) 'Sex and Social Structure' in 'Socialisation, Education and Women Exploitations in Gender Identity' by Karuna Chanana (ed.). Orient Longman, New Delhi; T.K. Oommen (2010), and so on. All these scholars have been perceived movement as a non-institutional collective response in favour of the collective cause in violent or non-violent manner. These movements are apolitical.
6. Dungdung (2013) observed that because of five reasons, media of Jharkhand, for example, is not faithful either to the tribals or to the interest of the state. These reasons are: (a) the builders and developers, who are mainly engaged in the real estate business in the state, also run TV news channels. They are strongly opposed to Chhotanagpur Tenancy Act (CTA) 1908, Santhal Pargana Tenancy Act 1949, and PESA Act 1996, which prohibit land transfer to them, hence they criticize these acts, (b) media has a clear corporate business interest in the name of development of Jharkhand, (c) nearly 90 per cent of journalists in the state are outsiders and from upper castes. They have mutual adjustment with builders and industrialists who are non-tribals and also from outside the state, (d) media still treat Jharkhand as a part of Bihar, hence, in most of the TV channels and newspapers of Jharkhand more time and space is provided to Bihar-related issues in comparison to Jharkhand issues, and (e) most of the consumers of Jharkhand media are originally outsiders and, therefore, their concerns are more important for the media in comparison to the concerns of the state and its original population, particularly tribals.
7. According to Guha (2011), some of the factors responsible for neglect of tribal concerns and the state of their pitiability are that they live in the resource-rich areas that have encouraged industrial houses to establish their plant as per their choice;

tribals failed to produce a fighter for their cause like Dr Ambedkar; they are geographically scattered and therefore not a strong political constituency for any political party; except the Northeast states, tribal students of rest of the country are notionally represented in top-level bureaucracy; their indigenous knowledge do not get space in the mainstream society except Santhali; no tribal language is recognized; tribals of central India are broadly residing in conflict-prone areas; and modern media is by and large insensitive to their difficulties. Because of the interplay of all these negative forces, they are neglected by all the development agencies. Rather in many cases, they are forced to become more and more pitiable. And this state of affair further contributes to protest and unrest in tribal areas.

8. Iyer (2013) rightly said, 'The spread of militant left radicalism in the central Indian states of Jharkhand, Odisha and Chhattisgarh is not a sudden eruption. It is also not primarily a law and order problem. It is a political movement which needs to be contextualized in the objective overall current situation of the people involved, which creates conditions for its emergence (p. 60).

References

Atal, Yogesh (2012). 'Tribal Unrest, State Policies and Empowerment in Contemporary India'. Keynote address (unpublished) in a nation seminar on 21–22 March. Bhopal: IGRMS.

Areeparampil, M.S.J. (2002). *Struggle for Swaraj*. Chaibasa, Jharkhand: Tribal Research and Training Centre (TRTC).

Barik, B.C. (2013). 'Globalization, National Development and Tribal Identity'. In S.N. Chaudhary (ed.) *Globalization, National Development and Tribal Identity*. Jaipur: Rawat.

Chaudhary, S.N. (2008). *Tribes and Their Indigenous Knowledge: Implications for Development*. Bhopal and New Delhi: Indira Gandhi Rashtriya Manav Sangralaya and Prathiba Prakashan.

——. (2010). *Tribal Economy at Crossroads*, Jaipur: Rawat.

——. (2012). *In Search of Sustainable Development: Scenario in a Tribal Village of Madhya Pradesh*. New Delhi: Serials Publications.

——. (2013). *Globalisation, National Development and Tribal Identity* (ed.). Jaipur: Rawat.

——. Mishra, M., and Sharma, M. (2013). *Adivasi Gramo Me Tikau Vikas Ka Yathartha*. New Delhi: Concept.

——. (2014). 'In Between Deprivation and Dependent Economic Development: The Case of Tribal Women of Madhya Pradesh'. In S.N. Chaudhary (ed.) *Tribal Women: Yesterday, Today and Tomorrow*. Jaipur: Rawat.

Cernea, M.M. (1988). *Putting People First: Sociological Variables in Rural Development* (ed.). London: Oxford University Press.

Desai, S.B.A. Dubey, B.L. Joshi, M. Sen, S. Shariff, and R. Vanneman (2010). *Human Development in India: Challenges for a Society in Transition*. New Delhi: OUP.

Dungdung, G. (2013). *Whose Country Is It Anyway?: Untold Stories of the Indigenous Peoples of India*. Kolkata: Adivaani.

Das, Vidya (2005). *PESA: A Reality, National Consultation on PESA Act*. Kashipur, Rayagada, Orissa: Agragamee.

Government of India (1956). *The Second Five Year Plan*. New Delhi: Planning Commission.

Guha, R. (2011). 'Apni Tradesio Se Azadi Ke Intezar Mey Adivasi'. *Dainik Bhaskar*. Bhopal. 15 August.

Iyer, K.G. (2013). 'Globalisation, Jharkhandi Identity and Rural Transformation'. In *Globalisation, National Development and Tribal Identity*. Jaipur: Rawat. 74–75.

Jharkhand Human Rights Report, 2001 (2011). Ranchi.

Manohar, D. (2001). *Bagh Ke Bacche Hai Ham (We Are the Children of the Tiger)*. Hoshangabad: Disha Samvad.

Nadkarni, M.V. (1987). 'Agricultural Development and Ecology: An Economist's View'. *Indian Journal of Agricultural Economics*. 42(3): 359–375.

Oommen, T.K. (ed.) (2010). *Social Movements: Issues of Identity and Social Movements: Concerns of Equality and Security*. Readings in Sociology and Social Anthropology. New Delhi: Oxford University Press.

Padel, F. (1998). 'Forest Knowledge, Tribal People, Their Environment and the Structure of Power'. In R.H. Groove, V. Damodaran, and S. Sangwan (ed.) *Nature and the Orient: The Environmental History of South and Southeast Asia*, New Delhi: Oxford University Press, 1998, 891–917.

Padhi, S. and Panigrahi, Nilkantha (2011). 'Tribal Movements and Livelihoods: Recent Developments in Orissa'. CPRC-IIPA Working Paper. No. 51. New Delhi.

Sisodia, Y.S. (2009). 'Panchayat Raj in Scheduled Areas after Implementation of PESA: Evidences from Western Tribal Belt of Madhya Pradesh. In S.N. Chaudhary (ed.) *Tribal Development Since Independence*. New Delhi: Concept Publishing Company, 2009, 226–243.

Sinha, Ratnawali (2011). 'Governance in the Scheduled Areas: Expectations and Realities'. *Man in India*. 91(3–4): 429–440.

Shah, G. (2004). *Social Movements in India: A Review of Literature*. New Delhi: Sage Publications.

Tripathy, S.N. (2013). 'Paradox of Development and the Plight of Tribes in India'. In *Globalisation, National Development and Tribal Identity* (ed.). Jaipur: Rawat.

Wood, J.R. (1993). 'India's Narmada River Dams: Sardar Sarovar Siege'. *Asian Survey*. XXXIII(10). October.

Visvesvaraya, M. (1920). *Reconstructing India*. London: P.S. King and Son Ltd.

9

Naxalism and the Problems of Development of Tribes

S.N. TRIPATHY

The Scheduled Tribe population represents one of the most economically impoverished and marginalized groups in India. Although scheduled tribes are a minority, they constitute about 8.2 per cent of the total population in India (Census of India, 2001). In recent decades in the tribal regions of the country, because of increasing unrest and violence being perpetrated by extremist forces in the name of tribal liberation, the normalcy of human existence is under severe tension. In such a scenario, any efforts initiated for the development by the government or other agencies are deliberately sabotaged so as to keep the flames of militancy at a high pitch. The intensity of the problem in tribal areas calls for an urgency in reviewing the causes for the rise of militancy and the need for reorganizing our policies with regard to indigenous communities.

In the above back drop, with the help of secondary sources of data, an attempt has been made in this chapter to portray the factors that contributed for the emergence of Naxalism and how the tribes fall prey to such Naxal activities and, finally, the policy measures required for the development of tribes and their economy.

In the context of tribes, the vulnerability of tribal populations to exploitation by minor government officials, as well as moneylenders, landlords, and other agents of vested interests, their illiteracy, and general ignorance of the world outside the narrow confines of their traditional environment, and so on is the contributing factors of Naxalism. However, the causes specific to the Naxalite movement are parts of an overall scenario of poverty, deprivation, oppression, and neglect in large parts of the country. Terrorism is the violent and illegitimate phase that terrorizes the nation from outside. On the contrary, the Naxalism is something which engulfs the country from the inside. Naxalism is the outcome of socio-economic deprivation among the tribes and downtrodden and their manifestations of discontents.

Contributory Factors for the Emergence of Naxalism

The underlying and foundational causes leading to unrest, discontent, and extremism have never been seriously studied or have been the subject matter of administrative or academic discourses in India. The massive influx of non-tribal populations has caused a complete fragmentation of tribal communities. This has further resulted in ineffectiveness of traditional authority systems due to the tribesmen's growing dependence on economic forces over which they have no control.

Land alienation, forced evictions from land, and displacement also added to unrest. Failure to implement protective regulations in scheduled areas, absence of credit mechanism leading to dependence on moneylenders, and consequent loss of land and often even violence by the state functionaries added to the problem. Moreover, land alienation over the decades, landlessness, and marginalization of the poor people turn out to be the main cause of tribes moving to other more developed regions of the country with a hope of a better livelihood.

The inability of tribes to cope with the many external forces, encountered by social attitudes rooted in a different system, developed a sense of insecurity in their mind. The prevailing illiteracy of tribes, their inability to read even the receipt given by an official, and compulsion to put their thumb impressions on document even though they are unaware about the contents of the document consequently victimize them of any fraud or misrepresentation, which more educated exploiters are used to devise.

Processes and causes contributing to continued tensions and alienation in the areas of unrest and discontent are widespread displacement, forest issues, unsecured tenancies, and other forms of exploitations such as usury, land alienation, and so on. In general, the contradiction between the tribal community and the state itself has become sharper, translating itself into open conflict in many areas. Almost all over the tribal areas, including Nagaland, Manipur, Tripura, Assam, Jharkhand, Orissa, Chhattisgarh, Maharashtra, Andhra Pradesh, and Kerala, tribal people seem to feel a deep sense of exclusion and alienation, which has been manifesting itself in different forms. The Report of the Expert Group on Prevention of Alienation of Tribal Land and Its Restoration (October, 2004) pointed out that the socio-economic infrastructure among the tribal people is inadequate, thereby contributing to their disempowerment and deprivation (GoI, 2004).

Apart from poverty and deprivation in general, the causes of the tribal movements are many: the most important among them are absence of self-governance, forest policy, excise policy, land-related issues, multifaceted forms of exploitation, cultural humiliation, and political marginalization.

A series of factors have contributed for the tribal unrest among them the important causes are enumerated as follows:

1. The laws laid down by the Constitution have rarely provided justice to the tribes in relation to forest revenue, excise, criminal, or civil laws. Virtually these laws were enacted to grab the resources of the tribes for the non-tribes in the pretext of national interest. These laws have inherently snatched away the tribal rights over land, forest, and resources, and, second, have failed to recognize the traditional legal system as well as the management practices of the tribes with regard to either resources or to the social systems. Even laws that are protective of tribal interests have not been implemented with earnestness as a result of which land alienation prevails as one of the most serious problems till date. The ignorance and docility of tribal people in confronting the exploitation of non-tribes has

shifted to gradual awareness of laws and assertion of their rights. Ironically, efforts to integrate the tribes into the mainstream civilization have resulted in cultural alienation, dehumanization, and deprivation of CPRs of tribes. Their right to live, as humans with dignity and equality, right over land, water, and forest resources, and right to freedom of expression have been violated resulting in impoverishment and marginalization of tribes.

2. Tribal communities have understood that the process of impoverishment and marginalization is the sequel of an exploitation process in the guise of national interest or national development. Hence, they have waged a crusade against the exploitative mechanism of deteriorating their life supporting system on their right over natural resources and CPRs to retain their identity. They desire to assert their right but do not accept the 'mainstream' ideology, which turns them into suppliers of cheap raw materials and cheap labour in order to gratify the greed and lust of others. While retaining their culture, identity, and actuary over the CPR, they also demand their due entitlement and share in national development and fruits of development. They demand that they need to be consulted in the decision-making process in the sustainable use of land, water, mines, and forest resources (CPR) with dignity to their community culture and identity in conformity with the PESA.
3. One traces the historical process of development intervention by the government in the tribal areas; one can perceive a very illogical, insincere, and shortsighted attempt at defining 'development' in the hill regions. Government policies have always been in contravention to the laws of the scheduled areas and have never been implemented. Moreover, the abundant resources of land, water, or forests have been utilized for the benefit of external societies and people but never for the development of the local communities. Further, there are evidences that depict that the tribes have been displaced with regard to the establishment of development projects such as irrigation, drinking water, electricity, or any other, and they even

experienced the plight of multiple displacement with meagre or no compensation for their loss of resources or livelihoods. The present policies of the government under the draconian law of Land Acquisition Act of 1894 to procure lands for the tribes so as to violate, circumvent, or amend the laws that protect the interests of the poor trials, falling over backwards to help private companies or industries, such as mining industries, tourism paper mills, film-, or wood-based industries, commercially prosper. The experience with such unscrupulous development policies of the government is repulsing the tribes, especially the unhappy youth into the tantalizing calls of extremist exhortations.

4. The reckless and indiscriminate exploitation of natural resources by the non-tribes who dominate the government machinery in the tribal area not only results in a threat to tribal survival but also leads to depletion of resources in the tribal regions. Directly or indirectly the non-tribes have total control over the lands and resources of the tribes who with the nexus with the politicians and police have been exploiting the tribes, which compels the tribes to seek the assistance and support the extremists who (extremist forces) in turn victimize the tribes in multifarious ways.
5. Despite positive political, institutional, and financial commitment to tribal development, there is presently a large-scale displacement and biological decline of adivasi communities, a growing loss of genetic and cultural diversity and destruction of a rich resource base leading to rising trends of dwindling forests, crumbling fisheries, increasing unemployment, hunger, and conflicts. The adivasis have preserved 90 per cent of the country's biocultural diversity protecting the polyvalent, precolonial, biodiversity-friendly Indian identity from biocultural pathogens. Extreme and indiscriminate demands of the urban market have reduced adivasis to raw material collectors and providers. The unprecedented rate and scale of invasion of tribal homelands for building mega dams, mines, pipelines, roads, energy developments, animal sanctuaries, reserve forests, and military

manoeuvres are astonishing. Thus, one of the earliest settlers on Indian subcontinent (adivasis/tribes) who have enriched its cultural history and heritage has virtually become refugees in their own land and victims of dominant cultural hegemony, human rights violations and development-induced displacement. Implicit in this exercise is the critique of the development policy pursued in the past as well as the search for an alternative strategy.

6. Development in itself is a highly complex phenomenon, and the complexity gets further compounded as we move on to the tribal context. Even the sub-plan strategy, which was once considered to be a positive and very useful device has not had the desired impact. Hence, in a country like India having a number of tribal pockets in different states with heterogeneous geophysical conditions and resource base, the strategies of tribal development have, of necessity, to be area specific and in tune with the peculiar socio-cultural ethos to be effective and meaningful.
7. Historically speaking, the inevitable sequel of all projects was displacement, and displacement has been a saga of marginalization. But considering the escalating needs of the people, it is not possible to abandon all projects. As such, what is imperative is to conceive the possible implications of displacement while examining the social, economic, and environmental aspects of the project as well as its viability. Of course, the cost–benefit analysis of the projects is usually undertaken before enforcement of a project, but the credibility of methods adopted, the procedures followed with regard to the evaluation of socio-economic costs involved in the projects, is subject to re-assessment. Even in most of the cases, a thorough scrutiny of costs in terms of loss of biodiversity or ecological damages is never examined nor the clearance from the department of environment and forests is adhered to. Displacement deprives the vital sustenance of the tribal people who are dependent on the land, forests, and CPRs for their livelihood and finally their long-term sustainability is also endangered. Whereas the tribes constitute 8.08 per cent of country's population, they are

40 per cent of the total displaced/affected persons by the projects (GoI, 2008: 22).

8. As tribal areas are also rich in mineral resources, the mining projects proposed in Orissa, Jharkhand, and Chhattisgarh have threaten the very existence of tribal people. Apart from the physical and occupational displacement caused by large projects, in the case of the Fifth Schedule areas, unless the tribes are resettled in the same scheduled tract, they will face deprivation of the special rights that have accrued to them by virtue of the schedule. The poor implementation of social sectors in government programmes has been attributed to the lack of mobilization and accountability, the absence of performance appraisal, nonexistence of a system of incentives and penalties, understaffing, poor working conditions, and large-scale leakages. These maladies can be corrected by bringing improved transparency, greater accountability, and streamlining the structures of government.
9. This has been due to the development paradigm as conceived by the policy makers which has always been imposed on these communities, and therefore it has remained insensitive to their needs and concerns, causing irreparable damage to these sections. The benefits of this paradigm of development have been disproportionately cornered by the dominant sections at the expense of the poor, who have borne most of the costs. Development which is insensitive to the needs of these communities has invariably caused displacement and reduced them to a sub-human existence. In the case of tribes in particular, it has ended up in destroying their social organization, cultural identity, and resource base and generated multiple conflicts, undermining their communal solidarity, which cumulatively makes them increasingly vulnerable to exploitation.
10. Naxalite movement's fundamental slogan has been 'land to the tiller' and that attempts to put the poor in possession of land have demonstrated much of their activity. CPR constitutes an important component of the natural resource endowment, which contributes significantly to the rural

economy and provides sustenance to local communities in rural areas. CPRs cover a wide basket of land, water, and vegetation resources consisting of community pastures, common dumping, and threshing grounds, watershed drainages, village tanks, rivers and rivulets, and waste-lands. The poor depends upon CPRs far more than the rich due to their lack of or low-productive assets, not enough work or purchasing power, particularly in the lean seasons. Therefore, the health of CPRs and ease of access are critical for these vulnerable groups.

11. The process of industrialization in India since the advent of 20th century, the Tata Iron and Steel Company, Jamshedpur (Bihar), The Bokaro Steel Plant (Bihar), The Rourkela Steel Plant (Orissa), has detrimental impact on the tribes resulting in alienation of land, displacement, and deprivation of this poverty-stricken community. Though the development activities in Orissa surged as early as 1950s, there were about 8,117 displaced families from 1,446 villages because of development projects during the period of 1950–1993. The UNDP estimates that till date more than 1 lakh people in Orissa have been displaced while 20 lakhs have been effected by development projects. Industrial projects such as Rourkela Steel Plant (RSP), The Hindustan Aeronautics (HAL), and National Aluminum Company (NALCO) have displaced people mainly the tribes (Fernandes, 1994; Tripathy, 2003).

In the tribal tracks of Andhra Pradesh, the Polavaram Project threatens to displace more than 1.75 lakhs people mostly the adivasis and will submerge 300 villages. The adivasis in their present habitat, that is, the schedule areas, enjoy a unique set of constitutional rights and privileges, which would no longer be available after they are uprooted. This project has been designed to impound water from Godavari and, apart from irrigating the coastal districts, it would also divert a portion of the stored water to the Krishna (Table 1).

The affected tribes have been deprived of modern fruits of development such as tap water, education, road, electricity, convenient medical facilities, and so on. The majority of the project affected families (PAFs) were involved in rain-fed agricultural activities for their own sustenance. There is partial employment in forestry sector. Since the area is hilly with difficult terrain, they are wholly dependent on vagaries of monsoon, and normally only a single crop is raised by them. Out of the PAFs of Madhya Pradesh who are re-settled in Gujarat, more than 70 per cent are tribal families. Majority of the total tribal PAFs are stated to have already been re-settled in Gujarat after having exercised their option. It is the contention of the state of Gujarat that the tribes in large number have responded positively to the re-settlement package offered by that state.

Table 1

Dams and the Displacement of Tribal People

Name of Project	*State*	*Population Facing Displacement*	*Tribal People as Percentage of Displaced*
Karjan	Gujarat	11,600	100
Sardar Sarovar	Gujarat	2,00,000	57.6
Maheshwar	Madhya Pradesh	20,000	60
Bodhghat	Madhya Pradesh	12,700	73.91
Icha	Bihar	30,800	80
Chandil	Bihar	37,600	87.92
Koel Karo	Bihar	66,000	88
Mahi Bajaj Sagar	Rajasthan	38,400	76.28
Polavaram	Andhra Pradesh	1,50,000	52.90
Maithon and Panchet	Bihar	93,874	56.46
Upper Indravati	Orissa	18,500	89.20
Pong	Himachal Pradesh	80,000	56.25
Inchampalli	Andhra Pradesh–Maharashtra	38,100	76.28
Tultuli	Maharashtra	13,600	51.61
Daman Ganga	Gujarat	8,700	48.70
Bhakra	Himachal Pradesh	36,000	34.76
Masan Reservoir	Bihar	3,700	31.00

Source: Satyajit Singh, *Taming the Waters*, OUP, 1997, and Government figures.

The Land Acquisition Act, 1894, has the provision that the government is not bound to provide a displaced person anything but cash compensation if the concerned person can show the evidence of his land title. Unfortunately, the tribes could not produce the same and as a result of which are usually deprived of the compensation. The elite have, therefore, through such pseudo-developmental activities impoverished the earth of its natural resources. The earth's impoverishment has meant that communities that depend upon the natural base for sustenance have been deprived of their resources. This alienation cannot be described in terms of loss of material livelihood only; it is most profoundly the loss of culture autonomy, knowledge, and power (Baviskar, 1995).

However, the voices of the displaced are no longer extraordinary. Echoed in virtually every displacement situations, be it Tehri, Narmada, Singrauli, or Koel Karo, only to name a few, they reveal what it means to be a 'displaced lot': loss of livelihood and traditional lands; demolition of homes; loss of social networks; severance from an ecosystem that sustained them earlier, and, above all, a feeling of powerlessness and insecurity for the future.

Displacement is a multidimensional phenomenon not confined to physical relocation; it reduces the 'quality of life' of the communities into sub-human conditions. This understanding of displacement highlights (i) the alienation of legal and customary rights of the individual and community and dislocation of the social and economic organization and (ii) the politics of legal and policy instruments that sanctions such disenfranchisement.

Cernea's impoverishment risk and reconstruction model proposes that 'the onset of impoverishment can be represented through a model of 10 interlinked potential risks intrinsic to displacement'. These are: (i) landlessness, (ii) joblessness, (iii) homelessness, (iv) marginalization, (v) food insecurity, (vi) increased morbidity and mortality, (vii) loss of access to common property, (viii) social disintegration, (ix) loss of access to community, (x) violation of human rights (Cernea, 1988).

For the government and its agents of development, cash compensation seems to be the only panacea for the problems induced by displacement and only policy for rehabilitation, whereas in practice it is the most inadequate means for rehabilitation. No procedure and principles are laid down to estimate the costs, showing the arbitrariness of compensation. Apart from loss of land, the villager suffers loss from CPR forest produce, village grazing land, community centre, social security, and so on. The problem is more acute with the artisans, some of them may own land, but their major income is from their profession within the known community. There seems no provision with regard to their rehabilitation. Besides, the landless and the tribes are probably the worst sufferers. The powerful exogenous forces of moneylenders, contractors, officials having their link with political personnel, and police could exert dominant control and gratify the selfish greed of exploiting tribes. The poverty stricken, illiterate, innocent, simple tribes fail to withstand the countervailing exogenous forces and becoming prey to all types of exploitations. Despite the vast expansion of the formal credit system in India, the dependence of the rural poor on moneylenders continues in some areas especially for meeting emergent credit requirements. Such dependencies are pronounced in the case of marginal farmers, landless labourers, petty traders, and rural artisans belonging to the socially and economically backward classes and the tribal population particularly in the resource-poor areas (Tripathy, 2007).

It has been observed that non-recognition of tribes over resources and restrictions on their use, alienation of tribes from the means of production, denial of due entitlement of labour, distressed payment of wages, and misappropriation of funds have kept the tribes in the web of misery and starvation. In tribal-dominated states in India, the life support system of the local tribes has been snatched away by non-tribes and state institutions, through the imposition of restrictions on the use of forests. As a result, tribal movement originated in fierce struggle of their rights (Tripathy, 2000).

The benefits of development have not percolated to the local tribal people, rather adversely affected their life style, leading to the violation of human rights, miserable living standard of tribes, restriction the community rights over natural resources, and their own forest resources, and, finally, culminated to identity crisis of the tribes. Thus, poverty of the local people is a great stumbling block for success of any programme in Orissa.

Much of the unrest in society, especially that which has given rise to militant movements such as the Naxalite movement, is linked to the lack of access to basic resources to sustain livelihood.

Despite the plethora of development plans, programmes, and activities initiated in the tribal areas, the majority of scheduled tribes still live in conditions of serious deprivation and poverty. The tribal people have remained backward in all aspects of human development including education, health, nutrition, and so on. Apart from socio-economic deprivation, there has been a steady erosion of traditional tribal rights and their command over resources.

Widespread practice of social discrimination, untouchability, domestic violence, and atrocities against the weaker sections is an index of the failure of the promises made to the oppressed people of this country. In this situation, it should not cause surprise that a large section of the people are angry and feel alienated from the polity. It is in this context that it has become necessary to identify the variety of causes of discontent and to seek ways by which the state could answer them in a humane, caring, and democratic way.

If the emphasis of this exploration is on the Naxalite phenomenon, it is not because other modes and forms of agitation are less important but only because the method of struggle chosen by the Naxalites has brought the problem to a head. Radical groups seek the justification for their methods of violence from structural violence which is implicit in the social and economic system. While not condoning the radical violence, an honest response to it must, therefore, begin by ameliorating the structural violence in the society. It has been conceived that the Naxal issue can be resolved only by involving tribes, downtrodden in the developmental activities. Unless they are benefited by development, jobs, services such as water, health, and road, and education, there is no prospect of solving the issue.

Developmental Intervention

In the above framework, the much-needed developmental intervention perceived as a multidimensional process, reflected in a wider perspectives such as improvement in the quality of life, achieving demographic transition, creating economic infrastructure, and much-needed investment in social sectors. The success story of inclusive growth, poverty reduction, and achieving socio-economic development depends upon the quality of governance. Inadequacies of governance may not be reflected from overall growth rates, but are clear from issues such as unmet demand leading to migration. It is, therefore, imperative that any analysis of government intervention in the tribal belt aiming at minimizing the discontents of tribes so as to mitigate Naxalism must not simply take into account growth; it must capture development in an equitable way.

The development paradigm pursued since independence has aggravated the prevailing discontent among marginalized sections of society. This is because development has always been imposed on these communities, and therefore it has remained insensitive to their needs and concerns, causing irreparable damage to these sections. The benefits of this paradigm of development have been disproportionately cornered by the dominant sections at the expense of the poor, who have borne most of the costs.

Development which is insensitive to the needs of these communities has invariably caused displacement and reduced them to a sub-human existence. In the case of tribes in particular, it has ended up in destroying their social organization, cultural identity, and resource base and generated multiple conflicts, undermining their communal solidarity, which cumulatively makes them increasingly vulnerable to exploitation.

However, there are organizations such as the Nehru Yuva Kendra Sangathan (NYKS) that organize National Integration Camps (NICs) with the objective to facilitate youth of the country to come together and share experience and interact together despite having diverse background of language, religion, culture, and traditions. There has been significant development of youth who have been associated with NYKS across the country. It is hoped that the placement-linked skill development scheme will show a 'new path' to the youths being targeted by Maoists. Recently, the Government of India has initiated a placement-linked skill development scheme targeting 50,000 rural men and women, mostly tribes, in 24 worst affected districts. At least 50 per cent of the candidates covered under the scheme will be women and special efforts will be made to proactively cover Particularly Vulnerable Tribal Groups (PVTGs) on a priority basis. The scheme is being implemented through training partners from the private and public sectors as well as non-profit organizations. The scheme aims at providing training for youth from identified districts for employment in the organized sector.

The new programme drew lessons from a similar scheme being implemented in two critical Left-wing extremism affected districts – West Singhbhum in Jharkhand and Sukma in Chhattisgarh – and Himayat programme launched to address the needs and aspirations of the youth in Jammu and Kashmir. Beneficiaries aged between 18 and 35 years with requisite aptitude depending upon the trade or job requirements are to be selected as per the participatory identification of poor.

There is no denying that what goes in the name of 'Naxalism' is to a large extent a product of collective failure to assure different segments of society their basic entitlements under the Constitution and other protective legislation. The processes and causes contributing to continued tensions and alienation in areas of unrest and discontent, such as widespread displacement, forest issues, insecure tenancies and other forms of exploitations such as usury, land alienation, and imperfect market conditions need to be identified, and suggestions are required to take up specific steps to reduce the tensions and causes of discontent.

Government of India's Policy to Control Naxalism

The salient features of government policy to deal with the Naxal problem, as outlined in the Ministry of Home Affairs Status Paper brought out in May 2006, are summarized as follows:

> (i) deal sternly with the Naxalites indulging in violence; political, security, and development fronts in a holistic manner; (ii) ensure interstate coordination in dealing with the problem; (iii) accord priority to faster socio-economic development in the Naxal-affected or – prone areas; (iv) supplement the efforts and

resources of the affected states on both security and development fronts; (v) promote local resistance groups against the Naxalites; (vi) use mass media to highlight the futility of Naxal violence and the loss of life and property caused by it; (vii) have a proper surrender and rehabilitation policy for the Naxalites; and affected states will not have any peace dialogue with the Naxal groups, unless the latter agree to give up violence and arms.

Concluding Remarks and Suggestions

The Constitution of India, which came into existence on 26 January 1950, prohibits discrimination on grounds of religion, race, caste, sex, or place of birth (Article, 15), and it provides the right to equality (Article, 14), to freedom of religion (Articles, 25–28), and to culture and education (Articles, 29–30). Scheduled tribes (STs) are supposedly addressed by as many as 209 articles and 2 special schedules of the Constitution – articles and special schedules that are protective and paternalistic. Articles, 341 and 342 provide for classification of scheduled castes (the untouchable lower castes) and STs, while Articles, 330, 332, and 334 provide for reservation of seats in the parliament and assemblies. For purposes of specific focus on the development of STs, the government has adopted a package of programmes, which is administered in specific geographical areas with considerable ST population, and it covers 69 per cent of the tribal population. Despite this, and after the largest 'modern democracy' of the world has existed for more than half a century, the struggles for survival of adivasis – for livelihood and existence as peoples – have today intensified and spread as never before in history. In the light of the above – backdrop, the following suggestions are forwarded to ameliorate the situation:

1. It is imperative that the government must recognize that the tribal people have a distinct socio-cultural life style and the administration need to understand this crucial cultural aspect while designing and implementing development programmes. Conflicts of customary laws versus universal laws, conflicts over control over resources, and tribal–non-tribal disputes in the tribal areas all over the country have led to the formulation of the Panchayati Exclusion in Schedule Areas (PESA) for the areas concentrated with tribes areas, which lays emphasis on the local

self-governance and powers to the gram sabha in scheduled areas.

2. The state government should, in all sincerity, implement this act without any dilutions to ensure that stability of administration is maintained. PESA is the single most important instrument for dealing with the economic and emotional alienation of the tribal people, which lies at the root of the growing menace of Naxalism. Its effective implementation would generate a deep sense of effective participation among tribal people in the conduct of their own affairs.
3. Literacy is essential as a first step towards enabling tribes to operate within the scope of the advanced communities dominating the economic and political scene. The rationale is that the disadvantages of illiterate tribes labour are multiplied in the case of those who do not even speak and understand the language of the dominant population. Therefore, they cannot communicate with officials except through better-educated fellow tribesmen acting as interpreters as a result, the real problem of tribes remain unsolved.
4. Panchayati Raj system was expected to give the oppressed communities, but with the empowerment of the local bodies as envisaged by the 73rd amendment to the Constitution remaining a mere promise in most states, and with the co-optation of the leaders generated by the Panchayati Raj Institutions in the corrupt political system, the hope has been largely belied. A very genuine empowerment of the local bodies and of the representatives of the oppressed communities within the system alone can fill this requirement.
5. Identify causes for persistent and abysmally low social and human development indicators and suggest steps for bringing these on par with the rest of the country in a time-bound manner.
6. Examine and suggest an appropriate strategy for ensuring peace and life with dignity and for resolution of conflicts in areas of chronic unrest.

7. Suggest measures to upgrade the levels of governance and strengthen public service delivery in these areas, through suitable administrative and institutional reform and mechanisms for prompt redressal of grievances.
8. Suggest measures for ensuring time-bound achievement of livelihood security, health and nutrition security, food security, and so on and also suggest changes in central and state legislations impeding the achievement of these objectives.
9. So long as the tribes and all other sections don't feel stakeholders in the development of the country, Naxalism will continue uncontrolled.

The symbiotic relationship between the forests and the local dwellers was not recognized and the forest became property of the state. The tribes who have a lifelong relationship with the forests – which are their very homes, their religion, and their culture – were conspicuous by its absence in the new frame. It is because of this basic lack of understanding, that there is state of confrontation and regime of destruction in almost all tribal concentrated regions of India, which in the final analysis means great injustice to the tribal people.

Despite PESA, as well as several other protective legislations in the tribal regions of our country, there has been extensive violation of fundamental rights and human rights of the tribal people. The second hindrance lies in the inability of the poor peasants to make their voice heard in the face of elite domination of the traditional power structures. The ingrained problem of elite domination can hardly be resolved, unless the poor themselves can exercise enough bargaining power and be organized so that their collective voice can be audible to the irrigation executives and bureaucrats. It is lamentable fact that the purpose of the PESA Act has not been completely understood either by the political leaders or by the bureaucracy. People at large are also not aware of the provisions of PESA Act except in those areas where the NGOs are seriously working with the people.

The tribes in many parts of the country fighting their battles to protect their right to life, but the state has no hesitation in using coercive force against the tribes who are struggling for establishing their rights. The state must rethink and re-look the root of the problem. The state must take into note that it has been entrusted with responsibility of protecting them, who can sustain on the good will and support of the state. In the absence of state support and practically repressive measures being adopted by the state machinery to snatch away their traditional rights and life support system, the tribes have no way out but to support the extremists and consequently they are unwillingly caught in the holocaust of a cross-fire. In this situation, if a dialogue has to be established with them for discharging, even though symbolic, the obligation as a part of the system and also in relation to the constitutional responsibility, there is no other alternative but to get directly linked with their struggle (Sharma, 1990).

Investment in social forestry, reclamation of agricultural land, provision of free and compulsory education, health services and guaranteed employment or source of employment with multiple livelihood options, and equitable sharing of resources with utmost priority for tribes will certainly ameliorate the situation and usher in an era of peace in the so-called 'disturbed tribal areas'.

References

Baviskar, Amita (1995). *In the Belly of the River*. New Delhi: Oxford University Press.

Cernea, Michael M. (1988). *Involuntary Resettlement in Development Projects: Policy Guidelines in World Bank Financed Projects*. World Bank Technical Paper No. 80. Washington, DC: World Bank.

Fernandes, W. (1994). *Development Induced Displacement in Tribal Areas of Eastern India* (mimeo). New Delhi: Indian Social Institute.

Government of India (2004). *Report of the Expert Group on Prevention of Alienation of Tribal Land and Its Restoration*. New Delhi: Ministry of Rural Development.

——. (2008). *Development Challenges in Extremists Affected Areas* (Report of an expert group to Planning Commission). New Delhi.

Sharma, B.D. (1990). *Report of the Commissioner for Scheduled Cates and Scheduled Tribes*. Twenty Ninth Report 1987–89. New Delhi: Government of India.

Tripathy, S.N. (2007). *Tribal Development: Issues and Policy Options*. New Delhi: Anmol Publishing.

——. (2000). *Glimpses on Tribal Development*. New Delhi: Discovery Publishing House.

——. (2003). 'Problems of Displacement and Development'. In S.N. Tripathy (ed.) *Economic Development and Problem of Displacement*. New Delhi: Anmol Publishing.

10

Securitization, Exceptions and Suspects

The Case of State-Maoist Interface in India

MOHAMMED SIIRAJUDDEEN

Mapping Governance Shifts

The state system around the world is in the phase of tumultuous transformations. Mapping of the same would bring into the fore, the status of governance on a global scale. It helps to discuss in detail the specificities which are unique to current era and also necessitate a conceptual distinction between the state and governance. The attributes of homogeneity, unity and sovereignty which characterized the conventional state system has now been transformed to heterogeneous, multi cultural, pluralistic one which forms the basics of the problematic of governance now. The change which brought about the anatomic shifts in the configuration of the state as an entity and governance as the functional aspect is fraught with contradictions and exceptions. The first specificity identified is the aspects of securitization. It became an overarching phenomenon which encompasses in itself various kinds of techniques making it different from the conventional militarism as a tool of defence governance. These methods of new kind included militarism in its crude form and surveillance, and various other newly employed technological tools. Securitization has been both outwards and inwards. The outward securitization regime is the one which explains the dynamics of securitization as specificity in the status of governance globally. It is this which determined the debates of Imperialism, hegemony, domination and invasion. If the securitization outward regimes and its consequences constituted the status of governance at global level, looking into India with this respect brings a different story of 'dualistic nature'. It is more about the securitization inwards dealing with internal challenges. That is to what extend the global narrative of securitization outwards in the context of 9/11 has influenced internal security? And what is peculiar in its contradictory course to that of the global one. This does not mean that the securitization strategy in India did not echo the global trends. What makes it different from the globally induced one is the 'pre-history' of the same which constitutes its conventionality in its nature as it at times amounted to the reflection of crude militarism as is evident in the conflict zones of Kashmir and Red Corridors.

Neoliberalization of politics with the pragmatic outlooks in the governance practice is the second specificity to be discussed. This has parallel as well as contradictory shifts in terms of its entrenchment and practices. Contrarily, the historical time period within which this turn has been inaugurated is completely different from that of the global story. The international factors contributed for the same was the demise of a 'hope of the alternative' as seen in the persistence of soviet model and its consequences across the borders. The internal contradiction to which governing practices succumbed to the modalities of neoliberalism is various ranging from crisis in economy, emergence of technocratic leadership in the echelons of governance, absence of potential opposition and weakness of movements resisting neoliberalism. Another parallel which can be traced from Indian shift to that of global is the movement of politics towards plutocracy and increase in power of wealthy and rich. Consequently, neoliberal politics reflected the impoverishment of masses reflected in widening inequality.

State-Society Interface: Global to Local

The absence of consensus on preserving democratic culture at global level in relations between the states is significant in the era of imperial securitization. The traditionally envisioned institutional global governance has crumbled and the ideal now became a distant dream given the power equations and emergent challenges in given framework, the result being 'political crisis' from global to that of the micro dynamics of individual state behaviours. Political crisis is then the cumulative effect. It is the sum total of specificities seen globally and is to be defined as the sociality of conditions in which governing structures are engulfed with at this juncture pointing the 'exceptionalism' reflected thereby. The uniqueness of the juncture is referred to as 'crisis' ridden because anomalies are in its totality. It is 'political' because the said juncture of 'difference' is a deep-rooted phenomenon influencing the politics from global to local. The crisis of politics resulted anomalies which are parallel and unparallel as far as India is concerned. The parallel trends include terrorism, mushrooming of identity politics in different forms, corruption and the loot of the public resources, diminishing accountability of the public institutions, and manipulation of public opinion. The differently trends with respect to India's political crisis includes emergence of new avenues of disciplinary state technologies, fragmentation of the political system, kinship-family dragging of political agencies, increasing repressive nature of the state apparatuses with respect to the internal challenges. Spiralling state repression internally is contradictory to the global shift. This rebuttal is not in the fact that the state is becoming repressive. What is distinct here is the exhibition of dissonance in the coerciveness domestically as a part of securitization inwards rather than outwards (rather than external reasons as in the case of US). The 'exceptionalism' is then reflected with the governing practices of extraordinary measures creating lawless zones. It is from this premise that the paper attempts briefly to address the questions of changing strategies of governance vis-à-viz the changing nature of state-society interface in India especially with respect to Maoist conflict in Central India. This would bring into lime light the conceptual aspects of why the state suspect certain sets of its own people? The framework will look into why different communities and groups are named, framed and implicated by State on various accounts. If so are only Maoists suspected? Or whether it is a parcel of the general contradictions entrenched in the status of governance which are networked globally. The paper therefore while particularly focusing on the State-Maoist interface, comparatively bring into brief analogies from the issues of political questions of Kashmir and Muslim question in India.

Securitization as Imperial Paradigm

Who all are suspects is a general question in an era when the state enters kitchen and kill its citizen, collude to build criminal impunity to the perpetrators of rape in Adivasi belts of Chhattisgarh, or when the state and its collaborators engage in racial attacks on ethnic minorities of North East India and persecute religious minorities. But the question turns bit complex when it is drawn in congruence with the commitment exhibited so far to resist such moves. We see a sea of sympathy and an acknowledged silence in academics, politics and activism going simultaneously. It is from this premise that we have to estimate the state coercion on vulnerable communities. The security is derived as an embedded concept with the emergence of modern nation state which manifested in earlier decades a crude militarization projected as the sole determinant, more importantly for guarding external sovereignty. What makes the securitization of the present era different is the way in which security is conceived with emergence of multiplicity of techniques as the tools where rather than militarization per se, a saga of methods such as surveillance, secrecy, spying, blaming, naming, and suspecting becomes central where none necessarily dominates in singular pattern but securitization thrives with politics and propaganda. Securitization drive is therefore ontologically different from the conventional militarism by encompassing in itself militarism in its crude forms along with new technologies of national security regime. And it is both 'inward' and 'outward', a distinction necessitated out of the new conditions of the interplay of global outward securitization regimes on the securitization inward dynamics of Indian State. Here the securitization outward is significant so as to read adventurism perpetrated by hegemonic states by erecting global regimes of Security with severe consequences for internal security dynamics of the states around the globe especially in the eventualities of the post 9/11 global discourse of 'war on terror'. Such an outlook in brief way points to whether imperialism as a category manifests or not and if so whether such a category is central or not? Similar is the key role securitization plays in state process steering disequilibrium caused by dominant ideology, thereby manufacturing hatred on vulnerable communities such as ethnic minorities and migrant working class.

Securitization in India

Militarization as an aspect of defence persisted with the state in India. It was conventionally seen on the lines of national security. While securitization as an all embracing project is the product of the new global security discourse, militarization persisted in its typical form the beginning. Militarism of all sorts in India has a long history which can be traced to the Vedic era. The development of an organized form of military state was developed through the necessities of the various political dynasties historically through the ages. Therefore, the trajectory of various dynasties was accompanied with militaristic advancements. It was with the coming of the British that militarism in modern sense got a stipulated substance. Independent India also in contingencies resorted to military actions. If it was the 'mission world war' which were the pre-independent militaristic external intervention, the battle grounds in the uneasy borders and voluntary UN task missions constituted the external militarism of independent India.

The most intriguing part of the coercive aspects of Indian State is the internal militarization which is a subject of controversies. The internal militarism is one of the tools to tackle the 'enemies within'. While it was the post independent assertion of internal sovereignty which invited military actions internally as seen in the operations ranging from Goa to Andhra Pradesh, many other political challenges emanating from 'Terrorism' and 'Separatism' historically, as well as to tackle the challenges of 'Naxalism' or 'Maoism' as internal security threats also reflected securitized excesses. The point however is how the securitization in India especially after 1990s and more notably after the global wave emanated out of the post 9/11 global security discourse, is different from that of the conventional military governance of defense as hitherto existed in India? How the securitization through comprehensive measures different? Did it succumb to the global narratives and ferocious propaganda?

Militarism and securitization even though ontologically different from each other pointing to different purposes of state actions, the global security regimes influenced India to inscribe militarism in its rudimentary form within the broader framework of an umbrella strategy of the securitization internally. As an all encompassing framework of guarding the territory and people, securitization as reflected globally, in India as well, implied a whole range of state practices containing threat to the order, both tangible in terms of institutions and flexible in terms of politics. It ranged from use of military, policing practices, intelligence, surveillance, spying, erecting mechanisms, legislations and plethora of other quasi state mechanisms. These complementary tools of discipline became a site of problematic in India today.

Dancing with Global: Domestic Implications

The global developments since 9/11 had severe impact on the state behaviour in India with respect to securitization. Like any other state, the initial reaction of India to terror strikes on the US World Trade Centre was of a sympathetic nature. India to that extend by identifying the global outrage on the incident declared high alert across most of its major cities and by expressing solidarity conveyed its deepest sympathies to the US and condemned the attacks.[1] In the immediate aftermath of the 9/11, US had sent its Pacific Command Chief to New Delhi with three specific military demands of assistance with respect to navy, air force and India's participation which the central government was unable to commit due to pressures from the coalition.[2] In sharp contrast to the initial reactions, 'in foreign policy, India moved much closer to the US, and the government even toyed with the idea of sending troops to Iraq at American request, until massive popular opposition made it desist. Though not formally abandoning India's traditional support for the Palestinian cause, it warmed up to Israel, and there was even occasional talk of an India-US-Israel axis'.[3] Therefore even after non-commitment of a comprehensive 'militarism' outwards, the policy establishments had hoped that the 'war on terror' under the leadership of the US would answer dual needs-of securing the borders externally and hoped to retard the edifice of terrorism within. Moreover, the inherent weakness of the state structures to face in isolation, the threats (elevated to global in nature) also induced the policy makers in India as was the case with Pakistan, and other Asian countries. The increasing number of terror strikes in South Asian countries including India as was evident in the attacks on Parliament in the just aftermath of 9/11 necessitated imminent cooperation by all possible means. The resultant global unity against terrorism helped India to pacify and nullify the threats posed by many international terrorist organizations.[4] 'On 21 October 2001, just over a month after the attacks in the United States, the governments of India and United States signed the Mutual Assistance on Criminal Matters Treaty, after which both sides expressed their determination to redouble efforts to eradicate the scourge of terrorism and to use this Treaty as an instrument to that end'.[5] It was not only the policy prescriptions of the government instead the articulations of the media, civil society and the commentators both within and outside added to the Indian journey of becoming an implicit partner in the global war on terror under US leadership. Years after the panic period of 9/11, invocation of the old spirit of such alignments began to prop up again. The observations of the US senator pertaining to that has been narrated by Tania Roy – 'Ten days, after the Mumbai attacks of 26 November 2008, Senator John McCain characterized the atrocities in terms of a borrowed metaphor, as "India's 9/11". McCain's strategic alignment of "India" with a sovereign American subject ('we', above) turned on a further conflation that remained implicit, even as its rhetorical effects appeared, at the time, to be overwhelming. In collapsing Mumbai into the memory of New York, McCain authorized an evident moral parity between two symmetrical, monolithic victims of global terrorism'.[6] Indeed, in the years since India allied implicitly itself with the United States in its big war, India has suffered at least one major terror attack every year at home.[7] The developments in India's relations with the US and Israel (the two countries which formed the bedrock of the Global Security regimes) through strategic partnerships is a different dimension of the securitization outwards which not only brought the security governance in India very close to the idiom of 'global war on terror' rhetoric but also explicitly linked the outward securitization regime in India to that of the one 'within' than ever before. It was after this that a series of moves such as diplomatic visits, joint statements, the Indo-US Nuclear deal, the Joint Naval exercise, and other defense pacts were mooted. At the same time India sought to develop an increasing proximity with Israel. It is a different matter that the long shaded India-Israel relationship was reworked by the right wing BJP-led government before 9/11 having implications on attitude to Palestine. The significance of the this bilateral engagement is that it eloped to a stage that India in the first decade of the 21st century transformed itself into a leading purchaser of armaments and striker of defence deals with Israel, a country which can be projected as the epicenter of US war projects in Middle East and South Asia. Relevance of the securitization through strategic partnership lies in the historic geopolitical contingencies integral to these countries as well as the 'convergence of the interests on the other'.[8]

Institutional Measures

In India securitization is featured with a manifestation of militarism and the institution of administrative mechanisms. A plethora new technologies right from the enactment of legislations to that of the establishment of agencies having national importance came as a part of internal security regime. The effect of global frenzy was clearly evident in the ordainment of Prevention of Terrorism Act (POTA) by invoking the spirit of Terrorist and Disruptive Activities (Prevention) Act (TADA) and giving it a reflection of the USA PATRIOT Act (USA PATRIOT). But coming of the Congress government even though gave a hope of repeal of the highly criticized provisions of POTA, contrastingly re-invoked the draconian aspects of POTA in the Unlawful Activities (Prevention) Act (UAPA) of 2004. The harsh provisions of these legislative actions were widely criticized in political circles, academia and by activists who came up with fact finding reports on its effects on ground. Along with these legislative measures policing practices in different parts of the country underwent fabulous changes in tandem to the counter terror wave and a premier agency named National Investigating Agency (NIA) was constituted in 2008 and the idea of National Counter Terrorism Centre (NCTC) were floated simultaneously aftermath of 2008 Mumbai terror attacks (popularly known as 26/11) that too taking influence from National Counterterrorism Centre of USA. By bringing the colonial legacy and contingent global spirits, new techniques such as strategic hamlets, Special Military Operations, and Special Police Zones are experimented in the country. The purpose is multifaceted with an overarching single agenda of containing the threat from within. The challenge of 'separatism' and the internal threat accelerated by the extremism exhibited by the Left of the political spectrum in India is one of the reasons of the state for strategizing 'normalization of the normlessness'.[9] 'Militarization of state and governance in India's tribal heartland, where the bulk of country's mineral and forest resources are located, is a great menace to democracy, perhaps greater than the crises in Kashmir or the north-eastern region were at their peak'.[10] In addition to militarization there are administrative measures like new policing tactics, continuation and enactment of controversial legislations like Armed Forces Special Powers Acts (AFSPA), Public Safety Act (PSA) in Kashmir and Chhattisgarh Special Public Security Act (CSPSA) to counter Maoism in Chhattisgarh, all which are misused that stemmed numerous instances of human rights violations. The developments to these sorts are captured by the writings of Ujjwal Kumar Singh and Nandini Sundar recently in academics.

Suspectism: The Maoist Case

Neoliberal development model pursued by the Indian State is fraught with plethora of opposition as it led to severe economic contradictions and social consequences. The paradigm is vociferously challenged by Maoists questioning the state sovereignty by other means in Central India. The full scale battle of the

Maoists for their self claimed cause of tribal population is a war against the sovereignty of the Indian state which according to them subjugated the peoples' sovereignty in the interests of the ruling class. Here the existing political freedom is conceived as 'non-freedom' in the face of the absence of economic democracy. State sought to throttle this challenge through force curbing civil liberties of the inhibiting population. Securitization here serves dual purpose primarily political as it put a check on challenge to state sovereignty and secondarily private as it ensured the designs of corporate interests of resource extraction in tribal areas. Therefore the spatiality of the Red Corridor and other contested zones meets in a common juncture when state's 'exceptionalism' renders the civilian space as a hub of 'non-persons'. In more clear terms, 'the heart of the conflict and repression is in the amoral political economy endorsed by the state and the departure of state policy from Nehruvian socialism in favour of a free market economy, the natural corollary of which is muscular and violent statecraft. The intimate connections between neo-liberal economic policy and a violently authoritarian state have been demonstrated in one country after another. The routine derogation of fundamental rights and human rights, large-scale displacement and dispossession of primarily indigenous tribal communities is an inseparable part of this process'.[11]

Central India is a home to substantial proportion of tribal population who were been excluded from the journey of development and widely articulated 'progress' since the dawn of independence. Like their brethren in any other part of India, the tribal population here also is a site of experiments of new development model driven by the neoliberal India since 1990s. In contrast to other oppressed communities, tribes of Central India are restrained from fruitfully using their concerns through the existing far absent democratic structures. The failures of the institutions and of the formal political system provided a space for Maoist revolutionaries to move into.[12] Moreover, the state in India treated the people of this conflict zone with zeal of contempt so as to clear the way for corporate greed. According to a compilation of case studies by Human Rights Law Network, the region provides entirely two different pictures. Primarily it is a place 'well known for its rich cultural heritage as well as for its abundant deposits of natural resources'[13] But as a result of the development model perpetuating displacement and dispossession, the state-corporate nexus is 'destroying the environment and shattering the lives of people in villages and cities, as well as indigenous tribal population who have lived for thousands of years in the forests'[14] This led to massive dislocation, displacement, rehabilitation and consequently ensuing plight of the affected people especially in Chhattisgarh. A project carried out by the International Institute for Environment and Development entitled Mining, Minerals and Sustainable Development (MMSD), shows that such displacements and rehabilitation augments risk factors giving a spiral of 'unemployment, homelessness, marginalization, insecure food provision, loss of common land and resources, increased health risks, lack of social articulation, and loss of civil and political rights'[15] and this model resulted 'accumulation by dispossession'.[16] All these moves are legitimized through the instruments of law meant to protect the interests of the 'corporate-bureaucratic-political nexus' at the cost of the indigenous population. It was in this context by dwelling on the examples of the havoc created by this process in the states of Chhattisgarh, Orissa and Jharkhand that a study conducted by 'The Perspective Team'[17] generalizes its odds by exposing that displacement and deprivation is always the method through which the state in India served the interests of the wealthy.

Matrix of Exceptionalism

Exceptionalism brought out by neoliberalism in Red Corridors bring into picture the generality of all contestations in the era of political crisis in Indian society which also takes into account the uniqueness of the particular terrain. Anomalies created by governance in India made the state more repressive than ever before. The repression meted out to the constructed 'other' is intense and always exhibited coercive will of the state which is a feature of all conflicted zones in India. This is also true for the tribal population of this region as is the case of people in Kashmir. Therefore, governance becoming more repressive is one of the instances which make a point for 'generality'. Economic reforms brought a paradigm of exclusive agendas and 'prosperity' under this schema is all about a pyramid reframe of the political system with plutocrats and political class[18] at the top, engineering ways for the 'normalization of exclusion' through the neoliberal exceptions as propounded by Aihwa Ong.[19]

Economic indifference of the state is divulged in the banished landscapes of Muslims and Dalits in India. Moreover the existence of a tussle over political goods in Kashmir and economic social goods in other areas of marginality in India tells the story of the non-inclusive decision making structures. In India, who is represented? is a problematic question. It took more decades to include a player for Indian cricket team from Kashmir. Bollywood is not a mere banal instrument of modernity constructing 'only Muslims' as pointed by Maidul Islam[20] but also is a no-admission area of the North East 'face' in the representation of the life of the nation until recently. The people caught up in the war zones of Maoist hunt are the ones who were under-represented in the mainstream of the social spaces of the nation for many decades. Then comes 'generally' the question as to, where is 'Muslim' in Indian Army? Therefore, the benchmark of 'representation and opportunity of participation' is a way through which political contradictions in different parts of India can be reckoned for a generalization.

War Frames for Local Threats: Characterizing the New Suspects

The last one decade in the political domain of India we witnessed a predatory usage of the terms 'terrorists', 'terrorism', as a common denominator to disqualify, their by suspect the loyalties of various groups in hundreds of cases. The term became a buzzword for the state and 'frames' were created to the extent that 'anti-nationals' to be fought tooth and nail. Along with the numerous cases of Muslims, the dissidents' of North East and Kashmir are being named, framed and victimized in many cases pertaining to terrorism, and the tribal groups of central India who are in all out contradiction with the state for being excluded in the journey of development are framed as terrorists. The arrests of human rights activists in various parts of the country, issue of Binayak Sen, detentions of members from different cultural groups, the arrest of Kashmiri Human Rights activist Khurram Parvez, the arrests and prosecution of journalists in Bastar and the recent police surveillance as well as draconian charges on academicians and students in various parts of the country and many unreported cases are the testimonies of 'constructed frames' complementing global discourse of threat perception and counter threat strategy. The trajectory of state hunt on dissident movements since 1980s shows this discourse becoming slowly entrenching deep into our social conscience. In the early 1960s 'Naxalites' were described as 'extremists' but then they later turned into 'terrorists'. Increasingly the term 'Naxalite' was used in a vituperative sense and gradually normalized in political circle as 'extremists'. Gradually at the national level the term 'terrorism' got prominence as a hegemonic discourse in the past decade and soon became the State language. Early in 1980s in the official account of the State all the 139 offences relating to the Maoist/Naxalite movement were described as offences by extremists and in 1989 witnessed an increased record of such offences with 592 cases in the state statistics of which 70 per cent were named as offences by terrorists.[21] In the 'Frames of War', Judith Butler discusses how the frames have been constructed as to how to represent the reality in public discourse,[22] so as to fit the state vocabulary. 'The frames of war often nudge politics towards a reality that suits such frames. Since it requires two opposing parties, reality is constructed in such a way that the frames of war look more legitimate'.[23] The parameters set by the new generalizations and the political subjectivity working in tandem to it conceived all opposition to the state as the act of 'terrorism' producing a reason for an abrupt use of draconian measures. It is here, Nandini Sundar's analysis of the State-Maoist conflict in India points to the official discourse of characterizing the movement, as 'terrorist threat'.[24]

Securitization Effects

Scholars of 'securitization' like Ole Wæver and Barry Buzan[25] maintains that military, political, economic, social, and environmental sectors are various sectors in which securitization thrive. Accordingly, if a subject is successfully securitized, it opens the channels of extraordinary methods to contain the perceived threat through multitudinous ways of militarism, emergency, draconian laws, and surveillance. State ideology therefore mobilizes the subject in the name of imminent threat and necessary unity. 'Overt securitization of social or political problems has often led to the neglect of the governance issues involved, as establishing the state monopoly on the use of violence (often through the adoption of extraordinary measures) becomes the main counter-insurgency strategy of the Indian state. This has unfortunately led to the fracturing and proliferation of conflicts rather than to their resolution'.[26] Centralization and brute violence turns out to be the state strategy then and 'one realize that at the bottom of all political questions is the issue of physical violence. From the most complex and abstract of issues of power to the most simple and banal issues of everyday conflicts, they are haunted by the prospect and possibility of breaking into physical violence. In these sites, the state and capital have responded with brute force without hesitation and with impunity. This remains essentially a question that draws equivalence between various dominant structures from the local to the global'.[27] Lokaneeta argues that violence and torture prevalent is part and parcel of liberal democratic discourse[28] which brings her close to the structural questions. It also convey to the fore, the significance of looking 'Why is it happening?' becomes important rather than a mechanistic description as to 'it is happening' in the first place. Similar is the colonial-hegemonic continuities of the nature of violence perpetrated by Indian state to contain threat in these terrains. As far as the Kashmir conundrum is concerned, it is a space where the hand of colonialism worked for the creation of 'conflicts of permanency' or in this context a buffer zone where the state in India has to show its presence time and again like that of Maoist zones. It is this normalized exception as ritualistic reality which Ajay Gudavarthy distinguishes from that of the exception of Agamben variety when he analyses the State-Maoist conflicts in India. That is the 'state today not only violates the law but would want its subjects to understand in no unclear terms that law is indeed being violated– fear cannot be but generated through lawlessness. This is an exceptionalism of a different kind from what Giorgio Agamben or Carl Schmitt have come to conceptualize, where what it wishes to re-impose is not the norm but to generalize normlessness itself. Sovereign power is sought in the willful and abject use of state power without norms. Normlessness is the only way state power actualises itself'.[29] Therefore, 'the state does not seek to legitimize its lawlessness as exception but in demonstrating its capacity to be lawless without seeking legitimacy. In not seeking legitimacy exception becomes real and comes to have its intended effects. It is no longer a condition where state of exception appears as a threshold of indeterminacy between democracy and absolutism'.[30]

The state's strategy of vigilantism as exemplified in the Ikhwanis of Kashmir and Salwa Judum of Bastar reflects the colonial continuities. It started in India with military use of strategic hamlets of regrouping the population by forceful displacements in Nagaland, Mizoram and Telangana. This was adopted in 1950s on the line of the Briggs Plan of the British in 1950 when they were at war against communists in Malaya.[31] State sponsored vigilantism to counter Maoism created sets of non-citizens in Bastar pointing 'state of exception'.[32] It is also a reminiscence of the fact that Hannah Arendt had hinted in her 'Origins of Totalitarianism'. By contextualizing the statelessness and helplessness of being refugees after the Second World War she describes the state of refugees flooding to the central Europe as in an 'abstract nakedness of being human' who lacked 'right to have rights'.[33] The state of affairs are no longer different in the battle zones of Kashmir where Ikhwanis had functioned as the agents of violence. Such spaces according to Nandini Sundar becomes the tangible sites of 'surveillance, search operations, starvations, forced labour, sexual violence, disruption of everyday life and infrastructure for sustenance, and the separation of human relationship'.[34] And the nakedness of being in contradiction to the dominant discourse of 'Indian nation', strips the sets of population in conflicted zones of Red Corridor from their basic right to have voice in the political space. This disconnected people from the very agency meant to overcome the state of being in the web of 'socio-political' and 'juridico-legal' exceptions meted out by the state, thereby making them the objects of experiments, voiceless, marginalized, non-persons, and 'the other' of the political community.

Maoists and Counter-Suspectism

Starting in the early 1980s, the Maoists established a strong base in Bastar, helping the villagers to resist the petty tyrannies of the bureaucracy[35] and politically with the emergence of CPI (Maoist) as dominant stream of Maoist/Naxal politics in Central India, the anatomy of the conflict changed. The amalgamation of two minor radical political streams had resulted in the consolidation of a strong Maoist presence in Chhattisgarh helped to streamline the movement around the Red corridors of Central India. Initially influencing the statist characterization of a simple law and order problem, gradually over a period of time the challenge emerged as a potential political question to be reckoned with. The situation severely affected normal life of the area in every aspect. Unlike the other cases, the regions of Maoist operations have an 'overlapping' and 'inward' dimension on the question of 'self-determination'. It is primarily overlapping in the sense that it is in contradiction to the sovereignty of the Indian state. The whole of the tribal front and self proclaimed agency of Maoist strategy combines to form a contingent opposition to what they call 'semi-colonial-feudal-landlord-bourgeoisie state'. Here the overlapping of the strategy within the territory confining to Red Corridors is not conceptually a total war against the Indian state. Instead this contradiction of the 'front' against the state constitutes the all out pan India movement of the Maoist front for the capture of state power. Here the success of the tribal-Maoist front may result pockets of liberated zones or liberated zones as it has been possible in Chhattisgarh. The movement in tribal heartland have inward looking dimensions because of the fact that the contradiction with the state machinery here is also a quest for self-determination for 'better off status' of life, thereby moving ahead to acquire the hitherto alienated rights and entitlements to the inhibiting population historically.[36] This inward dimension of the tribal self determination against the discriminative politics and the displacement anarchy of the development model show a positive connotation and liberation strength. Here the 'inward' dimension of the question of self determination stands in 'negotiation' terms with the Indian state having similarity to Sanjay Kak's formula of 'azadi' as freedom from the militarism.[37]

But the state response to demands in tribal belt is multi-faceted but primarily exceptional. Maoist program itself is a recipe for suspicious approach from the part of the government. The collision with Indian state and the consequent 'conter-suspectism' is inbuilt in the Maoist strategy. The document entitled 'Party Programme' gives light to goal of Maoist path of Indian revolution. Understanding of Indian independence as farce, seizure of state power in India, armed struggle, solidarity and connections with other armed groups within and outside the country, boycott of elections are the stated goals of the 'Maoist strategy' which keeps them as an 'anti-thesis' of the state in India.[38] Therefore, what deems the Maoist resistance an exceptional one and is under suspicion is nothing but the stated goals and the 'outlawed' articulations of propaganda rather than using the conventional method of mass mobilization to radically restructure the socio-political institutions which are oppressive to arrive at a solution. It is here, Partha Chatterjee's characterization of Maoist strategy gains importance. According to him, 'the Maoists in India carried in itself an alternative politico-economic praxis. This strategy at times sought to expel the governance institutions in their spaces of operations which obviously raised the question as to whether counter-suspectism thereby engineered takes the needs of the people into consideration'.[39] Pothik Ghosh on the other hand ponder the rationality of using the availability of the utility of the institutions of governance and participation in such avenues. For him, such arena of politics is limited because of what he calls the 'undemocratic exceptionalism' ingrained in the tenets of the formal liberal democracy.[40] It is by pointing to this dilemma that Lokaneeta brings Kannabiran's characterization of nature of the problem. That is 'the state needed to recognize that many of the armed movements, regardless of the ideology and strategy, represented politics, not terror, and required a political solution rather than further repressive action'.[41] Consequently, 'the crisis was mainly a result of the state's inability to respond to the grievances and demands of marginalized people and it was made worst by the increasing state repression of the movements'.[42]

Nation and Political Community

State-Maoist interface signifies the exclusionary political community in India. The bigoted approach in this aspect is predicated on the binary of 'us' and 'them'. Since Maoists are resisting corporate loot of resources in tribal belts, they are framed as anti-development, therefore 'anti-national' in congruence to the nature of Kashmir problem and the Muslim terrain. The Muslim case has a dimension of global aura aided by the 'anti-modern' and 'primordial' charge aiding suspectism. One discernible fact is that the question of Muslims and the contestation on Kashmir in India has been overlapping because of historic sociopolitical and cultural reasons and consequently when Kashmir is absent in 'political community', Muslims in India is relegated to margins in country's social space. Who belongs to Indian nation? is a fundamental angle when it poses uneasy questions to the ruling class. Anderson described nation as an imagined community emerged in the west supplying the modular forms from which the societies of the periphery or the non-west were destined to chose their module.[43] This conceptualization of the bestow 'nationalism' dossier as a project to be replicated was criticized by Partha Chatterjee in his dual political space in the colonial India as material and spiritual domain, Indian nationalism expressed its life politically with superiority in the latter, while the former belonged to the west.[44] Similarly, spiritual domain of the Indian nation itself was an exclusionary one which created 'otherness' in the political space. It is this side of Indian nation conceived right from the colonial time that Gyanendra Pandey questions. For Pandey 'Nationalisms have therefore commonly moved along the path of identifying the core or mainstream of the nation. Alongside this emerge notions of minorities, marginal communities, or elements, the fuzzy edges grey areas around which the question of boundaries geographical, social, and cultural will be negotiated or fought over'.[45] Indian nation before and after independence testified that 'otherization' of the non-dominant sections has been the story where the core of marginalities are questioned as not loyal, therefore 'anti-national'. Even though this discourse was inaugurated by the carriers of the cultural-communal articulations in pre-independent India, the post-colonial India encountered a different matrix where the cultural-social and religious expression of nationalism becoming subservient to the 'cultural-political' exclusionary nationalism which created 'suspects' through a concerted propaganda process of politicization. This has in contemporary times been stimulated by the political crisis of communalism and terrorism which has complementary relationship to the process of the new global 'cultural talk'.[46] While looking the changing contours of nationalism in India, Preeti Chauhan in her 'Anti-Terror Laws and the Construction of Suspect Communities', contents 'how the nation acknowledges certain imaginations, certain traditions, and certain narratives but leaves out others on its fringes, as suspect and questionable, depending upon contingencies of power and politics of the time'.[47] She also discusses the manner in which the notion of the criminal tribe was used as a ruling practice by the colonial government in India as an illustrative case whose plight had continued for many years after the independence as well.[48]

War on Political Will

Along with new tools of extraordinary measures starting from militarization to surveillance, the state strategy with respect to internal challenges in India undergone a sea change. The emerging global trends in the character of warfare which the security states are employing in tandem to the post cold war churnings are worth noting of. Conventional models of containment based on direct warfare, tactical maneuvering, invocation of transportation and communication with new technologies have all undergone changes with respect to the nature of political questions the state is facing now. The containment strategy of the Indian state had to therefore take into account the newer phase what Hammes[49] regard as the 'fourth dimensional warfare' which demands severe onslaughts on the 'political will' of the contending sides through a multiplicity of techniques other than direct military actions per se. As a result the space of Kashmir is transformed from a battle ground of mere national security to that of a political democratic question. Similarly, Chhattisgarh and other Maoist affected areas have turned itself from a mere threat to public order to a battle zone where the fight for economic democracy is articulated through contending 'political wills'.

The 'triangulations of neo-liberalism, nationalism, and militarism' in national security apparatuses has produced a prevailing condition of punitive containment for marked categories of the population, leading to the sedimentation of inequalities through patterns of social suffering and social death'.[50] New prescriptions effected by the changing nature of state warfare with respect to the rationality stimulated by this triangulation around the world since 1990s and more importantly since the advent of the 'global war on terror' also influenced exceptional mode of governance which the Indian state is exhibiting in the troubled areas of Red Corridor, Kashmir and with respect to the law enforcement on vulnerable communities including Muslims. There is a general agreement that the traditional state oriented techniques of securitization proved ineffective in the war on political will. It is therefore on the basis of experiments of privatized militias around the world and the use of market logic in conflicts since 2001 that non state actors as the agents of securitization for tactical combat was considered to be an efficient option. This shift is reflected in the new methods of exceptional governance through hired militias in different conflict zones which has also colonial precedents as discussed in the earlier paragraphs. While 'Ikhwanis' performed an agency role for the state in Kashmir, Salwa Judum and SULFA (surrendered ULFA) acted as new agencies of onslaughts in Chhattisgarh and Assam respectively. And, 'as India achieves global economic heft, the policing functions of the state, far from being whittled down, are being rapidly enhanced to deal not only with problems at the borders, but also with any form of resistance mounted by mobilized citizens within, whether these be communities protesting large-scale industrialization that displaces them and alienates them from their livelihood, or people who wish to call attention to the age-old socio-economic structures that are responsible for their historical dispossession'.[51]

Acknowledgements

A draft of this paper was presented at the Indian Council of Social Science Research (ICSSR) sponsored National Seminar 'Youth, Naxalism and Terrorism: The Politics of Development in Indian Subcontinent' held at Isabella Thoburn College, Lucknow, Uttar Pradesh, India on 21–22 February 2014. Author would like to acknowledge the suggestions from Dr. Ajay Gudavarthy, Associate Professor, Centre for Political Studies, Jawaharlal Nehru University, New Delhi, highly indebted to Mr. Vishesh Pratap Gurjar, Doctoral Fellow, Department of Humanities and Social Sciences, IIT Delhi, and Rupak Kumar, Centre for the Study of Law and Governance, JNU for their comments on the draft.

Notes

1. www.en.wikipedia.org/wiki/Reactions_to_the_September_11_attacks
2. Josy Joseph, 'Post-9/11, US sought India's military help for Afgha ops', www.articles.timesofindia.indiatimes.com/2011-09-11/india/30141684_1_threeservice-chiefs-chiefs-of-staff-committee-admiral-sushil-kumar.
3. See Prabhat Patnaik's observations at http://www.forumtiersmonde.net/fren/index.php?option=com_content&view=article&id=165%3Aindia-a-setback-for-neo-liberalism&Itemid=129.
4. See C. Raja Mohan, 'India and the War on Terror', http://www.hindu.com/2003/09/12/stories/2003091201571000.htm.
5. Recee Jones, 'Geopolitical boundary narratives, the global war on terror and border fencing in India', www2.hawaii.edu/~reecej/Jones%202009%20Transactions.pdf.

6. Tania Roy, 'India's 9/11-Accidents of a Moveable Metaphor', http://tcs.sagepub.com/content/26/7-8/314.full.pdf+html.
7. Recee Jones, 'Geopolitical Boundary Narratives, The Global War on Terror and Border Fencing in India', www2.hawaii.edu/~reecej/Jones%202009%20Transactions.pdf
8. Dr Biswajit Mohapatra, 'India-US strategic Partnerships and the Challenges of enhanced Cooperation', http://www.academia.edu/1214236/IndiaUS_Strategic_Partnership_and_the_Challenges_of_Enhanced_Cooperation_Presented_at_International_Conf_on_India_and_the_US_in_the_21st_Century_Building_a_New_Partnership_11-13_January_2012_at_Osmania_University_Center_for_International_Programs_OUCIP_
9. The interventions made by Ujjwal Kumar Singh and Ajay Gudavarthy and others in recent years point to an explanation to this effect through a reading of G. Agamben.
10. Praful Bidwai, 'Challenges for Left', Retrieved from http://www.frontlineonnet.com/fl2918/stories/20120921291811800.htm.
11. Kalpana Kannabiran, 'Development, Justice and the Constitution', http://www.thehindu.com/todays-paper/tp-opinion/development-justice-and-the-constitution/article2297261.ece
12. See Ramachandra Guha, 'Adivasis, Naxalites and Indian Democracy', Economic and Political Weekly, Vol. 42, No. 32 (11–17 August 2007)
13. Pallavi Chibber et al., 'Case Studies: Human Rights Violations by Transnational Corporations in Goa and Chhattisgarh', Human Rights Law Network, New Delhi, 2011. p. 56.
14. Ibid.
15. http://www.iied.org/sustainable-markets/key-issues/business-and-sustainable-development/mmsdintroduction.
16. David Harvey, The New Imperialism, Oxford University Press, 2003
17. The Perspectives Team, Abandoned: Development and Displacement' Perspectives, New Delhi, 2007, pp. 196.
18. Dipankar Gupta, *The Caged Phoenix: Can India Fly?*, Stanford University Press, 2010 (In this work Dipankar Gupta briefly

analyse the development of 'political class' as a separate class).

19. Aihwa Ong, *Neoliberalism as Exception*, Duke University Press, 2006.
20. Maidul Islam, 'Imagining Indian Muslims: Looking Through the Lens of Bollywood Cinema', *India Journal of Human Development*, Vol. 1, No. 2, 2007. Also available at, http://academia.edu/1215240/Imagining_Indian_Muslims_Looking_Through_the_Lens_of_Bollywood_Cinema.
21. Preeti Chauhan quotes from PUDR Report named 'Lawless Roads', in her 'Anti Terror Laws and the Construction Of Suspect Communities', A Dissertation Submitted to The University Of Delhi from The Department Of Political Science, in 2009 under the Supervision of Ujjwal Kumar Singh, p. 109.
22. Judit Butler, 'Media Death-Frames of War', The Books Interview By Nina Power, *New Statesmen*, 27 August, 2009, Shortversion. http://www.egs.edu/faculty/judith-butler/articles/media-death-frames-of-war/
23. Ajay Gudavarthy, 'Democracy Against Maoism and Maoism against Itself', *Economic and Political Weekly*, Vol. XLVIII, No. 7, 16 February 2013, p. 74.
24. Nandini Sundar, 'At War with Oneself: Constructing Naxalism as India's Biggest Security Threat', In Michael Kugelman ed. India's Contemporary Security Challenges, Washington, DC: Woodrow Wilson International Center for Scholars, 2011. Available at-http://nandinisundar.blogspot.in/2011/04/at-warwith-oneselfconstructing.html.
25. Barry et al. (1998) Buzan, Barry, Waever, Ole, de Wilde, Jaap (1998) Security: A New Framework for Analysis (London: Lynne Rienner)] www.allacademic.com/meta/p251976_index.html.
26. Shantanu Chakrabarti, 'Evolving Insurgency and India's Counter-Insurgency Options: Entering into the Age of Fourth-Generation Warfare?, http://www.isn.ethz.ch/ Digital-Library/Publications/Detail/?ots783=9c879a60-8a40-14e8-76c3-2c016ae9096c&lng=en&id=117096.

27. Ajay Gudavarthy, 'Democracy against Maoism and Maoism against Itself', *Economic and Political Weekly*, Vol. XLVIII, No. 7, 16 February 2013, see p. 70.
28. Jinee Lokaneeta, *Transnational Torture: Law, Violence, and State Power in The United States And India*, Orient Black Swan Private Limited, New Delhi, 2012.
29. Ajay Gudavarthy, 'Democracy Against Maoism and Maoism Against Itself', *Economic and Political Weekly*, Vol. XLVIII, No. 7, 16 February 2013, pp. 70–71.
30. Ibid.
31. Arundhati Roy, *Broken Republic: Three Essays*, Penguin Books, New Delhi, 2011. Arundhati Roy's mention on Strategic Hamleting can also be accessed at http://gaddeswarup.blogspot.in/2010/03/strategic-hamleting.html
32. Giorgio Agamben, *State of Exception*, University of Chicago Press (14 January 2005)
33. Hannah Arendt, 'The Origins of Totalitarianism', Published by The World Publishing Company, 1958.
34. Nandini Sundar, 'Interning Insurgent Populations: The Buried Histories of Indian Democracy', *Economic and Political Weekly*, Vol. XLVI, No. 6, 5 February 2011, pp. 50, Also available at http://www.epw.in/specialarticles/interning-insurgent-populations-buried-histories-indiande mocracy.html.
35. Nandini Sundar, *The Burning Forest: India's War in Bastar*, Juggernaut.
36. Nandini Sundar, *Subalterns and Sovereigns: An Anthropological history of Bastar*' Delhi, Oxford University Press, 2007 (2nd edition) (1st edition 1997, OUP 1999).
37. Sanjay Kak's conversation on Kashmir with David Barsamian for Alternative Radio, Colorado, US, www.alternativeradio.org
38. Party Programme, available at http://www.banned-thought.net/India/CPI-Maoist-Docs/ Founding/ Programme pamphlet.pdf.
39. Partha Chatterjee spoke on 'counter-suspectism' engineered by Maoists Militancy, 'Three Roads to Radical Democracy in India', Paper Presented at ICSSR sponsored International Conference, 'Changing Frontiers of Political Theory', 9-10

January 2014, Auditorium, SSS-1, Jawaharlal Nehru University, New Delhi.

40. Pothik Ghosh, 'A Generalised State of Exception and Maoists in India', *The Hindustan Times*, 8 April 2010.
41. Jinee Lakaneeta, 'Transnational Torture: Law, Violence, and State Power in the United States and India', Orient Black Swan Private Limited, New Delhi, 2012, p.173
42. Ibid.
43. Benedict Anderson, *Imagined Communities: Reflections on the Origin and Spread of Nationalism*, Verso, New Edition, London, 2006.
44. Partha Chatterjee, *Nation and its Fragments: Colonial and Post Colonial Histories*, Oxford University Press, Delhi, 1995.
45. Gyanendra Pandey, 'Can a Muslim be an Indian?', *In Comparative Studies in Society and History*, Vol. 41, No. 4, Cambridge University Press, October 1999, pp. 608–629.
46. Mahmood Mamdani, 'Good Muslim, Bad Muslim: America, the Cold War, and the Roots of Terror', Pantheon Books, 2004.
47. Preeti Chauhan, 'Anti Terror Laws and the Construction Of Suspect Communities', A Dissertation Submitted to The University Of Delhi from The Department Of Political Science, in 2009 under the Supervision of Ujjwal Kumar Singh, See p. 1.
48. Ibid.
49. Thomas X. Hammes, 'The Sling and the Stone: On War in the 21st Century', Zenith Press & Manas Publishers, New Delhi, 2006.
50. Haley Duschinski, *Anthropological Quarterly*, Vol. 82, No. 3, pp. 691–718.
51. Suvir Kaul, 'Indian Empire (and the Case of Kashmir), *Economic and Political Weekly*, 26 March 2011, Vol. xlvI, No. 13, p. 67.

11

Origin and Growth of Left-Wing Extremism in Schedule Tribes Dominated Areas of Central India

RAJNEESH KUMAR GUPTA

India has witnessed fast socio-economic transformation in post-independent period. Since the last two decades or so, the process of liberalization, privatization, and globalization is providing unprecedented challenges and opportunities. While a small, privileged section of Indian society has benefited from the opportunities offered by the new socio-economic order, governmental policies and programmes, and infrastructural development, a majority of Indians, particularly the downtrodden sections of the society, have not been able to effectively utilize these opportunities. Owing to historical reasons, attached socio-cultural stigma, and primitive way of life, schedule tribes have not been able to create for themselves a rightful space conducive to their advancement, in the complex and fast changing socio-cultural environment since they have been facing displacement in the way of the so-called development concentrated in building large dams, centralized industries, and recently popular idea of establishing SEZs.

Central India has highest concentration of tribal population. There are numerous distinct tribal communities, spread over in various parts of Madhya Pradesh, Chhattisgarh,

Bihar, Jharkhand, Odisha, and West Bengal. There is a fair diversity among them in terms of lifestyle, cultural traditions, socio-economic structure, religious beliefs, language and speech, customs, and so on. However, all of them have been severe victim of the process of development since colonial period. British forest laws were major blow on their livelihood and those were forced to look into other avenues for their survival. Further, they faced large-scale displacement in irrigation projects, dam construction, and industrial development and now in the way of establishing SEZs. Government has been often concerned for rehabilitation of displaced people but little efforts have been made to preserve their socio-cultural identities attached with their original habitation. Moreover, problems of illiteracy, poverty, hunger, heavy debts, and alcoholism still persist among them. This has led to dissatisfaction in younger generation which has been utilized by Naxal outfits. Thus, ongoing asymmetric violence in tribal-dominated habitations is not mere law and order problem but root cause of the problem is lack of pro-people developmental policies. Hence, a sustainable solution of the problem can be ensured only through meaningful dialogue and concrete efforts to address issues of tribes. This chapter attempts to make a comprehensive study on the problems of scheduled tribes in Central India and their linkages with asymmetric violence. This chapter is divided into three broad headings: Tribes in India: A Demographic Profile, Left-Wing Extremist Violence in Tribal Dominated Areas, and Left-Wing Extremist (LWE) Violence and Tribes: Interlinkages.

Tribes in India: A Demographic Profile

Anthropologically, the term 'tribe' refers to the aboriginal habitants living in natural and unpolluted surrounding far away from modorn civilization with their tradition values, customs, and beliefs. In the past, various studies have been conducted to study different aspects of tribes, and scholars have tried to define tribes in different ways. According to Thomas, 'A tribe is an indigenous, homogenous unit, speaking a common language, claiming ancestry, living in a particular geographical area, backward in technology, pre-literate, loyally observing social and political customs based on kinship' (Thomas, 1965). Majumdar observes 'a tribe is a collection of families or group of families bearing a common name, members of which occupy the same territory, speak the same language, and observe certain taboos regarding marriage, profession or occupation and have developed a well-assessed system of reciprocity and mutuality of obligations' On the other hand according to Bardhan, tribes are socio-cultural entity at a definite historical stage of development. It is a single, endogamous community with a cultural and psychological makeup.

Tribes in India are commonly known as *adivasi* (aboriginal), *vanvasi* (forest habitants), *girijan* (hill dwellers), *vanya jati* (forest caste), *adimjati* (primitive castes), and *anusuchit janjati* (scheduled tribes), and others. Article, 366(25) of the Constitution of India refers to scheduled tribes as those communities who are scheduled in accordance with Article, 342 of the Constitution. This article says that only those communities who have been declared as such by the President through an initial public notification or through a subsequent amending act of parliament will be considered as scheduled tribes. As per recommendations of the Lokur Committee, essential characteristics for a community to be identified as scheduled tribes are as follows:

1. indications of primitive traits;
2. distinctive culture;
3. shyness of contact with the community at large;
4. geographical isolation; and
5. backwardness (Ministry of Tribal Affairs, 2010).

The inclusion of a community as a scheduled tribe is an ongoing process and thus the number of communities identified as scheduled tribes is 698 in 2014 from merely 212 in 1950. The tribal population of the country, as per the 2011 census, is 10.45 crore, constituting 8.63 per cent of the total population of India. 'Tribal communities live in about 15 per cent of the country's areas, in various ecological and geo-climatic conditions ranging from plains and forests to hills and inaccessible areas' (Ministry of Tribal Affairs, 2010). However, they are not a homogeneous group and a fair diversity does exist according to their socio-cultural norms, physical features, livelihood, and moreover in stage of their development. Thus, they have been classified in various categories on the basis of race, language, religious belief, area of inhabitation, occupation, cultural contacts, and so on. Taking into account geographical factors, L.P. Vidyarthi identifies five geographical regions of tribal habitations in India:

1. Himalayan Region: With three subregions:
    (a) Northeastern Himalayan region
    (b) Central Himalayan region
    (c) North-Western Himalayan region
2. Middle Indian Region: It comprises Bihar, Jharkhand, West Bengal, Odisha, Chhattisgarh, and Madhya Pradesh.
3. Western Indian Region: It includes Rajasthan, Gujarat, Maharashtra, Goa, and Dadra and Nagar Haveli.
4. South India Region: It comprises Andhra Pradesh, Tamil Nadu, Karnataka, and Kerala.
5. The Island Region: The islands of Andaman and Nicobar in the Bay of Bengal and Lakshadweep in the Arabian Sea (Vidyarthi, 1981).

The 'Middle Indian Region' or central India is the major habitation of tribes and nearly 46 per cent of the tribal population of India is concentrated here (see Table 1). There are total 62 notified tribes in Odisha, 46 in Madhya Pradesh, 42 in Chhattisgarh, 38 in West Bengal, and 30 each in Jharkhand and Bihar.

Left-Wing Extremist (LWE) Violence in Tribal-Dominated Areas

The tribal-dominated areas of central India were traditionally known for rich cultural heritage and tremendous natural resources. However, currently they are more often associated with Naxal and asymmetric violence. The popular uprising of Naxalbari (West Bengal) in 1967 could be assumed as a convenient starting point of Naxal and asymmetric violence in India. 'The young and fiery ideologies of the Marxist-Leninist movement in India formed the CPI (M-L), envisioning a spontaneous mass upsurge all over India that would create a liberated zone' (Dixit, 2010). Though the United Front Government of West Bengal headed by the CPI(M) was able to contain the rebellion within 72 days using all possible repressive measures, in May 1968 a group of extremist Left leaders formed 'All India

Table 1

Tribal Demography in Central India

State	Segment	Tribal Population			Total Population			Percentage of Total Population		
		Male	Female	Total	Male	Female	Total	Male	Female	Total
Bihar	Rural	648,535	622,316	1,270,851	48,073,850	44,267,586	92,341,436	1.35	1.41	1. 38
	Urban	33,981	31,741	65,722	6,204,307	5,553,709	11,758,016	0.55	0.57	0. 56
	Total	682,516	654,057	1,336,573	54,278,157	49,821,295	104,099,452	1.26	1.31	1. 28
Chhattisgarh	Rural	3,577,134	3,653,948	7,231,082	9.797,426	9.810,535	19,607,961	36.51	37.25	36. 88
	Urban	296,057	295,763	591,820	3,035,469	2,901,768	5,937,237	9.75	10.19	9. 97
	Total	3,873,191	3.949,711	7.822,902	12,832,895	12,712,303	25,545,198	30.18	31.07	30. 62
Jharkhand	Rural	3,928,323	3,939,827	7,868,150	12,776,486	12,278,587	25.055,073	30.75	32.09	31. 40
	Urban	387,084	389,808	776,892	4,153,829	3,779,232	7,933,061	9.32	10.31	9. 79
	Total	4,315,407	4,329,635	8,645,042	16,930,315	16,057,819	32,988,134	25.49	26.96	26. 21
Madhya Pradesh	Rural	7,187,769	7,089,105	14,276,874	27,149,388	25,408,016	52,557,404	26.47	27.90	27. 16
	Urban	531,635	508,275	1,039,910	10,462,918	9,606,487	20,069,405	5.08	5.29	5. 18
	Total	7,719,404	7,597,380	15,316,784	37,612,306	35,014,503	72,626,809	20.52	21.70	21.09
Odisha	Rural	4,428,522	4,566,445	8,994,967	17,586,203	17,384,359	34,970,562	25.18	26.27	25.72
	Urban	299,210	296,579	595,789	3,625,933	3,377,723	7,003,656	8.25	8.78	8.51
	Total	4,727,732	4,863,024	9,590,756	21,212,136	20,762,082	41,974,218	22.29	23.42	22.85

Cont'd ...

... Cont'd

West Bengal	Rural	2,428,057	2,427,058	4,855,115	31,844,945	30,338,168	62,183,113	7. 62	8.00	7.81
	Urban	221,917	219,921	441,838	14,964,082	14,128,920	29,093,002	1.48	1.56	1.52
	Total	2,649,974	2,646,979	5,296,953	46,809,027	44,467,088	91,276,115	5.66	5.95	5.80
INDIA	Rural	47,263,733	46,820,111	94,083,844	4.28E + 08	4.06E + 08	833,748,852	11.05	11.53	11.28
	Urban	5,283,482	5,178,390	10,461,872	1.95E + 08	1.82E + 08	377,106,125	2.70	2.85	2.77
	Total	52,547,215	51,998,501	104,545,716	6.23E + 08	5.88E + 08	1.211E + 09	8.43	8.85	8.63

Source: www.censusindia.gov.in/DigitalLibrary/MFTableSeries.aspx (Accessed on 9 September 2014).

Coordination Committee of Communist Revolutionaries' (AICCCR) with two cardinal principles – allegiance to the armed struggle and nonparticipation in the elections (Kujur, 2008). But very soon, sharp differences emerged among them largely on account of ideology and control over the leadership of the movement. 'Government also looked at it as a law and order problem. It did not analyse the causes of the movement and the extent of mobilization of people' (Dixit, 2010: 21).

However, the Naxal movement continued to spread its base in different parts of the country and in 2006 Prime Minister Dr Manmohan Singh branded the Naxal threat to be the single largest internal security problem of the nation. As per the available statistics, 3,607 persons including civilians and security forces were killed in the Naxal violence between 2008 and 2012. This is no simple mathematics because it means more than double the deaths reported from Jammu & Kashmir and northeastern states collectively during the same period (Kujur, 2013). In the 2010 Planning Commission report on Left-Wing Extremist (LWE) states, 233 districts across 20 states were reported to be struggling with this menace with 67 districts being classified as worst affected.

A study of statistics released by Naxal Management Division, Ministry of Home Affairs (Government of India) reveals that there has been continuous decline in incidents of LWE violence. Nevertheless, tribal-dominated areas of central India continues to be worst affected from this phenomenon. A thorough analysis of figures indicates that during 2009–2014 (up to 15 August 2014), total 9,490 incidents of LWE violence were reported in which 3,548 casualties occurred. Out of these, 8,482 incidents and 3,187 casualties were in the selected geographical zone – central India (see Table 2).

Left-Wing Extremist (LWE) Violence and Tribes: Interlinkages

By going through above statistics, anyone can easily draw a conclusion that tribal-dominated areas of the region have become harbour of LWE. But in-depth study of the matter demonstrates that a systemic failure of the governmental approach and policies to address basic issues have generated

Table 2

State-wise Extent of Left-Wing Extremist (LWE) Violence during 2009–2014 (Up to 15 August 2014)

State	*2009*		*2010*		*2011*		*2012*		*2013*		*2014 (Up to 15 August)*	
	Incidents	*Death*	*Incidents*	*Death*	*Incidents*	*Death*	*Incidents*	*Death*	*Incidents*	*Death*	*Incidents*	*Death*
Andhra Pradesh	66	18	100	24	54	9	67	13	36	7	12	1
Bihar	232	72	307	97	316	63	166	44	177	69	111	26
Chhattisgarh	523	290	625	343	465	204	370	109	355	111	207	77
Jharkhand	742	208	501	157	517	182	480	163	387	152	234	59
Madhya Pradesh	1	0	7	1	8	0	11	0	1	0	2	0
Maharashtra	154	93	94	45	109	54	134	41	71	19	53	25
Odisha	263	67	218	79	192	53	171	45	101	35	79	20
Telengana	NA	NA	NA	NA	NA	NA	NA	NA	NA	4	9	4
Uttar Pradesh	8	2	6	1	1	0	2	0	0	0	0	0
West Bengal	255	158	350	258	92	45	6	0	1	0	0	0
Others	5	0	5	0	6	1	8	0	7	0	1	0
Total	2,258	908	2,213	1,005	1,760	611	1,415	415	1,136	397	708	212

Source: http://mha.nic.in/sites/upload_files/mha/files/LWEViolanceStatistics2014.PDF.

anguish among innocent tribal which has been utilized by the so-called LWE ideologues. As Raman Dixit writes:

> The Governments have enacted several laws to empower themselves to combat Naxals. The West Bengal Government enacted the West Bengal (Prevention of Violent Activities) Act 1970 to arm itself to repress the uprising. No particular national act has been enacted so far specifically to counter the Naxal … . However, in-spite of the government's muscle power and legal teeth, the Naxal movement has continued to spread its base because the rural poor and oppressed identify with its ideology. In other words, its inception, ideology, spread and sustenance are deeply rooted in socio-economic factors. (Dixit, 2010)

Throughout the history, tribes maintained their distinguish identity keeping themselves alienated from mainstream society. In fact they inherited egalitarian socio-economic norms and in many aspects such as impressive sex ratio, gender equality, and absence of caste-based restrictions, tribal are far advanced than our so-called modern society. However, this situation was challenged in the colonial period as British continuously tried to venture tribal-dominated forest areas for their vested interests. This resulted massive tribal upsurge in the late 18th and early 19th century. The Constitution of independent India made several provisions for the protection and well-being of tribes, and successive governments launched various schemes and plans for their welfare but actual practices have belied this hope. In fact,

> tribes today experience deprivation, oppression, exploitation and discrimination in almost every sphere of their life. The government response to the problems of scheduled tribes has either been lukewarm, indifferent or even hostile. Such an experience has been most strongly felt by the emerging middle class. That explains why there has been increasing assertion of an identity among tribes that now have a sizeable middle class. Underlying the new mobilization is the discriminatory treatment meted out to tribes by the dominant population or the state, which actually acts on behalf of the former. Hence there has been an increasing assertion by tribals for rights and control over land and other resources in the form of mobilization against alienation of land and state induced displacement projects. (Karegouda and Thakur, 2013)

Now let us discuss some of the problems of scheduled tribes that are generating anger among them, which caters conditions for popular support to LWE activities:

Unfair Forest Policies

Tribes have maintained a time immemorial relation with forest and always interact for their sustenance and try to recreate the forest with their traditional conservation systems. However, since the promulgation of Forest Act in 1878, forests were seen as a source of revenue generation for state, and tribals were treated like enemies of the forest. Even the New Forest Policy of 1952 'was the mere extension of government authority over forest to the detriment of tribal economy and life and changes in the rights of the tribal communities over the forest' (Chaithanaya, 2012). The Forest Act of 1988 had more tribal-oriented approach and allowed them to use forest produce for their livelihood. But the concept of exclusive state ownership of forest and recognition of industrial needs as national needs remained unfavourable for tribals. The Forest Act of 2006 is the milestone in the recognition of the tribal rights over forests and forest products.

> It attempts not only to correct a historic injustice committed by the colonial and post–colonial governments but also vest in forest communities as primary role in sustaining forest ecosystems by restoring their rights as well as their environmental duties. But law basically grants legal recognition to the rights of traditional forest-dwelling communities, partially correcting the injustice caused by successive forest laws in the past centuries. The law will not be able to resolve tribal people's human rights and livelihood issues without similar or greater advancement in law and administration in other areas such as land acquisition, development-induced displacement and political autonomy. (Chaithanaya, 2012: 109).

Displacement of Tribal

Displacement of any person from their native habitations causes severe pain to the injured party and no monetary compensation can be adequate to the loss occurred to them. Unfortunately, due to compulsory acquisition of land for construction of dams and roads, quarrying and mining operations, location of industries and reservation of forests for national parks, and other environmental reasons tribal people were continuously forced to leave their traditional habitations. Draft of National Policy on Tribals notes:

> Nearly 85.39 lakh tribals had been displaced until 1990 on account of some mega project or the other, reservation of forests as National Parks etc. Tribals constitute at least 55.16 per cent of the total displaced people in the country. Cash payment does not really compensate the tribals for the difficulties they experience in their living style and ethos.
>
> Displacement of tribals from their land amounts to violation of the Fifth Schedule of the Constitution as it deprives them of control and ownership of natural resources and land essential for their way of life. (http://www.prsindia.org/ accessed on 14 February 2014).

Land Alienation

Alienation of tribal land is a major issue that crippled their economic welfare. Alienation happened largely because of the moneylenders' trap in the tribal habitations. This was further propelled by the government's restrictions on access to forest land, traditionally the exclusive domain of the tribals. In executing government regulations on forest access, government officials resorted to harassment of the tribals. Loss of access to forest produce, which had constituted a significant part of their income and was also an integral part of their way of life, led to deep discontentment among the tribes (Dixit, 2010).

Poverty and Indebtedness

Poverty and indebtedness are two persistent features of tribal communities. Despite hard work, they find it difficult to meet even their everyday expenses. Many of them seek employment as daily wage worker in the local areas where payment is neither regular nor proper. Some of them undertake agricultural activities without modern technology and relies on 'shifting cultivation'. Other works as landless labours and gets only seasonal employment. As a result, a majority of them lives in absolute poverty (see Table 3) and frequently requires debt. In the absence of access to banking services, they take loans from moneylenders and landlords at a high rate of interest. When they express inability to repay their loan and interest, they are made to repay it by working as bonded labour at nominal wage.

Table 3

State-wise Percentage of Scheduled Tribes Population below Poverty Line for 1993–1994 and 1999–2000

S. No.	State	Rural		Urban	
		1993–1994	*1999–2000*	*1993–1994*	*1999–2000*
1	Andhra Pradesh	25.66	23.82	46.68	44.99
2	Assam	41.44	38.73	7.11	2.7
3	Bihar	69.75	59.68	35.76	39.47
4	Gujarat	31.2	29.11	35.47	36.66
5	Haryana	41.55	–	0	–
6	Himachal	63.94	5.73	0	–
7	Karnataka	37.33	25.49	62.05	51.37
8	Kerala	37.34	24.2	1.08	–
9	Madhya Pradesh	56.69	56.26	65.28	52.59
10	Maharashtra	50.38	43.56	61.06	42.98
11	Orissa	71.26	73.93	64.85	59.59
12	Punjab	27	17.99	0	12.95
13	Rajasthan	46.23	25.27	13.21	20.71
14	Tamil Nadu	44.37	43.2	30.08	5.22
15	Uttar Pradesh	37.11	34.06	36.89	13.27
16	West Bengal	61.95	50.02	19.41	31.88
17	All India	51.94	45.86	41.14	34.75

Source: Ministry of Tribal Affairs, Government of India. 2010. *Statistical Profile of Scheduled Tribes in India.* New Delhi: Ministry of Tribal Affairs.

Problem of Health and Nutrition

Traditionally, tribal life was close to the nature and they were able to manage quality food enough for their nutrition. But restriction to access forest products coupled with the depletion of forests and ban on hunting has resulted in malnutrition and undernourishment. The income of majority of tribal families is not enough to feed family members properly. This keeps them in the state of semi-starvation. Further, prevalence of alcoholism in many tribal groups keeps their health at risk. On the status of health and nutrition of tribes, Draft of National Policy on Tribes notes:

> Although tribal people live usually close to nature, a majority of them need health care on account of malnutrition, lack of safe drinking water, poor hygiene and environmental sanitation and above all poverty. Lack of awareness and apathy to utilize the available health services also affect their health status. In wake of the opening of tribal areas with highways industrialization, and communication facilities, diseases have spread to tribal areas. Endemics like malaria, deficiency diseases, venereal diseases including AIDS are not uncommon among tribal populations. However, lack of safe drinking water and malnutrition are well-recognised major health hazards. Tribals suffer from a deficiency of calcium, vitamin A, vitamin C, riboflavin and animal protein in their diets. Malnutrition and under-nutrition are common among Primitive Tribal Groups who largely depend upon food they either gather or raise by using simple methods. The poor nutritional status of tribal women directly influences their reproductive performance and their infants' survival, growth and development. (http://www.prsindia.org/ accessed on 14 February 2014).

Problem of Education and Awareness

Formal education is the key to all-round human development. Despite several campaigns to promote formal education ever since independence, the literacy rate among scheduled tribes was only 47.1 per cent in 2001. This is far below from the national average literacy rate of 64.84 in the same year. The female literacy rate was registered only 34.76 per cent compared to the national female literacy rate of 53.67 per cent (see Table 4). Describing low level of education among tribes, Draft of National Policy on Tribals notes that 'Alienation from the society, lack of adequate infrastructure like schools, hostels and teachers, abject poverty and apathy towards irrelevant curriculum have stood in the way of tribals getting formal education' (http://www.prsindia.org/ accessed on 14 February 2014). Lack of formal education has resulted in non-awareness among tribes with regard to constitutional protection, legal mechanism, governmental policies, and programmes launched for their benefits.

Table 4

Literacy Rate in India (1961–2001)

Year	All Social Groups			SC			ST		
	Male	Female	Total	Male	Female	Total	Male	Female	Total
1961	40.4	15.35	28.3	16.96	3.29	10.27	13.83	3.16	8.53
1971	45.96	21.97	34.45	22.36	6.44	14.67	17.63	4.85	11.3
1981	56.38	29.76	43.57	31.12	10.93	21.38	24.52	8.04	16.35
1991	64.13	39.29	52.21	49.91	23.76	37.41	40.65	18.19	29.6
2001	75.26	53.67	64.84	66.64	41.9	54.69	59.17	34.76	47.1

Source: Ministry of Tribal Affairs, Government of India, 2010. *Statistical Profile of Scheduled Tribes in India*. New Delhi: Ministry of Tribal Affairs.

Conclusion

In recent years, Left wing extremisms have emerged a major problem in various parts of India. Tribal-dominated areas of central India are worse affected regions of such incidences. Initially, it was looked as a mere law and order problem but now there is emerging consensus among scholars that root cause of the issues lies in historical injustice towards tribal people which continue to persist in various ways. The tribals have been severe victims of the so-called developmental process since the advent of colonial powers in the region. Unfair forest laws snatched their source of livelihood, and ongoing race of development is displacing them from their traditional habitations. Naturally, this has generated anguish among them which is being utilized by Left-wing extremists. We need to address basic issues of tribals for meaningful solution of the problem.

References

Bardhan, A.B. (1973). *The Tribal Problem in India*. New Delhi: Communist Party of India Publications.

Chaithanaya, E.P. (2012). 'Historical Injustice toward Tribals: A Reflection on Forest Policies of India'. *International Journal of Social Science and Interdisciplinary Research*. 1(11): 107–114.

Dixit, R. (2010). 'Naxalite Movement in India: The State's Response'. *Journal of Defence Studies*. 4(2): 21–35. Available at: http://www.prsindia.org/uploads/media/1167469383/bill53_2007010353_Draft_National_Policy_on_Tribals.pdf (Accessed on 14 February 2014).

Karegouda, M. and Thakur, J. (2013). 'The Status of Scheduled Tribes in India: Problems and Prospects'. *Indian Streams Research Journal*. 3(6): 1–4.

Kujur, R. (2008). *Naxal Movement in India: A Profile*. New Delhi: IPCS.

——. (2013). *Contemporary Naxal Movement in India New Trends. State Responses and Recommendations*. New Delhi: IPCS

Majumdar, D.N. (1961). *Races and Cultures of India*. Bombay: Asia Publishing House.

Ministry of Tribal Affairs, Government of India (2010). *Statistical Profile of Scheduled Tribes in India*. New Delhi: Ministry of Tribal Affairs.

Thomas, M.M. (1965). *Tribal Awakening*. Bangalore: Christian Institute for the Study of Religion and Society.

Vidyarthi, L.P. (1981). *Tribal Development and its Administration*. New Delhi: Concept Publishing Company.

12

Role of Media in Reporting Terrorism in India

Perspective of Complicity between Media and Terrorists

PALLAV MUKHOPADHYAY

The relationship between terrorism and Indian media is not at all unidirectional, rather terrorism reacts to and utilizes the Indian media in a way identical to that in which the Indian media react to and use the terrorist incidents. Statistically, terrorist incidents across the country are significant, both in terms of casualty and injury and in terms of the number of incidents reported annually. Extensive media coverage of any terrorist incident reach a vast audience, creating an impact in the mind of the mass without which few would know of terrorists' actions, motivations and key actors.

Aims and Objectives

The chapter follows the analytical approach of research and it includes host of observations and insights including case studies. This chapter has tried (a) to analyse the interaction of terrorism and the media, (b) to investigate how the media shape its role in covering the terrorist activities and whether the relationship between them potentially symbiotic, (c) to focus how can the media in a democratic society devise new methods of fair and credible reporting of terrorist activities without jeopardizing their responsibilities to the people.

Media's Effect on Terrorism

Alex Schmid offered three hypotheses that explain the media's effect on terrorism. The first, which is called the arousal hypothesis, indicates that any news story detailing some form of aggressive behaviour can increase the potential for more aggressive behaviour from members of the media's audience. A second hypothesis concerns what is termed as disinhibition. It suggests that violence portrayed in the media weakens the inhibition of the viewer to engage in similar behaviour, which in turn increases the person's readiness to engage in aggressive behaviour. The third one is termed as social learning theory. It suggests that if television depicts successful terrorist acts, then viewers will learn all about them. This will in turn increase the likelihood of terrorism. The media would thus be engaged in training individuals in terrorist behaviour each time it reported such acts.

Covering terrorism against India, the record of the Indian media is not all promising and creditable. This criticism applies more to the Indian broadcast media and less to the Indian print media. The Indian print media have the advantage of time in order to present a relatively more balanced reportage, which crystallizes in the time span between terrorist incidents and their reportage in print. The Indian broadcast media under the pressure of 24x7 competitive live coverage of terrorist incidents, absence of instant availability of Government releases and briefings on terrorist incidents and the prevailing doubt and confusion on the developing situation tend to indulge in speculative reporting. In this process, national security considerations are compromised and the Indian broadcast media end up as an unwilling tool of exploitation of various terrorist organizations' misinformation tactics. The Indian media, both print and electronic, seem to be confused when it comes to cover terrorism against India. This confusion becomes further confounded as the Indian media wrestles with itself as to what should be 'the role of the Indian media in terrorism'. Should it be 'the role of the Indian media in terrorism' or should the role of the Indian media be 'the role of the Indian media countering terrorism'. Since India has been subjected to terrorism for well over two decades now, the Indian media should rightfully perceive its role as 'the role of the Indian Media counter terrorism against India'. The Indian media would additionally be able to add more clarity and objectivity to its reportage and visual coverage. Targeting the terrorism controlled from abroad the Indian media in its print and TV coverage would not only be serving India's national security interests but also be assisting the democratic aspirations of the people.

Indian Constitution, Press Freedom and National Security

The Constitution of India does not mention 'freedom of the press' specifically in the Chapter on Fundamental Rights. Indian Constitution however clarified later that it was not necessary to mention it specifically as it is implicit in the right to freedom of speech and expression in Article 19(1)(a) of the Constitution. However, under the Constitution, during an emergency, fundamental rights including freedom of expression and speech can be suspended. In Article 19(2) of the Constitution of India, the freedom of the press can be restricted for reasons of sovereignty and integrity of India, the security of the state, besides some other reasonable restrictions.

Considering this issue this chapter would like to stress the following issues to the Indian media in their role while covering terrorism:

- With freedom of press, comes responsibility and accountability.
- In covering terrorist incident, national security imperatives and requirements should not be compromised in exchange of any misguided journalistic impulses for scoops, exclusives and sensations.
- Terrorists indulge in acts of terror and violence against the Indian state and its Constitution cannot seek refuge in the Indian Constitution for Human Rights protection. They have to face legal processes guaranteed by the Indian Constitution.

In light of the above, covering the terrorist situations, the Indian media is expected to exercise a large degree of self-restraint.

Combating Terrorism: Media's Role

The Indian media, despite many short comings, is a strong and valuable pillar of estate of the nation. Its scrutiny and surveillance of India's political leadership and policy has been an effective 'check and balance' to ensure that India's democracy is not endangered. Following the same spirit, the Indian media, both print and visual, should now look upon themselves as one more weapon of the country in combating terrorism which challenges India's national security and sovereignty. While the Indian Army, police, intelligence fight against terrorism with their arms and ammunition, the Indian media should battle against terrorism with the power of their pens and the impact of booms and visuals. In the coverage of terrorism which has a considerable effect in public mind since 2004, there is much to be expected from the Indian media in terms of their coverage and the desired impact that they should have normally been expected to create. The Indian TV media during the last five years seemed to err less on the side of national security perspective and more erring towards 'humanizing' the terrorists and their cause such as in Jammu and Kashmir by falling prey to the disinformation propaganda campaign of the separatists against India.

This arises from the Indian media's lack of grasp of the main and true intents of terrorism against India. Unless this is understood and recognized by the Indian media, especially the visual media, they would not have played an effective role in the coverage of terrorist incident in India.

Terrorism against Indian needs to be examined by the Indian media in the following perspectives:

- Terrorism is no longer confined to Jammu and Kashmir which aimed at the secession of the state from India.
- Terrorism against India is no longer militancy or terrorist activities, or insurgency arising from only domestic root causes.
- Terrorism against India is a full-fledged 'War against India' by applying all the instruments of war against India by a combined and coordinated application of militancy, insurgency and use of nuclear terrorism possibly in the future.

- Terrorism is no longer targeted at Indian security forces. Today, it targets the Indian people and Republic as a whole. It targets innocent civilian population and India's economic, financial, scientific and other strengths including its social and secular fabric.
- The root causes of terrorism against India by different jihadi terrorist organizations which continue strategically the war of terrorism to harm the very strengths of the Indian Republic.

Further while covering these terrorists' threats, root causes have to be discerned and highlighted. Root causes of terrorism should be explored by the Indian media. The Indian media's role in terrorism therefore should arise as a "Force Multiplier" of the Indian Army and police organizations as they battle terrorists' continuing and incessant threats against India.

Comparative Analysis of Terrorists' Exploitations of Media and the Country's Expectations from the Media

Prior of the analysis, excerpts from a US Congressional Report dealing with this subject may be observed, as these encapsulate the essence of the problems at issue, and these are:

- Terrorists, governments and the media see the functions, roles and responsibilities of the media covering terrorist events from differing and opposing perspectives.
- Such perceptions drive respective behaviour during terrorist incidents - often resulting in tactical and strategic gains or losses, to the terrorist operations and the overall terrorist cause.
- The challenge to the Government and the press community is to understand the dynamics of terrorist enterprise and develop policy options to serve government, media and societal interests.

Media Exploitation by the Terrorists

The terrorists commit violent act for gaining three universal objectives which they assess the media coverage facilitates. These are (1) arrest national and international attention, (2) gain recognition of their cause, and (3) gaining recognition, the terrorists think that with the help of media publicity, some degree of legitimacy would achieve.

Media exploitation by the terrorists focus on the following expectations: (1) media will provide publicity of their deeds and cause, aims and objectives, (2) in the process, media coverage would facilitate spread of terror and amplify fear and panic, (3) show up the impotence of the government and security forces to combat terrorism, and (4) exploit media as a tool for their coordinated and well-orchestrated disinformation strategies.

In case of the Indian media, external terrorist outfits and their terrorism surrogates exploit the liberalist impulses and spin approaches for human right violations by engineering situations in which security forces would be forced to act firmly. They take the opportunity to catch the fish in troubled water when media are in critical of government while exploring the root causes of terrorism. In fact, terrorism in India thrives on the 'oxygen of publicity' provided by the Indian media.

Indian Media's Role in Terrorism: The National Expectations

Combating terrorism is a challenging task for the security forces of the Indian Republic. The enemy is invisible. Though there are sleeper cells and modules of terrorist organizations within India and the Indian security forces have to battle this menace.

In such a climate, the Indian media needs to exhibit 'understanding, restraint, cooperation and loyalty' and by exhibiting these should act as a 'force multiplier' for India's security forces. The Indian media should guard against becoming a 'force multiplier' for terrorism machinery.

More specifically, the Indian media's expected role should be to (1) deny the terrorists a media platform for publicity, (2) avoid glamorizing and sensationalizing terrorists and terrorist incidents, (3) project terrorists as 'war criminals' and their nefarious terrorist act as acts of war against India, (4) prevent use of media as a disinformation tool of terrorists' tactics and strategy, (5) media should boost the morale of the security forces and so also their public image, and (6) media should restrain themselves from building pressures on the government and security forces for instant action or pressures in front of terrorists' demands especially in hostage situations.

Observation

Terrorism is not a passing phenomenon. This will continue as instruments of state policy against India fuelled by foreign states to destabilize India's secular fabric and communal harmony. Peace dialogues and confidence building measures are political expedients for both sides. Besides, India has to mount its pressure to combat terrorism in international bodies. The diplomatic stance needs to be strengthened more. But these cannot emerge as India's only weapons to neutralize or lessen foreign force backed terrorism against India. Indian media can assist in galvanizing the Indian people to vociferously demand strong counter-terrorism policies against external force's calibrated and coordinated terrorism against India.

During last decade revolutionary changes have taken place in the domain of mass media, especially in the news media. Tough competition and commercial pressures have increased by the time. Television has become the leading news medium, with newspapers only supplementary to TV's instant, live, emotional coverage. Critics argue that 'if the emotion you feel by looking at the pictures on TV news programmes is true, then the news is true.' Critics also opine 'television imposes its own perversions on the other information media, beginning with its fascination with pictures. And the basic idea that only what is visible deserves to be news'. Events which produce strong pictures naturally go to the top of the news priority though their importance is secondary in totalitarian perspective.

Recent changes in Terrorism

Terrorism has been practiced throughout history, but it has taken on special characteristics in recent decades, largely due to its interaction with the modern mass media. Brian Jenkins has commented that 'terrorism is a product of freedom, particularly freedom of the press'.[1] Brigitte L. Nacos acknowledged that 'getting the attention of the mass media, the public, and decision makers is the raison d'etre behind modern terrorism's increasingly shocking violence.'[2] Walter Laqueur said that 'the media are the terrorist's best friends, ... the terrorists' act by itself is nothing, publicity is all'.[3] In 1982, Grant Wardlaw had seen a symbiosis between terrorism and media. He later substantiated that 'there is no clear evidence that publicity (by the media) is responsible for significantly affecting the occurrence of terrorism'.[4]

Terrorism and Media: A Symbiotic Relationship?

Many authors have agreed more with Jenkins than with Wardlaw. Miquel Rodrigo has quoted three prominent modern thinkers, Umberto Eco, Jean Baudrillard, and Marshall McLuhan as proponents of an intimate causal relationship between the terrorism and mass media.[5] Though Rodrigo, himself, claims the member of the school of opposite view. Government officials have tended to link the media with terrorists' success or failure. British Prime Minister Margaret Thatcher once expressed her view as, 'Democracies must find ways to starve the terrorists and hijackers of the oxygen of publicity on which they depend'.[6] More recently, Peter C. Kratcoski has commented that, 'if one of the elements of terrorism is the wish to obtain publicity for a cause and create propaganda, the media has obviously overreacted in responding to this desire'.[7] French Sociologist Michel Wieviorka (1988) denied that terrorism and the media are in a 'symbiotic relationship,' arguing that terrorists relate to the media in any of four different ways, from 'pure indifference' to media, through 'relative indifference,' then to a 'media-oriented strategy,' and finally to 'coercion of the media'.[8] Paul Wilkinson directly challenged Wieviorka's four ways of the relationship, saying that channels of communication are always used by terrorists. Wilkinson says that 'if there is no aim to instill terror then the violence is not of a terroristic nature.' The 'instrumental relationship' between the terrorist and the media, which Wieviorka places only in his third category, is said by Wilkinson to be 'intrinsic to the very activity of terrorization' (Wilkinson, 1997).[9] J. Bowyer Bell saw the media-terrorist relationship as symbiotic, with the media coverage spreading the effect of a spatially limited act to a wide public (1978).

Views of Social Scientists and Terrorologists

Yonah Alexander says that the media provide terrorist groups with useful tools that serve their propaganda and psywar ends (1976).[10] M. Cherif Bassiouni says that the psychological effect of a particular violent act may be more important than the act itself, and that effect may be largely a creation of the media (1981).[11] Ralph E. Dowling characterized terrorism as a rhetorical genre, whose violence gives it access to the media that its perpetrators cannot achieve through ordinary forms of discourse (1986).[12] Walter B. Jaehning opines that terrorists recognize that their best route to public recognition is through appealing to traditional news values: drama, conflict and tragedy as fuelled by competition among the media (1978).[13] Patricia R. Palmerton sees the rhetoric of terrorism as in part depending on media coverage for its impact (1983).[14] Bell has said that the key to the success or failure of a terrorist act can be measured by its media coverage.[15] 'Once a terror-event is launched before the camera, the drama by definition is a success' (1978 as quoted by Hocking 1992).[16]

Models of the Terror-Media Relationship

Kevin G. Barnhurst has distinguished two models of the media-terrorism relationship that divide authorities on the topic (Barnhurst 1991). The culpable-media model sees 'a causal link with terrorism that calls for regulation.' The media are an intrinsic part of a vicious cycle: 'As media cover terrorism, they incite more terrorism, which produces more media coverage.'[17] But a second dilemma uncovered by this model involves a cycle of control: If government or the media censor coverage, the controls tend to harm the credibility of the government and/or the media. The terrorists… may resort to even greater violence. (Barnhurst, 1991).[18] On the other hand, the vulnerable media model sees the media as only victims, not causes of terrorism: Any control on coverage, even a natural one, will be ineffective because terrorists can shift to other forms of communication by striking vulnerable points in the infrastructure of liberal societies … although the mass media are involved, they present no escape from terrorism. (Barnhurst, 1991).[19] Barnhurst reviews some of the most significant research up to that time, but has to conclude that, although a causal link may exist it cannot be firmly established 'without falling into the post hoc ergo propter hoc fallacy' (Barnhurst, 1991).[20]

A 'New Age' of Terror?

Nacos has outlined a 'calculus of violence' that distinguishes among different 'target types that enter into the terrorists' objectives'. Domestic terrorists tend to target high-level political, diplomatic, military, or corporate leaders as immediate victims while international terrorism has mostly affected random victims who happened to be in the wrong place at the wrong time. In most instances the immediate victims' identities do not matter, but their nationality, their presence in certain locations, or their professions place them automatically into an identifiable 'enemy' category (Nacos, 1994).[21] In both domestic and foreign cases, however, the media are a significant factor, advertising the act and setting a media agenda focused on the terrorists' goals. Nacos quotes Donna M. Schlagheck that, 'the free press 'is the primary conduit connecting terrorists, the public, and governments,' and adds 'violent incidents can advance the terrorists' goals only if these kinds of incidents are widely reported' (Nacos, 1994, quoting Schlagheck 1988).[22]

The Power of Labelling

Journalists in their reporting of violent acts, can choose words that are either straightforward descriptions, on the one hand, or that contain implicit judgments about the act, on the other.

Media and the Social Matrix of Terrorism

Imbalances in the flow of news and information among nations have been spotlighted by advocates of a 'New World Information and Communication Order' (NWICO) since the 1970s. Alex P. Schmid and Janny de Graaf related this issue to insurgent terrorism in their book *Violence as Communication* (1982). Although recent developments such as computer based communication have brought the technologically less developed and more developed countries into closer contact than they were two decades ago, conditions in the two 'worlds' remain so dissimilar that mutual understanding still is difficult. Schmid and de Graaf say that their 'basic premise is that insurgent terrorism can be better understood if it is viewed in the first instance as communication rather than as mere violence'.[23] They therefore feel 'that this type of terrorism has to be explained in relation to the prevailing information order and the news values that are paramount within this order'.[24] The same authors point out that, while an international 'free flow of information' sounds like a principle that cannot be contested on democratic grounds, in practice it gave freedom of communication chiefly to those who controlled the media. Quoting A.J. Liebing, they note that 'freedom of the press is limited to those who own one' (Schmid and de Graaf, 1982; citing Mander, 1978). Since that control was centered in the West, chiefly under private management in the United States, the international media came to be dominated by western interests and perspectives and 'news values' that pandered to sensationalism and entertainment to the exclusion of the interests of poor people in the less technologically developed nations.[25] The serious needs of those nations are generally neglected in the Western media, prompting a violent response which will attract the attention of those media: We see the genesis of contemporary insurgent terrorism, as it has manifested itself in the Western World since the late 1960s, primarily as the outgrowth of minority strategies to get into the news (Schmid and de Graaf, 1982). A section of the society is of opinion that it is the time to enact a law that bans the media from publicizing the names of terror groups that claim responsibility for attacks. The punishment for publishing or reporting the prohibited information should also be made very stringent to strengthen disincentives against violation. Such legislation might provide a strong disincentive for terrorist organizations, which will then be compelled to resort to peaceful means to propagate their views or to espouse their cause.

Terrorists and Media Allies

After a terrorist attack claiming many lives and injure much more people, the press release issued by the terrorist groups claiming the responsibility of that incident gets prime time coverage. Naturally terrorists find it more effective to just kill a few people to advertise their cause. It is time for universal media guidelines for covering terrorist attacks. Besides, a large section of the mainstream media has to rectify the blind, thoughtless, mentality of its terminology like 'Islamic terrorism' or 'Islamic extremists' that condemn billions of peaceful followers of Islam into victims of discrimination and bias. Unfortunately leading dailies and senior journalists thoughtlessly use such libelous terms against an entire community, or millions of practitioners of a religion. There is no need for 'fatwas' to excommunicate terrorists. They have automatically excommunicated themselves. We need powerful, multi-lingual, creative mass media campaigns aimed at young people telling them the fact that they excommunicate themselves from their religion when they become terrorists. No religion condones violence. Those who kill innocent people are not mujahideen, but cowardly maniacs. The real mujahideen or holy warriors, are only those who bravely continue the inner fight to purify the mind. The mass media have to first understand and then convey this message instead of conveying terrorist publicity material and acting as their free advertising agencies. Journalists using indiscriminate generic terminology such as 'Islamic terrorists' or 'Islamic terrorism' or 'Hindu terrorist' actually feed a social and judicial bias that drives innocent victims of police harassment and social discrimination into violence. It becomes a vicious cycle bred by bias, for which global media professionals are culpable. Media personnel must realize their immense responsibility to save young generation from any particular community being turned into discontented cannon fodder for terrorism. Such terminologies actually create more terrorists amongst the followers of any religious community because of the widespread bias it generates against the community. To discourage terrorism, and to save our dear ones from probably being bomb victims, the mass media need to publicly ridicule the terrorists as cowardly, foolish, self-destructive human beings who kill innocent lives for no purpose. In a world order where no country is untouched by terrorism, media's coverage of terrorism activities is fast becoming critical. How much should be broadcast, whether broadcast of terrorist actions amounts to glorify terrorism and violence and whether it incites people, creates new recruits and gives publicity to terrorists who seek to grab world attention are issues of debate across nations in the post 9/11 world. While India is yet to frame its set of guidelines on coverage of terrorist acts despite such strikes in each and every months, there is increasing questioning of the media's conduct in the face of such attacks. The coverage of terrorist attacks provided by the Indian media, especially television, comes in for a fair bit of criticism. While some praise the media's courage in braving bullets to provide live footage, there is outrage too, with at least one prominent TV journalist derided as 'attention hog', or even as the 'worst senior journalist on the planet'.

Reporting Terrorism

The relationship between journalists and terrorists is complex. 'The media are important instruments of propaganda for the simple reason that they find terrorist actions newsworthy' (Weimann and Winn, 1994).[26] Interaction between the media and terrorism has intensified in the 21st century because of the increase of available information and round the clock news coverage. With news being presented in multimedia packages and delivered in innovative ways, terrorists have many more avenues for promoting their aims and objectives. At the same time, state-sponsored terrorism has a broader audience for mass propaganda campaigns and manipulation of news. Terrorism has...put pressure on journalists to cooperate with agents of the state (Herman and O'Sullivan, 1989).[27] The people's need to be informed has to be balanced by journalist's responsibility to prevent unnecessary harm. The paper identifies three issues when media sources provide news and information about terrorism. These are (a) interference, (b) cooperation and (c) commercialization.

Interference in State Operations against Terrorism

Journalists have become targets of terrorist activities and are repeatedly threatened for expressing opinions contrary to terrorist goals. Terrorists often describe journalists and the media who do not share their goals as traitors. According to terrorists the media are the mouthpiece for a strategy of news manipulation and instigation of war. Journalists have been targeted because of their views or what they have reported. It is just as likely that their notoriety makes reporters valuable as hostages regardless of their opinions. How reporters and photographers should act in tense terrorist situations is only one part of the equation for measuring journalistic responsibility. Another is how news managers decide under enormous pressure what should be aired live, what should be aired later, and what should never appear before the public. According to many in law enforcement, the public does not need to see tactical police activity (Shepard, 2000).[28] Many questions have been raised about the impact of the media on terrorism. The sheer volume of information provided makes a difference with regard to the outcome of terrorist events. In the Mumbai Terrorist attack on 26/11, the media became involved in the minute details. Because media coverage of the attack in Hotel Oberoi and other places was already in place, the attack became the centre of attention for the entire country. The condition of hostages increased nationwide support and sympathy for them and their families. The media coverage created the image of Ajmal Kasav, the terrorist arrested with arms.

According to Picard (1991), reporters can choose from four different traditions of reporting to relate terrorist events. In the information tradition, reports are expected to be factual and reliably documented. News about terrorism is notably poorly corroborated, although it may appear to be in the information tradition. In sensationalist tradition, coverage includes emotions, alarm, threat, anger, and fear. When the tradition is toward feature stories, the focus is on individuals as heroes, villains, victims, and perpetrators. Feature stories provoke readers with an actual person with whom to relate in emotional ways. Documentaries about terrorists and terrorism reveal a particular perspective and also support news industry agendas and pander to sponsor's interests. Explanations carry a slant and a viewpoint that reflect the people and organizations making them, though these individuals and groups may present themselves neutral.[29]

Critics insist that publication of the manifesto set a precedent that encourages terrorists to use the mass media to promote their political views.

Cooperation with Terrorists or with Government Control

Critics express their deep concern over media's cooperation and journalists' support for terrorist interests. Wilkinson (1997) asserts that it is intrinsic to the very activity of terrorization that some form of media, however crude, is utilized as an instrument to disseminate the messages of threat and intimidation.[30] Terrorists will receive benefits from the media through coverage of the incident. The three primary benefits that terrorists may expect are publicity to spread their message, opportunities to provide background and interpretation for their actions and a level of legitimacy that would otherwise be unobtainable (Becker, 1996).[31] Targets of terror do not lose their usefulness to terrorists even when violent incidents result in negative media coverage, public outcries against brutality, and widespread sympathy for victims. A nation enraged over terrorism either encourages or inhibits governmental responses in ways that may serve terrorist aims (Nacos, 1994), yet it is often difficult to see the gain obtained through media spotlights on terrorist events.[32] Slone (2000) found that media portrayals of terrorism, political violence, and threats to national security provoked anxiety in individual viewers.[33] The idea that media are the contagion of terrorism has been widely heralded. According to the theory of contagion, terrorism is cultivated and spread by media coverage. Media cooperation with law enforcement in support of government is more likely than media cooperation with terrorist aims.

Selling Terrorism: Commercial Interests in Media Reports

The mainstream mass media are large, profit-seeking corporations, owned and controlled by wealthy corporate heavily dependent on advertising for revenue and interlocked with other members of the corporate system. News about terrorism may be manufactured in several different ways. One is inflating the menace on the basis of modest, not very threatening, but real actions. Another is the false transfer of responsibility for a terrorist act to a convenient scapegoat. Terrorism is also manufactured in the private sector, sometimes in collusion with agents of the state, to incriminate organizers, resisters, activists and political enemies (Herman and O'Sullivan, 1989).[34] Although news of terrorist events is seldom outright fabrication, the stories may be manufactured from selected elements and assumptions, with the support of both commercial and government interests. Journalists are being asked to achieve an equilibrium between market orientation and a mission to bolster public confidence (Rosenfeld, 1996).[35] This balance has nothing to do with either validity or impartial reporting of events. The relationship between the media and terrorism is much too complex; it is controlled by the culture, not regulations from any single source.

Media's Role in Covering Maoist Terrorist Incident in West Bengal (2005–2011): A Case Study

The coverage of Maoist terrorist incident by various newspapers appeared as sensational and present scoops over other newspapers sidelining the most elementary sense of responsibility. If the highly armed terrorists are provided with information during an encounter it is bound to give them an advantage and make the task of the security personnel much more difficult. Unfortunately some newspapers provided detailed descriptions of the ongoing anti-terror operations. Most of the still photographers zoomed in their cameras at 'trouble spots'. Reporters, correspondents and photojournalists rushed to train and adjust their cameras accordingly the slightest movement of the Joint Forces. Such media hyperactivity could not have helped the security personnel who were risking their lives in a very complex and difficult operation against dangerous enemies.

The journalists, correspondents rushed to search for byte from the exhausted and traumatized village people who are the helpless victims of the Maoist terrorism. When they badly needed restraint, respect and mental support, microphones, tape recorders have been kept in front of their faces and flood of questions have flown. Those who had suffered personal tragedy and themselves still in shock were not spared by the so called conscientious newspapers. The camera panned in on their tears and watched their agony. Is this the victory of sensationalism over the sacrifice of essential humanity? The ghastly, tragic and horrifying incident of Maoist terror and its awful personal aftermath for the victims have been treated like a reality show. The militants knew from where the security forces were zeroing in. Lalgarh is not yet a 'liberated zone', much as Maoist propaganda and some giddy media would have it. The photographs published in Bengali and English newspapers exhibited Maoists who sat with their backs to the camera, flaunting automatic rifles, who talked of killing the class enemy, of assassinating the then Chief Minister. The newspaper's competitiveness compelled them to stress more on airing 'exclusives' in a time of a calamity that needed balanced, moderate and dispassionate representation.

Media Interfering in State Operations against Maoist Terrorism: A Debate

Journalists, newspaper correspondents, reporters, photo-journalists have become targets of terrorist activity and are repeatedly threatened for expressing opinions contrary to terrorist goals. Journalists may be targeted because of their views or what they have reported. How reporters and photographers should act in tense Maoist terrorist situations is one part of the equation for measuring journalistic responsibility. Another is how sub-editors, desk persons, assistant editors, leader writers overall editors decide under enormous pressure what should be print, what should be print later and what should never appear before the readers. It is essential that journalists observed the bombings as these occurred rather than reporting what terrorists directed them to announce after the incident.

When the Officer-in Charge, Sankrail, West Bengal, Atinndranath Dutta was kidnapped by the Maosists the newspapers became involved in the minute details. The kidnapping became the centre of attention for the entire state. The newspapers' coverage created the image of angry, violent

Maoist terrorists armed with rifles. Reporters, correspondents amplify, arbitrate and create their own rhetoric about terrorist acts. The demands of Maoists, their manifesto, news about their secret meetings have been published in newspapers. Critics label it as media cooperation. Critics argue that publication of their demands, portion of manifesto set a precedent that encourages Maoist terrorists to use the newspapers to promote their views.

Newspaper's Cooperation with Maoist Terrorists

The reports, features and editorials published in the newspapers knowingly or unknowingly cooperate with the interests of the Maoist extremists. According to the theory of contagion, terrorism is cultivated and spread by media coverage including newspaper. The fear is raised of irresponsible reporting by misguided and manipulated journalists.

Building Image of Terrorists as Martyrs

From the standpoint of propaganda and manipulating public opinion, journalists appeared useful. It has happened in covering the reports on exchange of bullets between Maoist terrorists and the joint forces. Careless use of words, phrases by the correspondents and journalists in few cases unnecessary build the image of terrorists as martyrs. Unfortunately, a few reports and features on Maoist terrorism have made Kishanji's image as larger than life. Sometimes a few stories have appeared upholding Kishenji as country's Robinhood. Maoist leaders are taking the advantage of this coverage. They use newspapers to promote their agenda. The reports published in newspapers after the release of O.C., Sankrail, Atindranath Dutta was presented in such a fashion that readers are compelled to believe that Kishenji was a person full of kindness and sympathy. His image was glorified.

The Study

Role of newspapers in covering Maoist terrorism in West Bengal was taken for statistical analysis for the period of three months (01.09.10 to 30.11.10). After three months the coverage of six English national newspapers (as representative) and six Bengali newspapers (as representative) was measured. In order to test if there is any significant difference in coverage between the English national newspapers and Bengali regional newspapers the 't' test has been applied.

Results and Discussion

Comparing the calculated value of t with the value of t in the Fisher and Yates' table for distribution of t against (n_A+n_B-2); i.e. (6+6–2); i.e. 10 degrees of freedom at $p=0.05$, it was found the latter (table value) to be 2.228. As the calculated, i.e. 12.76 is greater than table value it can be said that the difference between the samples A and B is statistically significant at 5% level. Thus, the difference between the role of English newspapers and Bengali newspapers in covering Maoist terrorism in West Bengal is statistically significant.

Observation

Maoist terrorism in West Bengal in recent years has upheld that terrorists are making a conscious and deliberate effort to manipulate the newspapers for their desired goals. Since majority of the newspapers are driven by market-economy and are based on competition and profit, it is inevitable that they become an integral part of any terrorist act. The newspaper coverage of Maoist terrorist activities clearly indicates that by providing extensive coverage of such terrorist incident the newspapers give the impression that they sympathize with the terrorist cause, thereby creating an atmosphere favourable to further violence. The newspapers often hinder the work of Police, Administration, Security Personnel and Forces combating terrorism, thus jeopardizing successful results of counter-terror attack. Newspapers have occasionally been helpful to the authorities in tackling the incident like Maoist terrorist strike. The newspapers without surrendering their prerogatives should help criminal justice processes in dealing with Maoist terrorism and vice versa the administration of justice officials should take cooperation of newspapers for professional assistance in handling the incidents and in limiting their derivative societal repercussions. Analysing the nature and complexity of Maoist terrorism, the determination of a proper role for the newspaper should not be left to their judgment alone.

Conclusion

It is a matter of concern that a section of newspapers has reduced news coverage into 'infotainment'. Sensationalism, trivialization and superficiality are now the hallmarks of a business of public service. Conflicting reports on casualties, defence resources, the number of terrorists, in-accurate news and information have increased our concern and anxiety. Irresponsible coverage encourages censorship. It would be tragic if the free fourth estate is punished because of its unethical, irresponsible behaviour. The newspaper should behave in a way that helps those who are performing their duties. We need powerful, multi-lingual, creative media campaigns aimed at young people telling them the fact that the terrorists excommunicate themselves from their civilized society. The mass media should objectively, accurately and credibly report about Maoist terrorist incidents minimize the public panic and anxiety and lose trust and confidence in both the press and government. Journalists need to publicly ridicule a terrorist as a cowardly, foolish, self-destructive human being who kills for no purpose.

Notes

1. Jenkins, Brian (1983). 'Research in Terrorism: Areas of Consensus, Areas of Ignorance'. In *Terrorism: Interdisciplinary Perspectives*, edited by E. Burr, D. Soskis, and W. Reid. Washington, DC: American Psychiatric Association.
2. Nacos, Brigitte (1994). *Terrorism and the Media*. New York: Columbia University Press.
3. Laqueur, Walter (1976). *Harper's Magazine*. 104.
4. Wardlaw, Grant (1982). *Political Terrorism*. London: Cambridge University Press.
5. Rodrigo, Miquel (1991). *Los medios de comunicación ante el terrorismo (The Media of Communication Confront Terrorism)*. Barcelona: Icariia.

6. Article in (1985) *The New York Times.*
7. Kratcoski, Peter C. (2001). Terrorist Victimization: Prevention, Control and Recovery, in *Studies in Conflict and Terrorism*, 24(6): 467–473.
8. Wieviorka, Michel (1988). The Making of Terrorism, Chicago: University of Chicago Press, p. 43.
9. Wilkinson, Paul (1997). The Media and Terrorism: A Reassessment. *Terrorism and Political Violence*, 9(2), 51–64.
10. Alexander, Yonah (ed.) (1976). *International Terrorism*. New York: Praeger Publishers.
11. Bassiouni, Cherif (1975). *Terrorism and Political Crimes.* Springfield, III, 43–46.
12. Dowling, Ralph E. (1986). 'Terrorism and the Media: A Rhetorical Genre'. *Journal of Communication*. Vol. 36(1), 12–24.
13. Jaehning, Walter B. 1978. 'Journalists and Terrorism: Captives of the Libertarian Tradition'. *Indiana Law Journal*. Vol. 53, No. 4, 717–744.
14. Palmerton, Patricia R. (1983). 'Terrorism in the Media: A Call for Rhetorical Criticism'. A paper delivered at the 1983 meeting of the Speech Communication Association, Mass Communication Division.
15. Bowyer, Bell J. (1975) *Transnational Terror*, AEI-Hoover Policy Study 17 Washington D.C.: American Enterprise Institute for Public Policy Research, 89.
16. Hocking, Jennifer Jane (1992). 'Governments' Perspectives'. In Paletz and Schmid, 1992, 86–104.
17. Volume 21 (2002) No. 1 *Communication Research Trends*.
18. Barnhurst, Kevin G. (1991). Contemporary Terrorism in Peru: Sendero Luminoso and the Media. *Journal of Communication*, 41(4), 75–89.
19. Ibid.
20. Ibid.
21. Nacos, Brigitte (1994). *Terrorism and the Media*. New York: Columbia University Press.
22. Ibid.
23. Schmid Alex P. and Graaf Janny de. (1982). *Violence as Communication*, 175.
24. Ibid.

25. Volume 21 (2002). *Communication Research Trends*. 1–9.
26. Weimann, Gabriel and Winn, Conrad (1994). *The Theater of Terror: Mass Media and International Terrorism*. New York: Longman, 112.
27. Herman, Edward S. and O'Sullivan, Gerry. (1989). *The Terrorism Industry: The Experts and Institutions that Shape our View of Terror.* New York: Pantheon.
28. Shepard, Alicia C. (2000). Safety first. American Journalism Review, 22(1), 22–28. Retrieved 7 June 2002, from www.ajr.org/Article.asp?id=518
29. Picard, Robert G. (1991). Journalists as targets and victims of terrorism. In Yonah Alexander and Robert G. Picard (eds.), *In the Camera's Eye*. Washington, DC: Macmillan-Brassey's.
30. Wilkinson, Paul (1997). The media and terrorism: A reassessment. *Terrorism and Political Violence,* 9(2), 51–64.
31. Becker, Jon B. (1996). The news media, terrorism, and democracy: The symbiotic relationship between freedom of the press and acts of terror. Retrieved 7 June 2002, from http://205.158.5.90/Iasd-eob/eob-tr2.
32. Nacos, Brigitte (1994). *Terrorism and the Media*. New York: Columbia University Press.
33. Slone, Michelle (2000). Responses to Media Coverage of Terrorism. *Journal of Conflict Resolution,* 44(4), 508–522.
34. Herman, Edward S. and O'Sullivan, Gerry. (1989). *The Terrorism Industry: The Experts and Institutions that Shape our View of Terror.* New York: Pantheon.
35. Rosenfeld, Shalom (1996). Blood-red Headlines Feed Terrorist Propaganda (IPI Report). Vienna: International Press Institute.

Index